Praise for *Elves, Witches & Gods*

"Travel with me now, from the history of Heathen magic, to snowy mountain top shrines and the sacred thread that connects Goddesses of the spun fiber Elves, *Witches & Gods* is a gripping journey that ries of the Gods and those that seek them with connection to the Gods and looking within your wait to see what Catherine Heath brings us next.

　　—Amy Blackthorn, author of *Blackthorn's Botanical Magic and Sacred Smoke*

"The Elder Heathen lived in an Animist world of spirits, ancestors, elves, magic, rich lore, and living Gods and Goddesses. Cat Heath teaches a real system of magic steeped in that elder world with all the real experimentation required to bring it to life today. She gives you a no-nonsense, practical step-by-step method to understand the lore, connect to these powers, and begin your magical journey in a way so few have explored in rich detail. Here you find the guidance and wisdom to become a Helrune."

　　—Lonnie Scott, coauthor of *Elhaz Ablaze: Compendium of Chaos Heathenry* and host of *Weird Web Radio*

"This is a lace up your boots, grab your sword and shield, and get down to business book on advanced Heathen magic. Cat has gone well past the introductory volumes to give the practicing Heathen a second level of magic. Her first part is a comprehensive overview of advanced basics that most never get to learn. By the time you reach her second part, practice, you are ready for lessons in fiber, herbs, oils, rituals, and all the other day-to-day practices that you perform during the year. If you weren't grounded in Heathenism before you will be now."

　　—Gypsey Teague, author of *A Witch's Guide to Wands* and *Steampunk Magic*

"In *Elves, Witches & Gods*, Heath surpasses the sum of all components of her research, magical work, and community efforts. Here in one book, Heath shares her knowledge she has attained of the deities and wights. Heath's descriptions are unique in that they include not only what to do when working with various beings or deities; they also provide cautions and warnings about what not to do. This book is a tremendous source of inspiration, insight, and information for Heathens of all tradition and experience levels."

　　—Robert Schreiwer, author of *First Book of Urglaawe Myths*

This book is dedicated to my daughter, Pod.
May you always keep your fierceness and never
dim your light. I love you and always will.

ELVES, WITCHES & GODS

About the Author

Hailing from the historically wild and lawless county of Lancashire, England, Cat Heath is a Heathen and Witch of over two decades of experience. A semi-nomadic type, Cat traded the windswept moors and ancient burial mounds of her homeland for a life on the winds, eventually coming to call Maryland home after a decade and a half of magical and mundane adventures across three continents.

She is the founder of the Cult of the Spinning Goddess and cofounder of the Open Halls Project. She also holds membership in the Shenandoah valley based Great Valley Kindred as well as the Troth. Cat has led ritual and taught classes both locally at in-person events, online, and as a co-presenter on the 2018 Land Sea Sky Travel "Hiddenfolk, Witches, and Elves" tour of Iceland. Further writings can be found at her home on the web seohelrune.com.

To Write to the Author

If you wish to contact the author or would like more information about this book, please write to the author in care of Llewellyn Worldwide Ltd. and we will forward your request. Both the author and publisher appreciate hearing from you and learning of your enjoyment of this book and how it has helped you. Llewellyn Worldwide Ltd. cannot guarantee that every letter written to the author can be answered, but all will be forwarded. Please write to:

Cat Heath
℅ Llewellyn Worldwide
2143 Wooddale Drive
Woodbury, MN 55125-2989
Please enclose a self-addressed stamped envelope for reply,
or $1.00 to cover costs. If outside the U.S.A., enclose
an international postal reply coupon.

Many of Llewellyn's authors have websites with additional
information and resources. For more information,
please visit our website at http://www.llewellyn.com.

ELVES, WITCHES & GODS

Spinning Old Heathen Magic in the Modern Day

CAT HEATH

Llewellyn Publications | Woodbury, Minnesota

FIRST EDITION
Second Printing, 2021

Book design by Samantha Peterson
Cover design by Shira Atakpu
Editing by Laura Kurtz
Interior art by Llewellyn Art Department

Llewellyn Publications is a registered trademark of Llewellyn Worldwide Ltd.

Library of Congress Cataloging-in-Publication Data
Names: Heath, Catherine, author.
Title: Elves, witches & gods : spinning old heathen magic in the modern day
    / Cat Heath.
Other titles: Elves, witches and gods
Description: First edition. | Woodbury, Minnesota : Llewellyn Publications,
    2021. | Includes bibliographical references and index. | Summary: "A
    book on Heathenry-based witchcraft, suitable for practitioners of all
    levels"—Provided by publisher.
Identifiers: LCCN 2020050982 (print) | LCCN 2020050983 (ebook) | ISBN
    9780738765358 (paperback) | ISBN 9780738765501 (ebook)
Subjects: LCSH: Witchcraft. | Magic.
Classification: LCC BF1566 .H39 2021 (print) | LCC BF1566 (ebook) | DDC
    133.4/3—dc23
LC record available at https://lccn.loc.gov/2020050982
LC ebook record available at https://lccn.loc.gov/2020050983

Llewellyn Worldwide Ltd. does not participate in, endorse, or have any authority or responsibility concerning private business transactions between our authors and the public.

All mail addressed to the author is forwarded but the publisher cannot, unless specifically instructed by the author, give out an address or phone number.

Any internet references contained in this work are current at publication time, but the publisher cannot guarantee that a specific location will continue to be maintained. Please refer to the publisher's website for links to authors' websites and other sources.

Llewellyn Publications
A Division of Llewellyn Worldwide Ltd.
2143 Wooddale Drive
Woodbury, MN 55125-2989
www.llewellyn.com

Printed in the United States of America

CONTENTS

FUNDAMENTALS, EXPERIENTIALS, REMEDIES, AND RECIPES

FOREWORD

When I heard that Catherine was writing a book, I was delighted. I respect her and all of the work she has done for the heathen community both locally and worldwide, even though her name itself is not yet highly known. "A book!" I thought. "I can't wait to see what she writes!"

Having read *Elves, Witches, and Gods*, I have to say that the wait has been worthwhile. Personally, I use scholarship to inform my spiritual practice. One of the first things I look for in a book is: is there scholarship and if so, is that scholarship accurate? This book certainly is. Catherine has researched magic, seidhr, charms, and Anglo Saxon as well as Old Norse practices, and her process is ongoing. The book is full of historically, culturally, and archeologically relevant information. Where she has had to divert from Old Norse and Anglos Saxon sources to fill in a "blank spot," she has done so using other Indo-European sources, which she has clearly researched as thoroughly as the others. While full of research, Anglo-Saxon and Old Norse terms (among others), Catherine takes the time to define and explain in a way that makes the terms resonate with the reader rather than leaving them dry.

This is the second thing I look for in a book: is it readable? While I am just as fond of researching dry tomes full of doctorate level prose, I think that in general, books should be accessible to many people. This book is just that. Catherine writes in a clear, open prose that feels nearly conversational in its tone. She explains her topics, research, and thoughts using a narrative that does not patronize—rather, the prose is straightforward and easy to understand.

Perhaps the best thing I can say about this book is that it is useful. Catherine uses a mix of scholarship and personal experience and tracks how she arrived at a belief, ritual, or other practice. This means that the book spans the gap between old and modern. When possible, she uses the source materials directly—for example, using Anglo-Saxon era charms to ward off illness. When she uses her own understanding and inspiration to develop a practice, she clearly states that she is doing so, which means that the reader receives a thorough understanding of the place scholarship has in the modern record. Above all, this book is practical. Catherine has taken the time to show the reader where beliefs, practices, spirituality, and her processes come from, and encourages readers to develop their own practices in each chapter.

Catherine is very clear that this book is not for beginners. This is for people who already have basic beliefs and magical practices under their belt. That said, Catherine does provide what she calls "foundations"—discussing such things as meditation, visualization, and other ways to develop a long-term practice and build on already existing practices. Chapter by chapter, each ritual builds on those that came before it, which shows how intertwined witchcraft, magic, and seidhr are. Working with the dead, with elves, and with gods can be very dangerous. This is not work for the faint of heart.

Elves, Witches, and Gods is, in my opinion, an essential book for any practitioner's shelf. It contains a wealth of information, practical foundational skill development, and advanced workings that help the reader both understand and practice on their own.

Patricia Lafayllve,
Author of *A Practical Heathen's Guide to Asatru*

INTRODUCTION

We walk up the ancient path toward the mound, our bags laden with offerings and magical tools. Drums and horns, mead and a stang, tealights in jars. The sun has still not found its rest, but we know it won't be long before she dies for the day. We know we have to hurry if we are to still have light while setting up.

When we arrive at the mound, we walk around, try to sense where the offerings would be best received, and eventually pour out our offerings on top of the mound in the dying light of the sun. We're a mixed bag of people today. The witch with decades of experience, the more eclectic Heathen friend, and myself.

It was the old tales that had inspired this adventure (as ill-advised as that might have been). I'd been doing this for a while—finding the old accounts of Heathen magic and trying them out. Pushing myself through wild, dirty, and sometimes dangerous exploits in order to better understand what I was reading. I was sure these practices could be resurrected. We just had to understand them first and there is no substitute for experience.

We climb inside the mound with our candles in jars, and set up in the largest chamber. At first we drum, unwilling to try and put expectations on the mound and anyone that might still be there. The sources I'd read had made this activity sound dangerous and I needed to understand why. What was it about the mound and being inside the mound that was dangerous to the living?

Time passes, but I'm not sure how much. Shadows cast from the warm glow of the candles dance on the walls, and the sound of drums reverberates around the small space. I begin to whisper fervent prayers, asking the dead to come and give us the knowledge we need. We'd fasted during the day so our perceptions are more intense, and soon we begin to feel as though we are getting some attention.

It's a woman who first makes herself known. She flashes before me in vision: auburn hair, homespun browns, and bright blue eyes. Her words are urgent yet foreign to me; I don't understand them. We continue to drum and pray.

At some point, I happen to look across at the witch in our party and see that he's looking suspiciously unlike himself. I ask him if he's okay, and tell him I can see a face superimposed over his own. He tells me he's fighting it. I choose to trust in him and his abilities. An angry scar and cruel smile now appears over his normally friendly and unmarred face, and I cannot help but think about how he is sat so close to the exit.

Should anything happen, we would have to go through him.

I don't get to think about this for long, though, because suddenly everything shifts and I know that we're no longer in a mound within the land of the living. We are now in Hel.

The witch friend becomes more restive with this shift, and I tell my other friend to make sure she is shielding if she isn't already. But then, my friend speaks the fatal words that make me pull the plug on the whole endeavor:

"How do I shield?"

I close down the rite as quickly as I can and shove the half-possessed friend out of the hole and into the night. We make our way down the path back to the car but we know we're being followed. We can hear the footsteps on the path behind us. My eclectic friend links her arm with mine. She thought she'd be up to this, that the things she'd encountered in her community were the extent of what was out there. But tonight she knows that's not true.

Three Strands of Heathen Magic

The Heathen worldview has always been inherently magical, even for the average person. For the "elder" (or historical) Heathen, the world was inhabited by both seen and unseen beings, all bound up in webs of relationship cemented together by gifting. It was also a world of knowing and power—of casual magic done covertly and overt ritual magic performed before audiences.

The image of Heathen magic in primary sources is rich and complex yet lacking in practical instruction. Written from the observer's perspective, Heathen-period accounts of magic concentrate on describing the spectacle. They focus on elements such as the platforms from which practitioners worked their "hardtwisted sorcery," or the clothes worn by a traveling seeress and what she ate the night before holding her seance. When it comes to the actual techniques and incantations used, however, they are unsurprisingly silent.

These period accounts give us the outer wrapping of the mysteries—a taste that always leaves you hungry for more and wanting to go deeper, but never the path to get there.

I was first infected with this hunger in the late nineties when I came across a mention of *seiðr* on an absolutely terrible Geocities website. The only way I can describe it is that something sparked to life inside of me when I saw the word. There was an impossible sense of familiarity but no details, just a maddeningly fuzzy shape that let me know that the information presented on the website was not what the practice had ever been.

I spent the next few years refining the methodology with which I would attempt to uncover and rebuild this practice. Around the mid-2000s I encountered the reconstructionist method and decided to apply it to my magical research too. One of the stories often told in Heathen reconstructionist groups (at least back then) is of a man who was trying to figure out if it was possible for medieval archers to shoot as quickly and accurately as historical sources suggested—to modern archers, it just didn't seem possible. However, this man took a different approach and began to copy the shooting style depicted in period art.

After some trial and error in working with the bow in the depicted way, he was able to accurately reconstruct the shooting style, and in doing so found that it was indeed possible to shoot as the sources described. My thought at the time was that perhaps some of the techniques used by those practitioners of old could be rediscovered by taking a similar approach.

Since then, my search for seiðr has taken me from the primary sources to windswept moors, weather-ravaged mounds, ancient forests, and on the road in travels as a nomad. I've created songs to pull and entice, trucked with spirits in the wilds, enchanted to bind, and along the way learned how to spin yarn. I've studied, experimented, and built practices around that experimentation.

The thing about Heathen magic is that when you begin to work in this way, *seiðrworker* becomes less of a label and more of a way of working to be kept in the "medicine chest," to be pulled out as needed.

The Heathen magical "medicine chest" is large and mostly unexplored. Most modern practitioners have something in the slots labeled "Seiðr," "Galdr," and "Runes," but little else. Sometimes there is no interest in the other slots, but all too often people are simply unaware that these other slots even exist. And while we do not always have much information on less well-known practices, the constellation of words describing different kinds of magical practices and practitioners in the primary sources suggest that those other slots did indeed exist.[1] If anything, historical Heathen magical practices seem to have been far more diverse (not to mention subversive) than their modern iterations.

As a general rule, magic, or the types of magic practiced by a culture, is not separate from the wider overarching worldview of that culture. In other words, when determining the likelihood of how a type of magic may have been practiced, it's important to make sure that it is congruous with the way that culture saw the world in the first place. When it comes to researching Heathen magic, matters are further complicated by the fact that not all Heathen cultures were preserved equally.

One key area in which we find this disparity particularly relevant to any study of Heathen magic is the sources on sickness and healing. The Norse and Anglo-Saxons seem to have viewed healing similarly—as an often magical skill—but the early English corpus is far more detailed in this area than the Norse. So I began to apply that same process of research and experimentation to the Anglo-Saxon magico-medical manuscripts. This avenue of research allowed me to both flesh out my view of the soul as well as extract a whole new group of magical technologies that, when reapplied to the Norse sources, helped me to make greater sense of them in turn. The galdr/galdor and herb craft born from that research constitute the second strand of magic in this book.

---

1. Neil Price, "The Archaeology of Seiðr: Circumpolar Traditions in Viking Pre-Christian Religion," *Brathair* 4, No. 2 (2004): 109–126.

The final strand of Heathen magic found here is a practice called "going under the cloak." This is perhaps the least commonly practiced form of Heathen magic, and if I'm being honest, we have less of an idea of how this practice was done than perhaps any other kind. The most that can be said about it is, at best, that it's a way of seeking wisdom as well as perceiving and possibly interacting with the hidden dimensions of a land. The practice as presented in this book is admittedly largely theoretical and experimental on my part. However, my experimentation has yielded good results, so I have included it as a demonstration of how magical reconstruction can look when historical information is sparse.

As an adjunct to the strand of seiðr, you will also find the work of the helrune. For me, the helrune is a völva who specializes in working with the dead and chthonic through intermediary technologies (including the body of the helrune herself/themselves) as her/their main practice.

What appears in this book is the result of more than a decade and a half of this work. Much of the knowledge presented here is hard-gotten and built upon the broken bones of countless mistakes. It is the result of research, experimentation, and evaluation. You will also notice that I sometimes include historical sources from other Indo-European cultures and that some of the practices given here are backfilled with them—this is due to the limited nature of Heathen-period sources, at least from the practitioner's perspective. As previously mentioned, the bulk of the sources pertaining to practices like seiðr are from the observer perspective only. There are thus times when the reconstructions of these practices require some backfilling in order for them to be workable enough for experimentation.

This is not a good book for those just beginning their journey into magic. There are some prerequisite skills I recommend developing before working with this material, among them: meditation, shielding, energy manipulation, and the ability to journey in trance. Additionally, I recommend becoming familiar with psychic hygiene practices and beginning regular purification practices before embarking upon this work. I have included information on all of these subjects in the Fundamentals section of each chapter, as well as in chapters 6 and 11. It is my hope that these sections serve as either a refresher or an opportunity to seat those basic skills within a Heathen framework rather than as an introduction.

The first section of the book is dedicated to an overview of the historical practice of these different forms of magic, the deities I personally work with, and cosmology. You will also find a chapter on what I consider the necessary underlying mechanics of Heathen magic. Here, we will explore concepts of "fate," "luck," and "soul."

The second section of this book contains practical instructions for performing these different forms of magic, as well as some rituals and recipes you can try out for yourself. This work is not inherently safe, but hopefully there will be enough to help keep you safe within these pages, at least in the beginning.

You will also find different types of practical instructions depending on what is being done and how difficult the activity can be. As one might expect, the practices described as "Foundations" are the bare bones of what is needed to work magically and include skills such as meditation, visualization, and energy work. Next are "Fundamentals," practices that teach you ways of staying safe and well as a magic worker, or the basic skills associated with a kind of magic. After that are "Experientials" (rites and rituals), "Recipes," and "Remedies" (troubleshooting activities) that you can do.

Finally, this book is not just a book of spells and workings to be followed religiously. This is a system with experimentation and diversity built in. The Heathen magic you come to practice will probably look nothing like mine, and that's wonderful! The more that people get out there and experiment, the more deeply our practices will root and grow. It is my sincere hope that you come away from this book with not only a knowledge of some underlying mechanics of Heathen magic, but the confidence to apply this process for yourself as well as the desire to grow.

The time to grow has come, so let us grow wildly.

Part One
COSMOLOGY

One

AN OVERVIEW
OF HEATHEN MAGIC

The Heathen magic that I practice is a thread of multiple strands all plied together to form the whole. As I mentioned in the introduction, there is this idea of a medicine chest that I pull from as needed. At times, I will work as a *seiðkona* ("seið-woman"); at other times I will be found covered by a cloak and still; and at others, I will be the galdoring healer chanting old incantations in long-dead tongues over mixtures of herbs. Some even call me *völva*, a kind of wand or staff-carrying seeress whose words can also bring about a fate as much as prophesize it. Most commonly, I am a mixture of all of the above and generally go by *helrune*, or a Heathen witch who works predominantly with the dead and chthonic.

This chapter gives an overview of the most important strands of the "thread" of Heathen magic that I practice, and some of the key concepts that I believe underpin them. As my journey into Heathen magic began with seiðr, it is among the high seats and spindles that I will begin.

Seiðr/Sīden

The Heathen community, and especially its magic workers, have struggled with question of what seiðr is for years. A simple answer would be that seiðr is magic, or more specifically, a magic of binding or pulling that was connected

9

with spinning in some contexts. Unfortunately, while that definition is accurate, it doesn't quite cover the entirety of what seiðr probably was.

As always, the problem with discussing seiðr is that there are no Viking Age "how-to" texts we can copy, and accounts of magic referred to as "seiðr" can often be puzzling. To further complicate matters, there are a number of distinctly modern practices that have arisen that are also commonly referred to as "seiðr", but that work from within a framework adapted from core shamanism.[2] The seiðr of the primary sources is a far more diverse set of practices than the high-seat-centered practice of modern groups.

The seiðr of the sources is a multifaceted art, that included not only the elements of prophecy and seership that we see today, but also the manipulation of luck, weather, and the minds of others. Practitioners were also reputed to be able to find hidden things (both in physical locations and in the minds of others), call fish and game, and heal the sick. They could summon spirits for questioning and perform acts of shapeshifting.[3] But as with all forms of magic, the same mechanisms that enabled the good could also be used to work ill. Seiðr was both beneficial and malefic, and practitioners were viewed with no small degree of ambivalence by those around them.[4] The seiðkona seems to have most commonly worked alone, but there were also those who worked in groups (most commonly with family members).[5]

So far, I have mostly discussed female practitioners of seiðr; however, there were also male practitioners. In fact, the earliest mention of seiðr appears in a poem allegedly written by a seiðmaðr ("seiðr-man") by the name of Vitgeir.

Men who practiced seiðr seem to have faced far more censure than their female counterparts and there are multiple accounts of them being burned alive in groups. Ynglinga Saga tells us that seiðr was generally taught to priestesses because it involved "great ergi" (shame, abomination) for the men who

---

2. Stefanie Schnurbein, "Shamanism in the Old Norse Tradition: A Theory Between Ideological Camps," in History of Religions 43, no. 2 (2003), 116–138.

3. Neil S. Price, The Viking Way: Religion and War in Late Iron Age Scandinavia, 1st ed. (Uppsala, Sweden: University of Uppsala, 2002), 64.

4. Leszek Gardeła, "Buried with Honour and Stoned to Death? The Ambivalence of Viking Age Magic in the Light of Archaeology," Analecta Archaeologica Ressoviensia 4 (2011): 339–375.

5. Thor Ewing, Gods and Worshippers: In the Viking and Germanic World (Stroud, Gloucestershire: History Press, 2010), 86.

participated.[6] Unfortunately, the matter of *ergi* and why it was considered so shameful is still not particularly clear, despite many years of theorizing by scholars and practitioners alike. Some point to the fact that Óðinn, a god particularly associated with seiðr, wore women's clothes while using seiðr. Others connect *ergi* to attitudes about homosexuality and social taboos against men taking the passive role in sex.[7]

Regardless of who was doing seiðr, there was always the implication of sexual deviance and promiscuity. These sexual overtones are never elaborated on in the sources beyond allusions to the goddess Freyja's promiscuity and apparent incest with her brother, Freyr. But the association between magic and sexual deviance were preserved in Norwegian legal history well into the sixteenth century.[8]

There are two main deities associated with seiðr (both of whom have already been mentioned in this chapter): Freyja and Óðinn. According to the *Ynglinga Saga*, Freyja taught Óðinn the art of seiðr. Both figures are paradigmatic in the sense that they serve as mythological "fix points" for human practitioners. Óðinn is in many ways the archetypal male seiðmaðr. Like his sisters in practice, he is peripatetic, moving from one place to the next to trade in wisdom. He too violates the sexual mores of (human) society and receives some censure for it in the form of accusations of shameful behavior and unmanliness.[9] However, when it comes to Freyja, the connection between deity and those who follow in her footsteps is made far more explicit in verses 21 and 22 of the thirteenth-century Norse poem *Völuspá*, or *Prophecy of the Seeress*:

She remembers that battle between people, the first in the world/realm
When they hoisted Gullveig up with spears on all sides
And burned her in the hall of Harr
Three times burned, three times born
Over and over, yet she still lives

---

6. Ibid., 87.

7. Ibid., 96.

8. Ibid., 110–111.

9. Ibid., 111.

> They called her Heidr at the houses where she visited
> The truth-telling seeress, she called upon spirits
> She made seiðr wherever she could
> She had a mind for seiðr
> She was always the joy of evil people/brides[10]

In these two short but powerful stanzas, we encounter a goddess of great power by the name of Gullveig who has the power to transcend death. But although she is horribly killed no less than three times, she is reborn and lives in the world as the seiðkona, Heiðr (again, an almost archetypal name for a peripatetic seiðkona who lives in the wilds).

Although there has been some debate as to the identity of Gullveig, I believe that she is none other than Freyja. Like Freyja, she is associated with gold, and her name has been variously translated to mean "woman made of gold," "gold-adorned woman," or "gold-adorned military power."[11] It is from her that Óðinn learned; it is in her that we see the true potential of seiðr as a magic that can transcend death, and it is a golden piece of her that we who practice this art carry within.

Perhaps surprisingly, some historical seiðr seems to have been spun. There are at least two accounts of spun seiðr in the primary sources, as well as at least another two accounts in which it may have been implied.[12] The etymology of the word itself also seems to support an association with spinning, at least originally. A more recent analysis traces the word *seiðr* back to the Proto-Germanic *saiða-* and the Proto-Celtic *soito-* ("sorcery"). These, in turn, are

---

10. Translation by author. Translated text is a composite of both *Hauksbok* and *Codex Regius* versions of *Völuspá*.

11. John McKinnell, "On Heiðr," *Saga-Book* 25, no. 4 (2001), 394–417.

12. Eldar Heide, "Spinning Seiðr," in *Old Norse Religion in Long-term Perspectives: Origins, Changes, and Interactions: An International Conference in Lund, Sweden, June 3–7, 2004,* ed. Anders Andrén, Kristina Jennbert, and Catharina Raudvere (Lund: Nordic Academic Press, 2006), 164–171.

theorized to derive from an earlier PIE root of *soi-to- ("string" or "rope"), which comes from the verb *seh₂i- or "to bind."[13]

There seem to have been three main magical actions associated with spindle-based magic. This kind of seiðr could not only ensnare and bind, but also attract things such as fish and game. This is the kind of seiðr that you could use to *pull things in*; roughly half of the accounts involving seiðr are related to attracting things and pulling them in. Sometimes those things are fish, sometimes they're people's minds, and sometimes they're resources. This concept of using thread-based magic to attract things was also retained in later folklore—as was the tradition of linking spinning and weaving implements with prophecy and magic in general. For example, in some places, a witch was believed to be able to steal a neighbor's milk by milking a length of rope, and it wasn't uncommon to depict witches riding upon distaffs instead of brooms.[14]

Practitioners of seiðr were also often associated with the carrying of wands or staffs used as part of their practices. In general terms, these staffs were either made of iron (often containing cremation ashes in the metal itself), or of wood. As one might expect, it is the iron staffs that have best stood up to the test of time, and archaeologists have had the opportunity to study a number of these possible seiðr staffs to date. Surprisingly, many of them have been found to resemble medieval distaffs (with others possibly resembling spears), but unlike actual distaffs of the period they would have been far too heavy (not to mention cold) for mundane use.[15]

For many modern practitioners, the staff serves as a representation of the world tree or a conduit through which the practitioner may travel in trance. However, there is good evidence that the Viking Age staff of sorcery was obtained from either an otherworldly source or created in a grave-field and contained the remains of the dead. After their human owners died, they were often also even named and subjected to the same apotropaic practices as the

---

13. Adam Hyllested, "The Precursors of Celtic and Germanic," in *Proceedings of the 21st Annual UCLA Indo-European Conference*: Los Angeles, October 30 and 31, 2009, ed. Stephanie W. Jamison, H. C. Melchert, and Brent H. Vine (Bremen: Hempen Verlag, 2010), 107–128.

14. Eldar Heide, "Spinning Seiðr," 166.

15. Leszek P. Słupecki, Jakub Morawiec, and Leszek Gardeła, "A Biography of the Seiðr-Staffs: Towards an Archaeology of Emotions," in *Between Paganism and Christianity in the North* (Rzeszów: Rzeszów University, 2009).

human owners themselves.[16] The clear implication here is that the staff was inhabited or alive in some way.

To round out our overview of historical seiðr (and perhaps also the matter of *who* it was that may have enlivened those staffs of sorcery), we need to return to the burial mound and another paradigmatic myth. Once again, we find ourselves with Freyja, but this time she is the *blótgyðja* or "sacrificial priestess" of her brother's cult in the *Ynglinga Saga*. Her brother and king of the land, Freyr, has died, but she and the rest of his followers continue to make offerings at his mound in order to maintain the "peace and good seasons" his reign is known for. As blótgyðja, it is Freyja who presides over these rites, and the peace and good seasons do indeed continue.[17] It is here, with the witch-priestess in charge of the rites of her elven-brother's mound cult, that we find our final mythological fix point.

We also potentially find the origins of the witch's familiar in early modern English magic in this place. The connection between elves and seiðrkonur is sadly one that has gone largely unexplored by modern practitioners but as you will see in later chapters, it was an important part of historical seiðr practice. This was especially the case in Old English sources where the seiðr cognate term *síden* was often collocated with the ælf compound ("elf") in order to form the term *ælfsíden*, and both witches and elves believed to be the cause of sickness.[18]

Seiðkona, Völva, or Helrune?

Before proceeding any further, I would like to take a few moments to delve into the parallels and differences between the seiðkona, völva, and helrune.

For the most part, the Old Norse terms *seiðkona* and *völva* seem to have been largely interchangeable. The only difference in some cases seems to have

---

16. Ibid., 205.

17. Snorri Sturluson, *Heimskringla: History of the Kings of Norway*, trans. Lee Hollander (Austin: University of Texas Press, 1964), 13–14.

18. Alaric Hall, *Elves in Anglo-Saxon England: Matters of Belief, Health, Gender and Identity* (Woodbridge, Suffolk, UK: Anglo-Saxon Studies, 2009), 119.

been that they were used in different social contexts and were also sometimes dependent on the age of the story being recounted.[19]

The biggest difference between the terms *helrune*, *seiðkona*, and *völva* is language. Unlike *seiðkona* and *völva*, *helrune* is an Old English word—taken from the Old English constellation of magical specialist terms. But the helrune (*helruna* for a man) was not limited to early England. In fact, the only attestation we have comes from a Gothic source, but it's a story familiar to anyone who has heard the tale of Gullveig.

In Jordanes's *History of the Goths*, the *halirunnae* were witches who were driven out into the wilds by the Gothic king Filimer. There, we are told, they "bestowed their embraces" upon the "unclean spirits" and birthed a people.[20] Like Gullveig and the Heiðr she became/birthed, the halirunnae made a similar journey from the halls of the tribe to wander the wilds. In both cases, the women seem to suffer persecution for their arts, though it is not entirely clear what the circumstances of Gullveig's repeated burnings were. In *Völuspá*, it is only the killing that is remembered. Because of this, some have argued that the burnings were part of an initiation ceremony and that Gullveig was more likely to have been propped up by the spears, not pierced by them.

Regardless of culture or source, the end result is the same: wandering witches who are noted for their sexual licentiousness (possibly) with otherworldly spirits.

As you can see, there is precious little information about the helrune and the magic she may have practiced, especially when compared with the sources that mention seiðrkonur or völur. However, there is this central idea of witches being driven out into the wilds (who are also connected with otherworldly spirits) present in both the story of Gullveig and the halirunnae. There is a very similar shape here, so I am inclined to think that the magic and function of the halirunnae were not so dissimilar from those of a völva.

There is, however, one important difference implied by the term "helrune." The first part of the word, *hel*, may be taken to refer to the realm of the dead,

---

19. John McKinnell, "Encounters with Völur," in *Old Norse Myths, Literature and Society: The Proceedings of the 11th International Saga Conference*, July 2–7, 2000, University of Sydney. Supplement, ed. Geraldine Barnes and Margaret C. Ross (Odense: University Press of Southern Denmark, 2000), 239–242.

20. Charles Mierow, *The Gothic History of Jordanes* (n.p: Literary Licensing LLC, 2014), 85.

the grave, or possibly the dead themselves. The second part, *rune*, is a little more complex, but recent etymology connects the word to "mystery," "secret," and "council," as well as (perhaps confusingly) to "bellow" and "roar."[21] There are a lot of ways in which these different meanings may be interpreted with regards to what a helrune actually was and did. After all, a person who seeks counsel from the dead is quite different from someone who is concerned with uncovering the mysteries of the underworld, and yet these are both possible interpretations of *helrune*. The most common translation for the word *helrune* is "necromantic witch," and it is here that we come to the crux of what differentiates the völva or seiðkona from the helrune.

The seiðkona we meet in the textual sources is one who exists in a world of revenants and graveside ancestor practices—there is a physicality here that is foreign to us today. Acts of necromancy in the textual sources only ever involve the raising of the dead in *physical* form. In other words, it is not the ghost of the dead person that is raised, but a reanimated corpse. And in all cases, the would-be necromancer is compelled to go to the grave site in order to work their art. This is not a practice that tallies well with the image of the itinerant seiðkona moving between farmsteads, exchanging food for prophecy. Moreover, the interactions between living and dead are quite formulaic in these accounts. There is a pattern of speech and interaction that may be observed across the different accounts, and these are quite different to what we find in accounts of oracular seiðr.

Because of these three reasons, we can be reasonably (or at least theoretically) sure that although the seiðworker of the textual sources may have summoned the spirits for her seership, those spirits were probably never human. Conversely, the *helrune* was intrinsically located among the dead and at the grave fields. But that is not to say that the seiðkona did not also find herself among the dead and grave fields, or indeed that she needed to make that journey despite what the textual sources say.

The archaeological evidence for practices involving the dead is somewhat contradictory to the textual evidence. Despite the physicality of encounters from the textual sources, the archaeological evidence reveals a world in which

---

21. Bernard Mees, "The etymology of rune," *Beiträge zur Geschichte der deutschen Sprache und Literatur* 136, no. 4 (2014): 527–537, https:doi.org/10.1515/bgsl-2014-0046.

people potentially did not need the presence of physical remains in order to interact with the dead. Instead, a range of what might be called "intermediary technologies" may have been employed to facilitate that necromantic contact, and given the role of (deceased) völur in the necromantic accounts of the textual sources, the völva herself may have been the most useful technology of all.[22]

Then as now, rather than finding a single "true" way of working or seeing the world, we find a dynamic and varied patchwork of practices and beliefs. Moreover, these beliefs varied by location and over time, and the names that people used to refer to magical practices often reflected not only specialization or current practice, but also concerns surrounding reputation and other social factors.

For those of us looking to reconnect with those threads of Heathen magic, it is the general "shapes" of belief and practice that are important. As with Óðinn's many epithets and titles, ours too can and should change as needed. So be a völva when carrying your elf-gotten staff, a seiðkona or seiðmaðr when enticing the spirits and spinning up a storm, and if the fancy ever takes you, a helrune or helruna when treading the paths of the dead. It's the work that matters, not the name.

Galdor/Galdr, Spoken Magic and Charms

For many modern Heathens, galdr is a form of magic that involves the chanting or singing of runes. Some even combine this chanting with holding their bodies in poses that emulate the shape of the runes. Historically, however, galdr (or *galdor* in Old English), although still a form of chanted or sung magic, was quite different.

The word *galdr* means "a song…but almost always with the notion of a charm or spell…hence…witchcraft, sorcery."[23] This definition accords well with the meaning of *galdor* in Old English. Rather than chanted runes, these were most commonly sung incantations, though written examples also exist.

---

22. Catherine Heath, *Waking the Dead: A Comparative Examination of Ancient Ritual Technologies for Modern Rites Introduction*, published 2009, https://www.academia.edu/39821235/Waking_the_Dead_A_Comparative_Examination_of_Ancient_Ritual_Technologies_for_Modern_Rites_Introduction.

23. Eirik Westcoat, "The Goals of Galdralag: Identifying the Historical Instances and Uses of the Metre," *Saga-Book* 40, vol. XL (2016): 69.

There are two main forms of galdr/galdor I have found: the first is in the form of a narrative charm, and the second as charms written/spoken in the poetic meter *galdralag*.

As the name suggests, "narrative charm" refers to a kind of charm that functions through the telling of a story. There are a few examples of this kind of charm in Old Norse sources, but they are plentiful in the Old English magico-medical manuscripts. In the manuscripts, these charms were often combined with herbal preparations and a series of ritual actions that all build layers of meaning into the charm.

Often the narratives found in the charms were mythological in nature, tapping back into a mythical time during which a similar set of circumstances was encountered and overcome. In much the same way as the story of Gullveig provides an origin story for the archetypal seiðkona, this was story-as-bridge to a possible cure, and one that was born within the sacred time of myth to boot.

The second form of galdr is the Old Norse poetic meter called *galdralag*, or "incantation meter." There is a power in poetry, and the ability to compose poetry was a highly regarded skill in Old Norse society. Far from the sedately wandering clouds of Wordsworth, this was an art in which the real was set down for remembrance or transformation, and then spoken or written into being. However, this was not the freeform poetry or rhyming couplets we so often see today. This was poetry in which words were pressed into meter and refined by the process—a trait shared with other magical poetry forms in neighboring cultures such as the Welsh.

Old Norse poetry was highly developed, and there are a number of meters known to modern scholars. There are, however, only two meters which are relevant for the creation of galdralag: *ljóðaháttr* (song meter) and galdralag itself. Scholars disagree on some of the specifics of what constitutes galdralag, but generally speaking, it is ljóðaháttr with some modifications that transform it into galdralag. For a magical poetic form focused on transforming circumstances, that the meter itself is constructed through the transformation of another meter—possibly the oldest one, even—is incredibly apt.[24; 25]

Going Under the Cloak

The final strand of magic in this book is one that I refer to simply as "going under the cloak," which means to practice a form of seership that involves, as the term suggests, covering one's head with a cloak. This was not the seership of the seiðr rite; the kind of information that is sought seems to be centered more around interactions with the unseen layer of a land both physical and otherworldly.

As far as forms of magic and seership go, few have played as pivotal a role in the history of a country as this practice has in Iceland. After all, it was due to a lawspeaker (a man charged with being a living repository of Icelandic law), going under his cloak in search of an answer to a seemingly impossible problem, that Iceland officially became Christian around 1000 CE.[26]

It's easy to think ill of this lawspeaker and the practice he engaged in to come to his answer. But the situation that faced Iceland—that he was tasked with finding a solution to—was truly difficult. A short version of this story is that Iceland was coming under increasing pressure to convert to Christianity by Norway, who was also threatening to cut off the trade that was the life's blood of the island. Moreover, to make matters worse, the Icelanders who were Christians had declared themselves to be "out of law with the others," a declaration that was far more serious than it may sound today. For the Icelanders, law was incredibly important. It was more than just a series of rules to be followed (although they most certainly had plenty of rules)—it was what bound Icelanders together as a nation. To be in law with each other was to be a whole nation, so for a sizable percentage of people to declare themselves out of law was a potentially disastrous situation.

The lawspeaker (a man by the name of Þorgeir Ljósvetningagoði), emerged from under his cloak at that fateful Alþingi (ruling assembly) at the

---

24. Jon Cyr, "Skald Craft: A Practical Guide to Understanding and Writing Poetry in the Old Norse Meters," Óðroerir, no. 2 (n.d.): 127.

25. See chapter 9 for basic instructions on how to construct galdralag.

26. Jón H. Aðalsteinsson, *Under the Cloak: A Pagan Ritual Turning Point in the Conversion of Iceland* (Reykjavik: Háskólaútgáfan, 1999), 79–81.

turn of the first millennium with a compromise that would save the island.[27] All Icelanders would officially convert but would be allowed to continue their Heathen worship in private. Unfortunately, this compromise would also be the killing blow for Heathenism in the land of fire and ice, and it would not be long before the "white Christ" (as the Icelanders called him) took root.

The question of what Þorgeir Ljósvetningagoði was actually doing under the cloak is one that scholars have discussed for quite some time. Some have suggested that he had already made the decision after cutting a deal with the Christians before going under the cloak in order to ensure the cooperation of the Heathens.[28] However, this ignores the other accounts of people going under the cloak (or simply lying down on the land as though asleep or dead) in order to either send forth the mind or shapeshifted form, or possibly even discover the far future.[29]

It is also possible that there was an element of spirit contact involved in some accounts involving the act of going under the cloak. As noted by Icelandic scholar Jón H. Aðalsteinsson, there are some important parallels between the accounts of going under the cloak and later Icelandic folk necromancy accounts. Moreover, in one of the sagas, there is the suggestion that not only was Þorgeir able to discover hidden information, but that his son was known for his "second sight." Could it be possible that Þorgeir's long sojourn under the cloak was due to his also consulting the unseen population of Iceland?

Unfortunately, what we know of this practice is very little compared with other practices. There are some similar accounts from Irish sources about the practices of poets and soothsayers in Ireland, and some interesting accounts of similar magic practiced by the Sámi. However, I include it here because this does form one of the strands of Heathen magic that I practice, and my years of experimentation have yielded some interesting results. I will share my method for going under the cloak in chapter 8.

---

27. A term used by Viking Age Heathens to refer to Jesus.

28. Aðalsteinsson, *Under the Cloak*, 106–107.

29. Ibid., 110.

Experiential: Interacting with the Sources

We've covered a lot of ground during our whirlwind tour of historical Heathen magic. But our work is not quite done yet here. A large part of my process for reconstructing and building magical practices involves interacting with the history and finding ways to pull it off the page in order to examine it on a deeper level. It's not enough to know what happened in the past.

There's a saying that "the past is a foreign country, they do things differently there," which in my opinion is absolutely correct. You wouldn't go to another country and expect everything to be the same as back home—there is bound to be a sense of foreignness and culture shock. And if you stay there for a while, you will need to learn the worldview of that culture in order to live well there. In a lot of ways, this is very similar to the process of reconstructing historical practices, except there is no way to visit the culture or even stay there. Instead, you must somehow learn from their world and find a way to work with what you find as authentically as possible in the now. Sometimes you may be lucky and encounter people who have inherited beliefs and practices that are discernibly rooted in that elder time, but most of the time you won't.

Take some time to sit with what you have read in this chapter. Is there anything in particular that grabs your attention? In my experience, even the research phase of this work is not entirely separated from the magico-religious; if you do this, you will probably be surprised by the amount of research leads you get in dreams or through incredibly strange circumstances that weirdly pan out. Sometimes the part of you that grabs your attention isn't just intellectual curiosity but a deeper knowing—it's a good idea to pay attention to that.

Another thing to ask yourself is if anything feels familiar. The past may well be a foreign country, but from my experience of years of nomadic living, I can assure you that even places you've never been to before can feel strangely familiar. Take some time to sit with it, and again pay attention to any dreams. For a Heathen, dreaming is more than the mind working through emotions or events of the day. Instead, dreams are a place where the mantic and otherworldly may be encountered. You may be surprised by what surfaces during your nocturnal adventures.

One thing I like to do when still in this stage of the process is to take scenes from the primary sources and visualize them as well as I can. This is not a trance practice for me, but more of a thought experiment, a way to help lift the people from the pages. A good example of an account you can do this with is that of Þorbjörg Litilvölva from chapter 4 of *Eirik the Red's Saga*. Simply read the account a few times in order to cement the various details in your mind, then close your eyes and try to visualize it in as much detail as you can. How would it have felt to have been present at that rite? What might the songs have sounded like? What of the völva?

Finally, be sure to write down all your impressions, research, dreams, and thought experiments. If you do not already keep a journal, this is a great time to start. Don't worry about putting your research in there or separating out the research from the spiritual. If anything, it's a good idea to keep it all together (albeit labeled clearly so you know which is which), so you can see that interplay that I mentioned when it occurs. Over time, the journals you keep will become some of the most important magical books you own.

Two

THE DEITIES OF HEATHEN MAGIC 1: THE SPINDLE AND SPEAR

In the field of religious studies, there is a theory that all of the important ritual activities of humans may be traced back to the mythological actions and activities of the gods.[30] We've already discussed this to some degree in the story of Gullveig/Heiðr, the account of Freyja as the blótgyðja of her brother's mound cult, and the many magical activities of Óðinn. It may only be a theory, but it does seem to hold true for Heathen magical practices and the deities who were believed to have founded them.

In the previous chapter, we entered a world of wandering witches, elves, necromancers, and seers who quite literally changed the course of a nation's history. In this chapter, we're going to take a look at two of the main deities from whom those practices originated at some point in "mythic time," their cross-cultural analogs, and what they reveal about the practices themselves.

---

30. Taittiriya Brahmana (1, 5, 9, 4) quoted in Mircea Eliade, *The Sacred and the Profane: The Nature of Religion* (New York: Mariner Books, 1959), 98.

The Spinning Goddess

The story of the deity I refer to as the Spinning Goddess is a long and winding one. But before getting into the details of that story, I'm going to take you back to where it all began for me.

Meeting the Spinning Goddess of Magic and Fate

The first time I met the one I now call the Spinning Goddess, I was on a snowy mountain in Germany. My husband and I had decided to take a trip there after I translated a folktale about it and the "folkloric being" said to live there. There had been a draw for me from the beginning. There was just something about the stories of that mountain and the folkloric being that called to me and compelled me to learn how to spin yarn. Though relatively recent, the stories felt heavy with the ages; even at a distance, I couldn't help but get the feeling that those folktales were scratching at something much older.

So there we were with our dog, carefully picking our way over this icy, snow-covered mountain. The landscape was craggy and paths slippery, and we passed the dog between us in order to negotiate the most treacherous parts. Our GPS had failed us miserably and was leading us everywhere but where we wanted to go. Eventually, after two hours of wandering through the ice and snow, we decided to give up. Incredibly, that's when we found her, rising up from the low mists of the Frau Holle Teich.

To describe the scene that awaited us is not easy, but I shall try. The Teich is a pond on a mountain, but it was frozen over that day. Jutting out into the pond itself was a small piece of land that appeared as an island, and upon it, a statue made by a local chainsaw artist that somehow looked ancient despite its recent provenance. Tall pines towered above the pond, and reeds bordered the frozen water. And there was mist that rose like steam from the ice, wrapping around her and adding to the overall ambiance of the place. It was both otherworldly and deeply holy—the kind of "holy" that steals a person's words and makes you err on the side of caution with silence in case you misspeak.

I detached the silver berkano rune I'd brought as a gift from the chain about my neck and then set about making my way across the frozen ice toward what I thought to be a small island with the statue.

My original plan had been to get to the foot of the statue, make an offering, and then take a photograph. But when I came to kneel at the foot of that statue and look up into her eyes, my plans fell to dust. There was this absolutely unbelievable sense of presence that was frankly earth-shattering. It was deep, it was resonant, it was like being dragged downward through the waters of both the Teich and time itself. It was both terrifying and amazing, and there was this fierce love there too. It was "awe" in the truest sense of the word. I knew then that it was no mere "folkloric being" that I knelt before but a deeply rooted goddess who could have taken my life at any moment should she have so chosen.

I prayed and promised, mumbling and incoherent, my camera forgotten in my pocket. I found myself bowing my head out of compulsion and buried the silver rune in the snow at the foot of the statue in the hope that the spring melt would eventually carry it into the waters.

Finally, I began to make my way back over the ice to my husband, but the goddess was not yet done with me. A sound I can only describe as being dark, like something rushing up from the depths, seems to emanate all around me as I moved over the ice, and I rushed to the bank and back to my husband's arms.

Then we stood and waited for a while to see how the offering had been accepted. There was a sense of expectancy in the air, like she was considering what I had given and the promises I'd made. Suddenly, the moment of tension broke and the fog cleared as the sun burst through the trees to shine down on the statue, bathing it in the most splendid light. The atmosphere of the Teich changed completely and we knew she was pleased.

When we left, we found that despite our hours of wandering, we had been less than five minutes from where we'd parked the car, and we laughed.

The Goddess's Own Story

We begin our story with a mystery. It's the mystery of a goddess of spun magic who never seems to wield a spindle. Our story begins with Freyja, the original teacher of seiðr, and as I hope to demonstrate, one of the faces of the being I now know as the Spinning Goddess.

There is, in my opinion, a suggestion of something *older* in the practice of seiðr (and Freya). Moreover, this "older" is not something that is limited to the Scandinavian world either. As we discussed in chapter 1, seiðr is attested outside of Scandinavia and may be traced back to a Proto-Indo-European word that, if correct, is incredibly compatible with the picture of seiðr as recorded in the primary sources. Before exploring those roots further, we must return to Scandinavia and Freyja.

When we first encountered her in chapter 1, it was as the promiscuous priestess who presided over the rituals of her brother's mound-cult and who taught a certain one-eyed god the art in which "the greatest power is lodged." We also encountered her as the Gullveig who overcame death only to be "reborn" as Heiðr, the archetypal seiðkona and mythological mother of witches. But could we really picture her at work with distaff and spindle as her human daughters were depicted as doing?

Though admittedly sparse, the evidence for a spinning Freyja is not entirely absent; if anything, it is certainly no weaker than the evidence for the more stereotypical spinning Frigga. Neither Frigga nor Freyja are depicted as spinning in the primary sources, yet both are associated with distaffs in Scandinavian constellation names. In some parts of Scandinavia, Orion's belt is known variously as *Friggerock* ("Frigga's distaff"), and *Frejerock* or *Fröjas Rock* ("Freyja's distaff").[31] Unfortunately, we cannot take these constellation names as evidence, as no one seems to know how *old* those constellation names are. They were recorded by Grimm in the nineteenth century (where most modern Heathens encounter them), but the trail seems to dry up after that. That said, these names *do* demonstrate that Freyja was associated with spinning at least in the minds of the people who first used these names (however far back that was).

Slightly more convincing is the name *Hörn*. Like Óðinn, Freyja also had multiple *heiti* (names), and as with Óðinn, these reflected her attributes and associations. The name *Hörn* is believed to derive from *Hörr* or "flax." Connected to this idea (and also inhabiting the same group of names as Gullveig) is the kenning for "lady," *hörveig*.[32]

A collection of epithets isn't the only attribute that Freyja shares with Óðinn; she too wanders (albeit for *seemingly* different reasons). Snorri tells us that she "has many names, and this is the cause thereof: that she gave her-

31. Jakob Grimm and James Stallybrass (trans.), *Teutonic Mythology* (London: George Bell and Sons, 1882), 302.

32. Richard Cleasby and Gudbrand Vigfusson, *An Icelandic Dictionary* (Oxford, 1874), 311.

self sundry names, when she went out among unknown people seeking Óðr."[33] The name Freyja (an epithet that simply means "lady") is never attested outside of Scandinavia, but when you have a deity who in the primary sources is both said to travel and go by many names, this does not necessarily present as big of a problem as one might think. The theme of the seiðrworker who comes from outside Norse society is not uncommon in the primary sources, and I believe Freyja is no different in this.[34] More importantly, I believe that these foreign origins do far more to explain both the spinning connection largely missing from the Norse sources, and why it makes sense that seiðr was often spun.

The Methodology of Our Quest

But how does one trace a goddess of many names and wanderings when (presumably) not all of her names were recorded in Scandinavian sources? The only approach that makes sense here is a comparison of attributes. As the etymology of *seiðr* is limited to Indo-European linguistic groups, it makes sense to limit a comparative study to those groups. Moreover, although the earliest (theorized) etymology is Proto-Indo-European, we have no written sources in this language and so must rely on the textual and archaeological evidence of Indo-European descendant cultures.

As for what attributes we might look for, the most obvious associations are spinning, witches, and magic. However, Freyja also bears the epithet *Valfreyja* ("Lady of the Slain") and was said to receive half of the battle dead, taking the first pick over Óðinn. Her deceased entourage does not seem to have been limited to the battle dead either, and we find mention of other people going to the halls of Freyja in death too, suggesting that her halls play host to at least some of the dead.[35] Although she is not typically thought of as a death goddess, it would not be unreasonable to add this to the list of attributes. Finally, there is mention of Freyja in connection with childbirth in *Oddrun's Lament*. In this, a woman by the name of Oddrun chants "mightily," magic charms to

---

33. Snorri Sturluson and Anthony Faulkes (trans.), *Edda* (North Clarendon, VT: Tuttle Publishing, 2003), 30.

34. John McKinnell, "On Heiðr," *Saga-Book* 25, no. 4 (2001): 398.

35. Lotte Motz, "Freya, Anat, Ishtar, and Inanna: Some Cross-Cultural Comparisons," *Mankind Quarterly* 23 (1982): 199.

aid another woman in childbirth and Freyja is mentioned in conjunction with Frigg. So I include "childbirth goddess" in the list of attributes too.

Comparing Goddesses

This is quite a specialized and seemingly disparate list of attributions. And yet, there are a number of Indo-European goddesses who fulfill the criteria of being goddesses of spinning, magic, childbirth, witches, and death.

The Classical World

Among the ancient Greek deities, it is Artemis who best fits our criteria, or rather the Artemis who was worshipped at Brauron, Greece. The remains of the former sanctuary have yielded ample physical evidence of a connection between Artemis Brauronia and spinning. Artifacts such as spindles, spindle whorls, loom weights, and a kind of thigh guard used for preparing roving all make a strong argument for Artemis as a spinning goddess. She was, as Homer once wrote, the "goddess with the golden distaff."[36]

So strongly was Artemis connected to childbirth and the female reproductive system that people would leave votive offerings of silver reproductions of female reproductive parts at her sanctuary.[37] Expectant mothers in particular would take measures to gain her favor in childbirth, believing death to be a certainty without it. For the poor mother who died in childbirth, death would bring the greater horror of becoming new prey to Artemis and her Wild Hunt.[38; 39] She was both a helper at birth and huntress of the dead (or at least of the dead she considered her rightful prey).

But deities in the Classical world rarely remained wholly themselves, and in the late classical period, the goddess with the golden distaff was syncretized with Hekate, the goddess of witches and magic. Syncretism was not uncom-

---

36. Susan Guettel Cole, *Landscapes, Gender, and Ritual Space: The Ancient Greek Experience* (Berkeley: University of California Press, 2004), 214.

37. Ibid., 214.

38. Ibid., 212–213.

39. Kris Kershaw, *The One-Eyed God: Odin and the Indo-Germanic Männerbünde* (Washington, DC: Journal of Indo-European Studies, 2000), 37.

mon in the ancient world, and this would not be the only time Artemis would find her sphere of influence expanding in this way.[40]

The next major change of how Artemis was understood by those who worshipped her would take place in Rome, at the *lectisternium* of 217 BCE. The lectisternium was a Roman ceremony of propitiation in which a meal was laid out for the gods, and then figures representing the gods were brought in and set to recline on couches so as to participate in the meal. During the lectisternium of 217 BCE, the Roman state officially identified Roman deities with their Greek counterparts, and reified them in ritual. From that point forth, the Roman Diana would be considered to be equivalent to the Greek Artemis (regardless of the clear differences between the two), "in perpetuity."[41]

Once again, Artemis found herself with the witches. It's easy to understand why the Romans identified Artemis with Diana. After all, Artemis had already found herself at Hekate's crossroads with that initial round of syncretism. For the Romans, Diana was the obvious equivalent for a huntress goddess of witches. But we are still left with the mystery of why the Greeks themselves felt it appropriate to identify Hekate with Artemis. What was it about Artemis that placed her firmly enough in the realm of the witch that she became a goddess of witches? In my opinion, it was her association with spinning that marked her so, because as we will see, spindles and spinning have long been the sign of the witch.

But first, we must move from the Greeks to the Slavs, and to another (albeit unlikely) analog in the figure of Baba Yaga.

The Slavic Peoples

You would be hard pressed to find a more stereotypical "folk horror" witch than Baba Yaga. She is an oft-horrifying figure who lives in a cottage that stands on chicken legs—the Bone Mother who lives in the birch woods. Out of all of our criteria, she is most easily connected with witchcraft and death, but the connections with spinning are also not so hard to find. Her cottage is sometimes depicted as having a spindle or spinning wheel fixed through the center that she uses to spin the thread of life from the bones and entrails of

---

40. Michael Maas, *Readings in Late Antiquity: A Sourcebook* (London: Routledge, 2000), 175.

41. Charlotte R. Long, *The Twelve Gods of Greece and Rome* (Leiden: Brill, 1987), 235–237.

the dead.[42] She is undoubtedly fearsome, a shape-shifting witch of possible ancient origins. So far, she fulfills all but one of our criteria, but I believe it is also possible to connect her with childbirth too.

One theory holds Baba Yaga to be the "low cult" representation of the Slavic goddess, Mokosh (from Russian *mokryi*, "wet," "moist"), and Mokosh herself to be of the "high" aristocratic Pagan cult.[43] Like Baba Yaga, Mokosh is also associated with spinning, or rather her association with the Christian Saint Paraskeva-Piatnitsa ("Saint Friday"), connects her with the practice. Saint Paraskeva-Piatnitsa was associated with certain spinning taboos, and adherents of East Slavic popular religion would leave offerings to her in wells of woven fabric. Unlike Baba Yaga, Mokosh was associated with childbirth.[44; 45] Between these two possible low/high cult aspects of the goddess, our criteria has been met; we once more see the collocation of spinning with magic and witches.

Frau Holle, Frau Percht, and Related Figures

This collocation is even stronger and more overt once we get to Germany and the figure/s of Holle or Holda. Like Freyja, she is (largely) known by a number of regional names, including Frau Gode, Frau Wode, Frau Herke, and Perchta. Unlike Freyja, there are no Heathen-period attestations of this goddess. The earliest possible mentions of any of her names date back to the eleventh century. Despite this, there is still a lot of evidence that the figure of Holda (under her various names) is the "survival form" of a much older Germanic goddess.[46]

Reweaving the threads between who the goddess Holda once was and the figure in which she now survives is no small task. As a short summary of the

---

42. Mike Dixon-Kennedy, *Encyclopedia of Russian and Slavic Myth and Legend* (Santa Barbara, CA: ABC-CLIO, 1998), 23–28.

43. Andreas Johns, *Baba Yaga: The Ambiguous Mother and Witch of the Russian Folktale* (New York: Peter Lang, 2004), 59.

44. T. Gamkrelidze et al., *Indo-European and the Indo-Europeans: A Reconstruction and Historical Analysis of a Proto-Language and a Proto-Culture* (Berlin: Mouton de Gruyter, 1995), 498.

45. Johns, *Baba Yaga*, 59.

46. Erika Timm, *Frau Holle, Frau Percht, und verwandte Gestalten: 160 Jahre nach Jacob Grimm aus germanistischer Sicht betrachtet* (Stuttgart: Hirzel, 2003), 38.

main arguments, scholars point to the fact that in around half of the earliest mentions of this goddess, she is referred to as *Diana*, despite the fact that Diana was never associated with spinning. This, they suggest, was *interpretatio christiana*, or the continuation of the Roman practice of equating the deities of other cultures with their own, only through Christian eyes.

The smoking gun of evidence comes from the *Passio Minor* of the *Passion of St. Killian*, an eighth-century text detailing the efforts of St. Killian in converting the people in the area of Würzburg to Christianity, and some of the original religious practices he came up against.[47] One such practice was the worship of the Diana of Würzburg, a deity to whom the people were very attached and attributed their prosperity.[48] It is important to note here that we can be reasonably certain that the scribe who committed the *Passio Minor* to paper was doing so within *living memory* of Heathenism. His grandparents had probably practiced the old faith, and so it is likely the scribe heard of this goddess and her practices firsthand.[49] Because of this, we have to assume that the *interpretatio christiana* use of the name *Diana* was not without foundation. She must have been sufficiently similar enough to the syncretized Diana of the late Roman era for the comparison to have been made. As I've previously mentioned, Holda was referred to as "Diana" in around half of the pre-1500 sources. From the available sources, we can say without any doubt that this Holda/Diana fulfills every single one of our criteria. Given the use of the *interpretatio christiana* epithet Diana, it is logical to assume that whoever this Diana of Würzburg was, she too must have had those same attributes. But which Heathen goddess could she have been?

Here is where we look to the clues in the names *Frau Gode* and *Frau Wode*. The curious thing about these names is that although they're only attested relatively late and reflect a fifteenth-century naming convention wherein married women were named after their husbands (e.g., "Mrs. Woden"), the interchangeability of the name *Gode* and *Wode* is far older.[50; 51]

---

47. Ibid., 284.

48. Ibid., 208.

49. Ibid., 284.

50. Ibid., 72.

51. Ibid., 213.

So now we are looking for a wife of Wodan (per the naming convention), from an era in which the letters *g* and *w* were interchangeable in German.

Incredibly, this is where our path actually becomes easier. There is a text that was composed around the same time as the *Passion of St. Killian* in which Wodan is referred to interchangeably as *Wodan* and *Godan*. The story is relatively well-known too, and concerns how the Langobards received their name. It is the *History of the Langobards* by Paul the Deacon, and it gives us the name of Wodan's wife, *Frea*.[52]

Etymologically, this *Frea* is identical to the Old Norse; on the other hand, *Frigga*, the continental Germanic goddess who survived in Holle, seems to have been far more of a "great" goddess, with elements of both Frigga and Freyja within her makeup.[53] From the attributes of her probable survival form, Holle, we can gain a holistic view of this goddess, because where Heathenism ended after the rise of Christianity, the rites and cult of this goddess continued in German folk tradition.[54]

The goddess Holda (by whichever name she is known) fulfills our criteria in every way. She is a spinning goddess, and involved in both the teaching of the art, as well as enforcing the many taboos that once surrounded it. To the industrious, she was the bringer of rewards, but to the lazy she brought only punishment. She was also known as the goddess of witches, and witches were believed to meet up at her sites. Her footprints can be found in the rants of church fathers, court records, and folklore alike.[55] She was also a goddess of birth, and in some places was believed to hold the spirits of the children yet to be born in a local spring. As a leader of the Wild Hunt, she was also strongly associated with the dead, and more specifically, dead warriors. In short, this goddess fulfills our criteria perfectly.[56]

---

52. Ibid., 301.

53. Ibid., 211.

54. Lotte Motz, "The Winter Goddess: Percht, Holda, and Related Figures," *Folklore* 95, no. 2 (1984): 152–153.

55. Ibid., 153–156.

56. Gardenstone, *Göttin Holle: Auf der Suche nach einer germanischen Göttin: Frau Holle in Märchen, Sagen, Legenden, Gedichten, Gebräuchen und in der Mythologie,* (Norderstedt: Books on Demand GmbH, 2006), 76.

Weaving the Threads Together

At the beginning of this section, we began with the mistress of seiðr, Freyja, and the mystery of how she could be so heavily associated with a kind of magic that was often spun. Then we moved further afield into the wider Indo-European world with a list of criteria derived from Freyja's various characteristics. We were in search of analogs in other Indo-European cultures—goddesses who had the same attributes as Freyja, but with the additional criterion of "spinning."

Among the Greeks we found Artemis (and due to later syncretism, Hekate and Diana too). Among the Slavs were the possibly high-cult and low-cult emanations of a singular goddess known to their cultic adherents as Mokosh and Baba Yaga respectively. Finally, we found ourselves back in the Germanic cultural sphere, spinning up magic on a mountain with Holda under her many names.

Along the way, we found that a deity of spinning could easily become a deity of magic and witches, and that if anything, the very presence of spindles and spinning seem to have been enough to suggest witchcraft. Moreover, again and again, we find those spindles and witches seated comfortably alongside the milestones of childbirth and death. But why? What was it about the act of spinning that linked it so strongly with not only magic, but also birth and death?

Key Concept: Spun Fate in the Indo-European World

To understand these connections, we must first understand how spinning relates to fate in the Indo-European world. If there is one thing our search attributes have in common, it's "fate"… whatever that is.

When you get down to it, birth, death, childbirth, and magic are all matters of fate. So if we are to gain a better understanding of the Spinning Goddess and the underlying logic for spun magic, then our investigation must include at least a cursory examination of fate as understood by Pagan period Indo-European cultures.

The concept of fate as something that was spun was quite widespread across the Indo-European world. And while it was by no means a universal concept, we do find evidence for a belief in spun fate among Indo-European cultures stretching from Asia Minor and Syria to northwestern Europe.[57] Usually these beliefs center around a triad of fate-spinning goddesses that spin the fates of people at birth. For example, Greek and Roman writers described fate as something that was apportioned by a triad of goddesses who collectively spin a length of life-thread for each person.[58] Similar beliefs also existed among the Slavic peoples.[59]

However, Scandinavia, where our story first began, proves yet again to be a curious exception. Even though sources attest to a triad of goddesses associated with fate (the Nornir/Norns), unlike their classical and Slavic counterparts, they are arguably never depicted spinning, but instead score the fates of men onto tablets.[60] With the Nornir as with Freyja, we find ourselves with *almost* all of the same elements as found in other Indo-European cultures but with the spindle conspicuously absent yet again.

In spite of this notable exception, there generally seems to be a clear connection between cultures in which fate was conceived as being spun and the existence of distaff-wielding goddesses of magic. When viewed from this perspective, the humble spindle and distaff—those tools so conspicuously absent from the fate shapers of the North—are nothing less than the tools of fate herself.

Fate, Death, and Spun Snares

So far we have discussed spun fate as it pertains to the beginning of human life. And as the final fate of all living beings, an examination of fate would be incomplete without some discussion of death. Death is the ultimate expression of fate, so it would be logical for spinning to feature here too; but is it possible to make such a connection with the available evidence?

In some ways, the connection between spinning and fate, or rather the *finished products* of spinning, are clearer at the end of life than at birth. In multiple IE cultures, we encounter this idea that the resistant dead must

---

57. Gamkrelidze and Vjaceslav, *Indo-European and the IndoEuropeans*, 498.

58. George Giannakis, "The 'Fate-as-Spinner' motif: A study on the poetic and metaphorical language of Ancient Greek and Indo-European (Part I)" in *Indogermanische Forschungen. Zeitschrift für Indogermanistik und allgemeine Sprachwissenschaft* 103 (1998): 1–27.

59. Ibid., 25.

60. Norse/Germanic ideas of fate discussed in greater detail in chapter 5.

be *ensnared* with some kind of ligature and then dragged downward to the realms of the dead.[61] This ligature may take various forms but in all cases must be something that is strong enough to counter the will to continue living and ensure the dead leave at their proper time. In many cultures, the ligature is some kind of snare or halter but this is by no means universal. Once more, we find that the Norse sources differ here too (though only slightly)—instead of snares, it's unbreakable *hel-ropes* that drag the dead down to Hel's realm.[62]

Regardless of the ligature's form, it was (at least in Europe), the final product of something that was spun. In other words, it was the "final things" of the thread-creation process in much the same way as death is the "final things" of life. It is a form of binding magic that uses a snare, cord/rope, or halter.

And it is here that we return to Freyja and the magical art she is best known for, because as we saw in chapter 1, there are three probable meanings of the word *seiðr* that will sound incredibly familiar to us now: "snare," "cord," and "halter."

"The Art in Which the Greatest Power is Lodged."

In this section, we've uncovered a goddess or set of goddesses concerned with spinning, childbirth, death, witches, and magic. We've unveiled the spindle and distaff as the tools of fate, thus presenting a rationale for why it makes sense for goddesses of magic to also be goddesses of spinning *as well as* of birth and death. And in the final things of this section, we encountered the unbreakable ligature and came back full circle to the snares and halters of seiðr, a magic described as "the art in which the greatest power is lodged."

The Spinning Goddess of Seiðr

Unfortunately for the newcomer to Heathenry, the image most often encountered of the goddess of seiðr is far less nuanced than the material presented here might suggest. Most often, Freyja is presented as being little more than the goddess of love and sex … and little else. But even in these seemingly shallow

---

61. Bruce Lincoln, *Death, War, and Sacrifice: Studies in Ideology & Practice* (Chicago: University of Chicago Press, 1991), 78.

62. Ibid.

associations, there are lessons to be learned from contemplating love and sex within the context of this goddess.

Take love, for example. Love is the only force that can rival death. It's the only thing that can bind us to life (if only temporarily), even when the snares draw near. People have fought wars for love, and died trying to protect loved ones. Love is a force that inspires as well as maddens—and in the hands of a goddess, perhaps it can even make nothing of death.

And what of sex? In all likelihood, sex was a part of seiðr. After all, both Freyja and Óðinn were known for their promiscuity, and people involved in magic in later court cases seem to have automatically been assumed to have also been promiscuous just by virtue of practicing magic. But as easy as it is to focus on the sex, perhaps it wasn't the point.

The Christian world seems to have always had issues with sex, so it is unsurprising that it can be hard for people from predominately Christian societies and cultures to combine sex with magic and ideas of sacredness without getting caught up in ideas of sin *or* making the sex the point of focus. A good model for us here is the way in which tantra is perceived by many Americans. Most people in North America primarily associate tantra with sex and little else. And while it is true that traditional forms of tantra *can* include sexual practices, the true point of tantra is enlightenment. Even worse, when we narrow this entire path down to sex, we miss the countless hours of meditation, prayers, rituals, chanting, and mastering the inner energies. Tantra can teach a person how to bend reality in incredibly visceral ways, yet the only thing people in the West take away from it is the sex. See what I mean? The sex becomes the point in much the same way that it seems to have become the point in the sources on Freyja.

The goddess who stands before us is mighty indeed. She is a far-faring goddess of many names who I believe lost her spindle at some point along the way. She stands both at life's beginning and end, and she shows her children all the things that are left to play for in between (as well as how to play for them). She's much reduced from her former station yet can thrive as easily on the edges and in the between places as up on a throne in receipt of adoration. Death has no meaning for her, and even when the world has burned to ashes, I believe that she will still continue to exist in some form. After all, it's not like she hasn't faced the fires before.

The "God of the Roads," Óðinn/Woden

The next deity we're going to look at in this chapter is the first deity I ever encountered—the first one to reach beyond the printed word, take root in my heart, and inspire me to prayer. Much has changed since my first halting prayer to him in the bedroom of my childhood, but this god has more or less remained a constant in my life since then.

Introduction to a Mad God

For many modern Heathens, Óðinn is a spear-carrying god of kings and the aristocracy, a god of warriors and poets, and a god of magic and death. As one of the best attested gods in Norse mythology, his modern cult is quite prominent, and as with other modern deity cults, adherents who count themselves among his followers typically fall into those spheres of influence in some way.

But for all of the available information on Óðinn, he is not without his mysteries. The primary sources for Norse mythology were written by *skalds*, or poets, who wrote of the god as they saw him (or how their aristocratic patrons needed him to appear).[63] As the god reputed to have stolen the mead that conferred the gift of poetry, and (unintentionally) brought it into the human world, it's unsurprising that the voices of the wordsmiths are the loudest.[64] But what of the god of magic and death? What would the magic workers (both living and dead) have written of him had they a greater voice to do so?

If there is one thing that always seems to hold true with the Allfather, it's that he is who he needs to be, and because of this, it can be difficult to know and understand him enough to work with him magically.

The names we use in our lives are important, and for the average person, they become attached to that sense of self that almost all of us carry. However Óðinn famously has many names or *heiti*.[65] Moreover, these are not just situational names, or names plucked randomly from the air like an inept spy looking for cover might do in some B-movie. From a magical perspective, his

---

63. Terry Gunnell, "Pantheon? What Pantheon?" *Scripta Islandica, Isländska Sällskapets Årsbok* 66, (2015): 55–56.

64. Snorri Sturluson and Anthony Faulkes (trans.), *Edda* (North Clarendon, VT: Tuttle Publishing, 2003), 61–64.

65. Neil Price, *The Viking Way: Religion and War in Late Iron Age Scandinavia*, 2nd Ed. (Oxford: Oxbow Books, 2019), 63–68.

names are an *identity* taken up and worn as a mask, only to be dropped unceremoniously when the next mask is needed. They are *who* he is in the moment.

That's not to say that there isn't a core there…that there isn't something intrinsically him—there is. But as we will see, it too is mutable and inhabits a constantly shifting field.

To begin with his name, Óðinn and its cognates in Old English and Old High German can be traced back to a continuum of different meanings that refer more to different states of mind rather than any concrete identity. These in turn nestle alongside ideas of possession (in the sense of being possessed), and rest on the outer robes of the Proto-Germanic *woðanaz, or "seer/prophet." The óðr in Óðinn speaks of madness, frenzy, and fury, as well as mind, feeling, and poetry, and the Old English Woden has always been similarly *wōd* ("mad").[66]

A mad, possessed and ever-changing seer is far from the idea of Óðinn-as-king or warband leader. Yet in my experience, it is this Óðinn, the peripatetic seiðmaðr dressed as a woman who trucks with spirits and makes prophecies with clever words, who has the most to teach us about magic.

Óðinn's magic is often word magic. It is the galdr/galdor incantations chanted to heal a horse or bring about the fall of a ruler. It is the words that ensnare the listener and persuade them to take the desired action. It is in the poetry, story and song that sets down memory to shape past reality, as well as changing our current reality. For me, his connection with language runs even deeper than his legendarily skillful use—he is the *source* of that particular stream.

In the Old English rune poem for the rune *os*, we are told that *os* (a word that may be translated as "mouth," but perhaps more properly as "god") is the source of all speech. The question of *which* god remains a mystery in this poem, but the corresponding Icelandic rune poem is less coy and reveals the identity of this god to be *Gautr* (one of Óðinn's names), the "lord of Valhalla." In other words, it is Woden/Óðinn, the giver of both breath-soul and inspiration to humankind, who is the source of all speech.[67]

---

66. Kris Kershaw, *The One-Eyed God, Odin and the (Indo-) Germanic Männerbünde* (Washington, DC: The Institute for the Study of Man, 200), 69–74.

67. Marijane Osborn and Stella Longland, "A Celtic Intruder in the Old English 'Rune Poem'" in *Neuphilologische Mitteilungen* 81, no. 4 (1980): 385–387.

Like the Spinning Goddess, the God of the Roads also has potential cross-cultural analogs, with scholars such as Enright linking him with the Gaulish Lugus, Roman Mercury, and eventually, the Irish Lugh.[68] Kershaw, however, more controversially goes further back in time, connecting him with the Vedic god Rudra, indicating a deeply ancient provenance for this god of many faces.[69]

At the beginning of this chapter, we began with the religious studies concept that all paradigmatic activities and actions had their origins in the activities and actions of the gods. We saw this in chapter 1 with the magical children of the witch goddess who took up the spindle and distaff, and we see it now in the practitioner of galdr/galdor who wields the god-given gift of wordcraft to make best use of the god-created gift of speech.

Óðinn is most often associated with death, but he's a god of beginnings too. In *Völuspá*, it was Óðinn and two companions, Hœnir and Lóðurr, who created the first man and woman out of logs of ash and elm. We are told that Óðinn's gift was Qnd/önd, or what might be thought of as a "breath-soul." This is not the only example of this god creating life in wooden effigies either. The Old English texts attest that *Woden weorhte weohs*, or "Woden made idols." But these were no simple effigies or statues. There is a tradition of religious idols that are *alive* or at least possessed in accounts of Heathen magic. So to make those idols was no simple matter of carving. Similarly, this too was a form of magic that was copied by humans (or at least that's what the sources tell us). In the Icelandic texts, there are several accounts of witches making *trémaður* or "tree men"—men made of wood and clothed as men, that were then enlivened with magic and set to (usually murderous) tasks.[70]

The most famous beginning that Óðinn is associated with is the winning of the runes. This story from *Hávamál* is deeply evocative, setting its scene at the foot of a windswept tree and an agonizing act of self-sacrifice committed in the hope of winning power.[71] Here the god hangs on the tree and is pierced by a spear for nine days and nights. There's a lot of debate about how this form of

68. Michael J. Enright, *Lady with a Mead Cup: Ritual, Prophecy and Lordship in the European Warband From La Tène to the Viking Age* (Dublin: Four Courts Press, 1996), 227–228, 276–278.

69. Kershaw, *The One-Eyed God*, 180–200.

70. Richard North, *Heathen Gods in Old English Literature* (Cambridge: Cambridge University Press, 2006), 88–97.

71. Carolyne Larrington (trans.), *The Poetic Edda* (Oxford: Oxford University Press, 1999), 34.

self-sacrifice could have given him the knowledge of the runes. For some, it was the pain of the ordeal itself that somehow enabled him to attain an altered state of consciousness in which the runes were revealed. For others, it's the proximity to death that confers the knowledge. Given the existence of modern-day people who have returned from the dead with greater knowledge or previously unlearned skills, I tend to agree far more with the latter interpretation.

Moreover, there was a tradition of gods going to dead seeresses for mantic wisdom. For example, the entire poem *Völuspá* is purportedly the prophecy of a dead völva who was raised by Óðinn. There seems to be an implication here, that death gives a suitably gifted person access to greater knowledge and sight. Yet only the dead may pass beyond the gates of Hel (and presumably obtain those secrets). In *Hávamál*, we are told that Óðinn won the runes after nine nights upon the tree and that he snatched them up from a downward direction. This accords well with the description of the nine-day journey "downwards and northwards" to Hel in *Gylfaginning*.[72] Could it be that the runes themselves come from the dead and that it was from just beyond the gates of Hel that they were so perilously snatched?

Finally, Óðinn is a god of the dead and necromancy. He is the *Drauga-dröttin* (god of revenants), the *Hangatýr* (god of hanged men), a leader of the Wild Hunt, and Lord of the Slain in Valhalla.[73] In *Hávamál*, we are told that he can carve and color the runes so that a dead man may walk and talk with him, and he is depicted raising dead seeresses and hanged men alike.

The Óðinn found in this book and in the kinds of Heathen magic I practice is an inspired teacher of magical arts: a god of many masks, who teaches the virtues of being who you need to be at the time, and what it is to endure in order to get what you want or need. He is a god who works with a "by hook or by crook" philosophy, and nothing he does is without purpose. He is a god and he is a mystery, and he's got one hell of a sense of (gallows) humor.

---

72. Snorri Sturluson and Anthony Faulkes (trans.), *Edda* (London: J.M. Dent, 2003), 50.

73. Morgan Daimler, *Odin, Meeting the Norse Allfather* (Alresford, Hampshire: Moon Books, 2018), 13–14.

Experiential: Building Relationships with the Gods

For a Heathen, all relationships are founded on gifting and reciprocity, and this is equally true for relationships with gods as it is with other humans. Stereotypically, we Heathens offer mead to our gods. But for the following ritual, I have included the suggestion of a bottle of wine for the Spear god as well as gifts such as handspun yarn or homemade bread shaped in the form of a man for the Spinning Goddess. In the *Prose Edda*, wine is named as being both food and drink for Óðinn,[74] and over the years, I've found the Spinning Goddess to enjoy both homespun yarn and homemade bread men as gifts.

If you are new to Heathenry (or even this form of Heathen magic), you may not already have a representation of the Spear God and Spinning Goddess. If this is the case, then a simple noose made of yarn will suffice. As a form of ligature, the noose can be taken to symbolize both Óðinn-as-gallows-god as well as the binding seiðr of Freyja.

There are a number of ways in which we can create sacred space in modern Heathen ritual. However, for this ritual, I have chosen a method based on the Old Norse practice of landtaking. A landtaking was performed by early Icelandic settlers by carrying fire or lighting fires at key points around the boundaries of their land. Functionally, this ritual served to delineate human-inhabited space from the wilds where the unseen beings of the land lived. As our ritual is focused on Holy Powers, this circumambulation should be sunwise (clockwise)—there is a longstanding tradition of moving with the course of the sun when seeking healing or blessings from the Holy Powers, which is precisely what we want here.

The ritual instructions below include indoor and outdoor variants. I would recommend that you perform this ritual outside if you can, preferably next to a flowing body of water. However, there is nothing wrong with performing this ritual indoors if you need to.

⟶⟩∘ Offering Ritual ∘⟨⟵

You will need

> A candle (a candle in a jar if working outside)
>
> A large offering bowl

---

74. Faulkes, *Prose Edda*, 33.

A bottle of wine for the Spear God

A gift of either handspun yarn or homemade bread shaped into the form of a man for the Spinning Goddess

Mugwort incense (if working outside)

An offering for the land spirits (milk, water, cornmeal, bread are all good options depending on where you are)

A representation of the Spear God and Spinning Goddess

The tools of whichever form of divination you are most comfortable with

Instructions

1. Heathen altars are generally quite simple, often consisting of little more than representations, some form of fire, and an offering bowl for drink offerings. If you are working outside, simply arrange the offerings, representation/s, and bowl on the ground at the center of the space where you wish to work. If working inside, try to find space where you can circumambulate and set up your altar there. You can either set it up on the floor, or upon a small table commandeered for the purpose. There is no standardized way of setting up an altar in Heathenry. Most people tend to place the bowl before any deity representations, but this may not be practical with the space you have, so do your best. Once you have set up your altar, open the bottle of wine so that you have it ready for when it's needed (if it is the kind of bottle with a cork, recork it so that it doesn't spill if you accidentally knock it over during ritual).

2. If you are outside, begin by making a small offering to the local *wihta* (an Old English word I use to denote all manner of unseen beings). Explain in your own words what you are doing and give them assurances that you will return the land to them when you are done. It's important to show this kind of respect to the hidden people in the land as they can make things very difficult for you if you do not. When making this offering to the local spirits, my preference is to pour out or scatter the offering directly onto the ground a short distance from where I intend to work. I like to think of it as almost setting them up with snacks at a safe distance from the action.

3. If you are inside, burn some mugwort incense and carry it around the space in a clockwise direction to cleanse and bless the space. Mugwort is a purifying herb that was credited with being able to drive out all evil in the old English magico-medical manuscripts.[75]

4. Next, take a few moments to take three deep breaths. Let the concerns of the mundane world fall away and rest your attention wholly on the ritual. When particularly stressed, I have found it useful to perform a cycle of nine breaths instead of three. During the first three breaths, I concentrate on systematically dismissing the irritations of life. During the second three, I center myself in the here and now. And during the final three breaths, I focus my mind on the ritual ahead.

5. Once you have dismissed those mundane stresses, light the candle and walk the boundaries clockwise, visualizing a barrier of fire appearing around your space as you do so. There are no records of any spoken charms when performing a landtaking with fire.[76] However, I have included the following charm because in addition to it aiding concentration, there is also a long tradition of spoken magic in Heathenry:[77]

Fire I bear
Bright it burns
And ask for peace from all
Fast flee the enemies
Evil be gone
This space is now safe from all harm
This space is now hallowed and hæl.[78]

6. Once you have hallowed the space, bring the candle to your altar at the center. As I believe the Spinning Goddess taught the art of seiðr to the

---

75. Stephen Pollington, *Leechcraft: Early English Charms, Plantlore and Healing* (Hockwold-cum-Wilton, Norfolk, UK: Anglo-Saxon Books, 2003), 215.

76. Jón Hnefill Aðalsteinsson, *Going Under the Cloak*, 24–25.

77. See chapters 5 and 10 for more information on magical speech.

78. *Hæl* is an Old English word meaning "healthy," "holy," "whole," "lucky."

Spear God, I begin by inviting her as the first teacher with the following words:

High lady
Life-giving one
Shaper of luck with spindle in hand
Slayer of death
Desirous of wisdom
Far-faring Freyja, propitious and fair
Far-faring Freyja, come hear my prayer

As you speak this prayer, try to think about this goddess in as much detail as you can. Visualize her and think about how she looks to you. Build this image, and think about how much you would like her to hear your prayer/invocation and make her presence known at your rite. This is the *inner action* that must be present for the *outer action* of speaking the invocation to work. When you have visualized her to the best of your ability, then turn your attention to the Spear God and do the same, calling to him with the following invocation:

Raven god
God of the roads
Tree-bound taker of runes
Life-breather
Inspiration's breath
Wise wanderer, you travel with the winds
Wise wanderer, wind your way to me.

7. Explain that you want to found a relationship with them and why. Make the offering by pouring the wine into the offering bowl and holding up any non-liquid offerings in a gesture of offering before setting them to the side of the bowl.

8. Perform your divination. In this context, divination is a way to communicate with the Holy Powers and see what they have to say in return. Use whichever form of divination you are most comfortable with.

9. Thank the deities and then walk the boundaries counterclockwise to return the land to the spirits. Make a small offering of thanks to the wīhta (a small handful of cornmeal will do). Be sure to pick up any trash and leave the place as you found it.

A Note About the Disposal of Offerings

Generally speaking, offerings to the local spirits or wīhta are poured or scattered directly onto the ground, and offerings to the beings you're worshipping are poured into the bowl, then poured out in an appropriate place after the rite. However, depending on your location and its environment, you may not be able to dispose of your offerings in this way without damaging the local nature. In these cases, you may wish to offer incense or water to the local spirits (sweet scents like Nag Champa are usually well-received) and find some way of transporting any offerings made back home with you for disposal. When I do this, I consider these offerings to have already been accepted and consumed and dispose of them as I would any other kind of rotten food or drink in the home.

Building Shrines

If you receive positive omens or divination from your rite, you may want to set up a shrine to these deities in your home. Heathen shrines tend to be quite simple, consisting only of idols/statues and offering bowls. Many Heathens like adding other items such as drinking horns, items found in nature, candles, and incense. I like to have some kind of fire present when I pray to the gods because I believe fire and water are important mediums through which prayers and offerings may be conveyed to the Holy Powers. This seems to have been a belief shared by historical Heathens, as there is archaeological evidence that they sometimes burnt their offerings or deposited them in bodies of water.[79; 80]

---

79. Gunnar Andersson, "Among Trees, Bones, and Stones: The Sacred Grove at Lunda," in *Old Norse Religion in Long-term Perspectives: Origins, Changes, and Interactions: An International Conference in Lund, Sweden,* June 3–7, 2004, ed. Anders Andrén, Kristina Jennbert, and Catharina Raudvere (Lund: Nordic Academic Press, 2006), 196–197

80. Julie Lund, "Banks, Borders and Bodies of Water in a Viking Age Mentality," *Journal of Wetland Archaeology* 8 (2008): 53–72.

From a more reconstructionist perspective, it is not individuals who worship the gods but communities. The underlying idea here is that the gods are not interested in the business of the average Heathen. However, the gods have always been more interested in the business of magic workers, so it's good to foster that individual connection. In my experience, if you are a magic worker, they will come into your life anyway, often in incredibly visceral ways. Sometimes they come to teach you things (and then ensure you end up in a series of situations that require you to practice that skill). Other times, they have a task they want you to work on.

House shrines play a very important role in the maintenance and deepening of relationships with deities such as the Spinning Goddess and Spear God. On the most basic level, they are a point of contact, a space set aside, and a seat for the divine to come and inhabit during ritual. But shrines are not the only ways in which you can connect with these deities.

Connecting Through Thread

One of the most powerful ways in which you can connect with the Spinning Goddess is to learn to spin or take up another form of fiber art and set aside a period of time each day to practice your chosen art as a devotional activity. Spin/knit/sew/crochet/weave your prayers, and know that you are learning to work with the tools of "fate" herself.

This is especially important if you are a cisgender man and *most* especially if you believe the fiber arts too "womanly" for men to do. That sense of transgression and taboo is an important part of working with these deities and this kind of magic. It represents a barrier that must be torn down in your mind and sense of self that would otherwise hinder you.

Connecting Through Breath

In my opinion, the best places to connect with the Allfather are high places, outside on a windy day, or in places where the dead reside. At this stage, you might want to forego hanging out in graveyards and instead stick to high places and windy days until you are more settled in this way of working.

Since he breathed life into the logs that became people, I associate him with the wind. Some of my most powerful experiences with the Old Man have been in the high windswept places. The practice of connecting with the

Spear God in these places is both the easiest and hardest thing in the world. Just go outside, call to him, make an offering and wait. Pay attention to your breath and the wind around you. Allow your breath to merge with the wind; rest in that sense of connection. This is something that connects all things that have a breath-soul. It is my belief that we all exist in that oneness and that our breath-souls return to that oneness with our last exhale. From there it returns to the trees from whence we came (at least in myth), is then renewed, and breathed in by the next life to take its first breath.

When I do this and the Old Man makes his presence known, time seems to slow down and become weightier. The world around me feels more real, and I feel as though I'm touching something greater. Often there are animal or bird omens too. My heartbeat becomes loud in my ears, and I am in no doubt that it is this god I am experiencing.

Fundamentals: Balance I

For most people, finding a sense of balance is important; it's the healthy thing to do. And for practitioners of magic, this is especially the case. When you work with magic, you are working with energies and emotions that can easily knock you off your center. If left unchecked, these uncontrolled energies and emotions can eventually get you into trouble, which is one of the reasons magic has always been considered dangerous.

Of course, magic is dangerous in other, more external ways. But sometimes the greatest dangers come from within. It can be as simple as the paranoia that you're always being cursed or paralysis caused by the fear of not doing it right. More dangerously, it can be the result of ramping up personal energies and their inevitable effect on your emotions. Practices that promote and maintain balance are an incredibly important part of any magical practice, regardless of tradition.

When it comes to sources on Heathen magic and how it was performed, we have *nothing* regarding any practices we might think of as magical self-care. And yet, the symptoms of energetic and emotional imbalance are relatively common among practitioners, making it clear that some practices are required.

Modeling Progression and Balance

In my opinion, it's no coincidence that each Heathen god described in this book can be readily associated with a part of the body. Óðinn is most closely associated with the mind, Freyja with the heart, and her brother Freyr with the reproductive organs.[81]

Although not Norse or Germanic in origin, these body parts closely mirror the positions of the three "cauldrons" from the seventh-century Irish text known as the *Cauldron of Poesy*. And the similarities don't stop there.

The first cauldron is *coire goiriath*, the "cauldron of warming" and is located in the womb/reproductive area. The "warming" metaphor features heavily in the languages of law and religion and is associated with heat, religious observance, piety, and the sun. It is the cauldron of sustenance from which everything else comes.

The next cauldron is *coire erma*, the "cauldron of motion." This is the cauldron of progress and is thought to be located in the chest. Bound up in concepts surrounding this cauldron are ideas of motion and turning. It is the cauldron upon which all other progress rests.

Finally is *coire sofis*, or the "cauldron of good knowledge" that might be understood as poetic knowledge, considered to be located in the head.

The *Cauldron of Poesy* tells us that not all the cauldrons are upright (and therefore capable of functioning to their fullest capacity). All people are born with the first cauldron upright, and it is said to be the source of knowledge in youth, something we may even think of as being gifted to us by our ancestors. For most people, the other two cauldrons must be turned if the powers associated with them are to be acquired.

Here is where the similarities come in—as we will see in greater detail in chapter 3, the mound, its lord Freyr, and his elven subjects are the source of magic and inspiration for witches. This parallels the upward track from coire goiriath to coire erma. Unless the cauldron of warming is upright and full, there can be no progress upward for any of us.

At coire erma, we reach the turning point that allows for continued upward progress. In a sense, this mirrors the role of Freyja as initiatrix and teacher of the mysteries. Of greater interest are the prescribed ways for turn-

---

81. See chapter 3 for more on Freyr.

ing this cauldron upright. Both joy and sorrow are said to be the main ways in which this cauldron may be turned, but only certain categories of joy and sorrow are effective. In other words, they have to be sufficiently strong or passionate emotions to work.

It is here we begin to walk the knife's edge of emotion in magic, as one of the requirements of the *Cauldron of Poesy* for progress is also the most dangerous.[82] This danger intensifies as we continue upward to coire sofis and what might be thought of as Óðinn's realm. Similar conditions to those that turn the cauldron of motion also turn the cauldron of knowledge, but here the poem also relates other measures—among them, divine inspiration.[83]

Despite this admittedly very modern and eclectic interpretation of the *Cauldron of Poesy* with regards to the three deities we have encountered so far, I find this to be a useful model for magical practice because not only do the order and function of the cauldrons mirror the order in which Heathen magic is transmitted and the potential path for development; it can also provide a way for diagnosing areas of imbalance and working with them.

Magic isn't just about affecting the world around you and your way of seeing it. It can affect the body in very visceral ways too. People who are out of balance, or who need to purify whatever they have going on in order to offload some of the more negative elements they may be carrying around, might end up with a racing heartbeat, unable to sleep, and feeling nervous. They may become wrapped up in mind and come to neglect the heart and her brother, the reproductive core. Alternatively, they may become caught in the chambers of the heart, or fail to see a path that leads much further than raw carnality.

For most people, sensing this kind of imbalance isn't that hard. Aside from the physical symptoms listed above, most of us at least have a sense when our lives are spinning out of balance. We can often tell how balanced we are by our actions, emotions, and the kinds of things we focus on. However, I've found that there are times in life when that recognition of imbalance isn't conscious but rather subconscious, which is where tools like body scan meditations can be useful.

---

82. See chapter 6 for a full discussion on some of the dangers of emotion in magic.

83. P. L. Henry, "The Cauldron of Poesy," *Studia Celtica* 14, no. 15 (1979/1980): 114–129.

⇥ Scanning the Spheres ⇤

For the following exercise, you will need to find somewhere comfortable to sit where you will not be disturbed. This is a relatively quick exercise that, once mastered, can be performed as you go about your day-to-day life as a kind of check-in. But for the first few times you do this, I recommend doing so in a place where you can take the time to really build up the visualization and fully contemplate what you see.

You will need

10 to 15 minutes when you will not be disturbed

A place to sit comfortably in an upright position

Practice

1. Begin by seating yourself comfortably in an upright position. You can also do this while lying down, but I do not recommend it as there is a greater danger of falling asleep.

2. Once you have seated yourself comfortably, take 9 deep breaths. If possible, you should inhale through your nose and out through your mouth. As you breathe, visualize yourself exhaling as much stress, tension, and distracting emotions as you possibly can.

3. Now close your eyes and imagine your body as it is. Try to visualize yourself as clearly as you can, and in as much detail as you can. Really take the time to build this visualization up. You want it to be as realistic as possible, so really lean into small details like how your hair is, what you're wearing, and the expression on your face as you sit.

4. When you have visualized yourself as clearly as you can, allow the surface details (e.g., hair, clothes, face, etc.) to fall away until you're left with a shimmering ghostly shape. My favorite way to do this is to imagine my physical layer of imagery being rolled up like paper on a flipchart to reveal the next layer underneath.

5. Using visualization, begin the process of adding three spheres to this subtle layer: one seated in your pelvis, one at the heart, and the final one in your head. You may already see them at this point, or they may come into view organically and require no conscious effort to construct them.

Although you are working with the non-physical body here, the process of constructing these spheres requires both visualization and physical sensation working in tandem. As you begin to visualize the spheres, try to attune yourself to any emotions and sensations in each of the areas occupied by the spheres and allow them to shape your spheres accordingly. Your spheres can be whichever color or colors you feel to be most appropriate, and vary in size and brightness depending on prominence.

6. When you feel like you have your spheres right, take a few moments to contemplate them. How do they look? Are any of the spheres brighter, bigger, or stronger than others? If so, which one/s? Why do you think that is? How has that manifested in your thoughts/emotions/health/behavior/life? What about your color choices? Make a mental note of what you see and the conclusions you come to at this point.

Keeping Track

At the end of chapter 1, I encouraged you to begin keeping a journal. I'm just going to reiterate that here. One of the most important roles that journals play in magical practice is that they help you to remember and keep track of interactions, messages, and any oaths made to gods and other numinous spirits. I would encourage you to avoid making any oaths to numinous powers at this point. Oath-making to a Heathen is an incredibly serious matter that, if done badly, can negatively affect your luck for years to come. So, you should never rush into making oaths, and especially not with numinous beings.

But oath or not, you will still likely find yourself making short-term promises of offerings or work that you will do. It can be all too easy to forget these promises, and with each forgotten promise, your word becomes worth a little less the next time you try to give it. So again, if you haven't already started it, begin your journal.

It'll save you a lot of trouble down the line.

Three

HEATHEN DEITIES II: FREYR AND THE ELVES

Seventeenth-century Scotland could be a brutal place for a witch. For the accused, the odds of proving one's innocence were next to impossible, confessions were routinely coerced by means of torture, and more often than not these trials ended with death at the stake. You're probably wondering why I'm beginning this chapter with seventeenth-century witch trials, but the reason will soon become clear.

In such an environment, it's hard to imagine someone voluntarily turning themselves in to the authorities and confessing their witchery. Yet that is what a Scottish woman by the name of Issobel Gowdie allegedly did in 1662.[84]

Over the course of six weeks, Issobel provided her interrogators with four confessions that have since become famous among witch trial confessions. Because although they did contain details that conformed to the usual narrative found in these documents, the confessions of Issobel Gowdie seem to have touched upon something much older than the fevered imaginations of celibate churchmen. Instead, Issobel spoke of fairies and nighttime flights with her coven during which she would shoot her victims with "elf-arrow-heidies" or "elf-arrows." These, she told her interrogators, were from the "elfes howsis" (i.e.,

---

84. Alaric Hall, "Getting Shot of Elves: Healing, Witchcraft, and Fairies in the Scottish Witchcraft Trials," *Folklore* 116 (April 2005), 31.

burial mounds), shaped by the Devil himself then passed on to the "elf-boyes" for finishing.[85]

Unbeknownst to Issobel's interrogators (who seem to have repeatedly tried to steer Issobel away from talking about fairies), Issobel was describing a truly old pattern of practice. It is one that may even be traced back to the Heathen period, reflected in the cult of the dead mound god Freyr, and the witch-priestess Freyja who led his cult.

In this final chapter on the deities of Heathen magic, we're returning from the wide-faring roads of the wandering witches and wending our way back to the mounds. There we will meet with the mound god Freyr and his subjects: the elves from whom Heathen witches traditionally derived their sight and power.

Freyr, God of the World

Freyr (or "Lord") is a god of many layers. On the surface, he's a god of the harvest who fell madly in love with a giantess (who may or may not have symbolized an enclosure of earth).[86] He's a virile god, one of the vanir (the tribe of gods concerned with wisdom, nature, and magic), and often depicted with a large phallus.[87] A god of plenty, brother to Freyja, and apparently elf enough to have received Álfheimr (the realm of the elves) as a "tooth gift" when he was young.[88] He was considered a "god of the world" and renowned for his ability to deliver peace and good seasons even from within the burial mound if given proper worship.[89]

Like his sister, he was not limited to Scandinavia, and if anything was probably far more deeply rooted among the early English than he was among the Scandinavians. To Anglo-Saxons, he was a mythical progenitor and known as *Ing*, a name that is thought to have meant "man" (from the Proto-

---

85. Alaric Hall, *Elves in Anglo-Saxon England: Matters of Belief, Health, Gender and Identity* (Woodbridge, Suffolk: Boydell Press, 2009), 114.

86. Richard North, *Heathen Gods in Old English Literature* (Cambridge: Cambridge University Press, 1997), 253–255.

87. Ibid., 30.

88. Hilda Ellis Davidson, *Gods and Myths of Northern Europe* (London: Penguin UK, 1990), 98-99, 156.

89. Ibid., 92.

Germanic *inguz).[90] He is the best attested of all the Heathen gods in Old English sources.

Liminality and Transgression

Ing was a *wild* god, whose cult was conducted via a wain (wagon) moving throughout the land spreading his (likely) sexually licentious form of worship.[91] This was ritual as sympathetic magic that ensured the fertility of the land through the fertility of wombs.

He is a god of blurring boundaries and transgressing social norms—both a god and an elf, and somehow living and dead. The alleged lover of his sister and apparently possessed of a giant phallus, he is inherently masculine yet at the same time also tied to concepts of emasculation.[92; 93] He becomes sick with love. Thus weakened, he sends his servant Skirnir to woo the giantess Gerðr in his place. Instead of immediately agreeing to marriage, Gerðr rebuffs Freyr's servant until he threatens to curse her with an "unbearable desire" (among other things); in the end she is "won" by magic rather than strength and might. But most importantly, Gerðr is able to sow the seeds of Freyr's future destruction at Ragnarök by taking his sword (a classic symbol of masculinity) as a condition of marriage.[94]

This double-edged sword of virility and effeminacy was not just limited to the god himself either. His human ritual specialists at the cult center of Uppsala were also similarly tied to concepts of effeminacy, reputedly cross-dressing and participating in ritual drama, as well as making "effeminate gestures" to the "unmanly clattering of bells."[95]

---

90. North, *Heathen Gods*, 26–30.

91. Ibid., 46–48, 260–264.

92. Ibid., 254.

93. At least by the standards of the time. For a more complete treatment of some period ideas pertaining to gender, see Carol J. Clover, "Regardless of Sex: Men, Women, and Power in Early Northern Europe" in *Representations* no. 44 (Autumn, 1993): 1–28.

94. Larrington (trans.), *The Poetic Edda*, 61–68.

95. Hilda Davidson, *Gods and Myths* (London: Penguin UK, 1990), 96.

A Challenging God

While a beloved god (in the Heathen period as now), Freyr can be a difficult god regardless of your political or social beliefs. Some modern people may find the transgressive nature of the god and his followers with regards to gender expression pleasing and potentially indicative of ritual roles beyond the gender binary, whereas others may find it discomfiting. Then there is the matter of sexual coercion to reckon with—Freyr did not gain Gerðr's acquiescence to marry through any of the usual means, and were it not for the threat of curses that included uncontrollable sexual desires levied by his servant, likely would not have.

Unsurprisingly, modern worshippers of Freyr have long struggled to reconcile the story of his marriage, often digging into the deeper symbolism of the story in search of answers. This story is heavily symbolic, and it has long been clear that it is not simply a story of sexual coercion. The most common explanation is that the story of Freyr and Gerðr is an example of *hieros gamos*, a myth of marriage between the god of the sky and a goddess of fruitful earth that results in a rich harvest.

As a god of fertility and harvest, Freyr is associated with the sun and rain, and said to control both.[96] Gerðr, on the other hand, is intrinsically connected with the earth, and the etymology of her name relates to words like "farm" and "enclosure."[97] When she finally yields, she imposes a waiting period of nine nights upon her suitor before she agrees to "grant pleasure to the son of Njǫrðr" (Freyr), and when they meet, they do so in a grove named *Barri*, "for barley."[98]

Freyr and the Cycle of Birth and Rebirth

As a notoiously virile god associated with peace and good seasons, the themes of sex and sexuality are inescapable when it comes to Freyr. In my opinion, it is this same virile, generative power that enables him to continue regardless of death, much in the same way that his equally sexual sister repeatedly rebirths

---

96. Alaric Hall, *Elves in Anglo-Saxon England*, 38.

97. Ibid.

98. Ibid., 196.

herself after being burned as Gullveig. The story of Freyr is as cyclical as the harvests he ensures. It is a story of life, death and possibly even *rebirth*.

The topic of rebirth can be somewhat controversial among modern Heathens. Admittedly, attestations of this phenomenon are far from common in the Old Norse corpus. However, there are attestations, and not only is rebirth attested, but it seems to have been connected to the mound and its *elves*.[99] When viewed from this perspective, the burial place of Freyr is both grave and womb, gestating new life in much the same way as seeds from the previous year may be planted in tiny earthen graves and grown anew. For völur, it is with the elves and the mound where we predominantly find our focus when engaging with the mysteries of Freyr. In this place—at the old site of death and rebirth—we find the origins of the partnership between witches and elves.

From Godly Álfar to Spirits of Mound and Land

Belief in the elves seems to have been an important part of the Heathen-period worldview. However, despite this, many modern Heathens (at least in Anglophone communities) seem to find them confusing. The problem, if we can indeed call it that, is that elves are not easily classified as either gods, otherworldly beings, land-spirits, or a category of dead human, and there have been many changes in elf-beliefs since the Heathen period. To cut a long story short, the álfar that were known to Heathen period Icelanders are largely not the same as the álfar known to modern Icelanders, and the ælfe of the early English sources are different again.

The very earliest mentions of elves seem to situate them as being conceptually similar to gods. We see the formula *æsir ok álfar* ("gods and elves") used multiple times in the Eddas—often seemingly in place of the more typical *æsir ok vanir* ("gods of the æsir tribe and gods of the vanir tribe"), which has led some scholars to suggest that the term *álfar* might be thought of as being synonymous with *vanir*.[100]

The early English sources demonstrate a similar conceptual link between gods and elves. However, there was also a repositioning of the elves in terms

---

99. Hilda Ellis Davidson, *The Road to Hel* (New York: Greenwood Press, 1968), 139.

100. Alaric Hall, Elves in Anglo-Saxon England, 35–36.

of function and gender in these sources. The traditionally divine and holy elves were made monstrous and Other; by the late eighth/early ninth centuries, they were even equated with Satan and demons.[101]

Similarly, by the ninth century, the previously all-male beings gained female counterparts in their ranks. These newly-elven sisters seem to have been the product of early English scribes in search of English equivalents for Latin terms for different numina; it was often the simplest solution to declare these numinous powers elves regardless of their traditional genders. So for example, a dryad was called a *wood-elf*, and a naiad a *sea-elf*.[102] In order to make these glosses work grammatically, a new gender of elves had to be created in order to accommodate these glosses.[103]

Conversion came to Iceland much later than it did England and brought considerably dramatic changes to how the álfar were understood by Icelanders. The wise and holy elves were demoted once more. But instead of being made demons like their counterparts across the Atlantic, they instead eventually became a class of hidden spirits in the land. By the thirteenth century, the concepts of "elf" and "land-spirit" began to merge, and by the fourteenth and fifteenth centuries the álfar were well on their way to becoming the folkloric beings we know today.

What the Elf?

If you were to ask most people in the anglophone world to describe an elf, you would probably come away with a description of one of Santa's elves. This is, after all, the most common folkloric expression of elves in pretty much every modern anglophone culture today.

However, this limited view of what an elf is can make it very difficult for Heathens in those places to conceptualize elves in an authentic way, let alone work with them. The cultural frameworks that once existed for understanding and recognizing these beings in encounters are no longer there. So how can we come to understand what is meant by the term "elf"?

---

101. Ibid., 71–72.

102. Ibid., 78–79.

103. Ibid., 94–95.

The first most important thing to realize about elves is that they do not easily fit into one single category of being. We humans tend to prefer tidy concepts and struggle with liminality, but elves defy the need for easy labels and boxes. We have already encountered elves as both god-level beings, and as Hiddenfolk in the land that are not so dissimilar to fairies. There is, however, a further subcategory of álfr that has not yet been covered. This is the deceased human who is worshipped as an álfr after death in exchange for the traditional bargain of "peace and good seasons."[104] An álfr may be one (or more) of these different types of beings depending on how powerful they are, the places with which they are associated, and origins.

So if being an elf is not necessarily dependent on originating from an elven race, just what is it that makes an elf, then? What is it that connects these different types of being and unites them under the label of "elf"?

The simplest answer to this question is that they all tend to have the same (or sufficiently similar) characteristics. An álfr can seemingly be of any origin, and can come from many places if they demonstrate sufficiently elven traits. We have already seen this to some degree in the previously mentioned old English elf glosses. Numina-like dryads and naiads originate from outside the Germanic world yet seem to have been considered sufficiently similar enough with their reputation for beauty and sexual seductiveness to be glossed with ælf despite the gender difference.[105]

We have already covered the main characteristics of elves to some degree in the discussion on Freyr. In many ways, he is the archetypal elf. In the older sources, elves are inherently connected with sexual deviancy, fertility, and the mound.[106; 107] They are also inherently masculine, yet challenge traditional ideas of masculinity with their reputation for beauty as well as conventionally effeminate traits and behaviors.[108] And like Freyr, they were often depicted in partnership with witches as a possible source of supernatural power as well as

---

104. Ibid., 26–27.

105. Alaric Hall, *Elves in Anglo-Saxon England*, 94–95, 157–161.

106. Hilda Roderick Ellis Davidson, *The Road to Hel* (New York: Greenwood Press, 1968), 111–115.

107. Alaric Hall, *Elves in Anglo-Saxon England*, 34–38.

108. Ibid., 157–161.

prophetic knowledge.[109] But before further exploring the connection between elves and witches, there is one final element of elf-lore that we must discuss: hierarchies.

Freyr, Elves, and Hierarchies

Freyr seems to have been more than an elven archetype. In *Grimnismal* we are told that Freyr was the lord of Álfheimr, and that he received that realm as a "tooth gift" (Álfheimr is quite literally the "land of elves").[110] In other words, he seems to have been considered a ruler of the elves (or at least that particular group of elves).

There is an undeniable implication of hierarchy here, one that is also echoed in the eighth-century idea of Satan and his demons being akin to elves and their king, as well as Issobel Gowdie's seventeenth-century devil shaping arrow heads with the "elf-boyes" in the "elfes howsis."

Scholars have long remarked on the similarities between the álfar and the Irish *aes sídhe* (fairies, "people of the mounds"), and I believe that some of those similarities are worth looking at here in order to gain a better understanding of elves and the hierarchies implied in these examples.

Both the aes sídhe and the álfar are associated with mounds and have experienced a decline from divinity to land-spirit in the collective imagination over the years. Moreover, both groups are associated with magic and witches, and the ability to harm as well as heal.[111] However, where they differ is that there is a clear concept of hierarchy among the Irish Fair Folk that is only inferred in Old English and Old Norse sources. The idea that there are some among the aes sídhe who are *royalty* is well-documented in Irish folk tradition. Most pertinent for us, however, is the idea that one of the ways in which a witch may gain a familiar is by being assigned one by fairy royalty.[112]

It is my belief that similar concepts of hierarchy apply to the álfar too, and that there are "big" álfar who are deities like Freyr, as well as "smaller" álfar

---

109. Ibid., 112–115, 148–155.

110. Ibid., 36.

111. Alaric Hall, *Elves in Anglo-Saxon England*, 172–175.

112. Morgan Daimler, *Travelling the Fairy Path* (Alresford, UK: Moon Books, 2018), 90.

who are less powerful in the grand scheme of things. It's with those lesser-ranking álfar that we witches typically work.

Elves and Witches

At the beginning of this chapter, we began with Issobel Gowdie, the seventeenth-century witch famous for her accounts of partnering and working with elves. For Gowdie, the elves with whom she worked were co-conspirators in magic, forming for her the tiny arrows that she would then use to shoot people while out with her sister witches on their nocturnal flights over the land.

The *shape* of what Gowdie described to her interrogators would have probably sounded incredibly familiar to the tenth-century English healer tasked with removing that same elf-gotten shot or ailments from his or her patients. The early English magico-medical manuscripts contain numerous cures for elfshot and the various kinds of elf-disease, as well as for mitigating the effects of ælfsīden, or "elf-seiðr."[113] There is a continuity of magical tradition here that stretches from the Old English and Old Norse sources, all the way to the court records of early modern Scotland. This tradition is one that may be traced back to Freyr-as-mound-elf and Freyja, his sister witch and priestess of his cult.

Experiential: Offering Ritual

In the historical sources, the relationship between witches and elves is a key element of the witch's practice. However, relatively few modern practitioners of Heathen magic (at least outside of Iceland) work with the elves in this way, and almost none of us are open about our practices. This can make it very difficult for people who are interested in entering into a magical partnership with elves to get started, but there are two important reasons why so few speak openly about these practices. The first is that this kind of relationship can be very visceral and therefore poses greater risk to the practitioner. The second reason is that so few people in the anglophone world would recognize an elf if they were to encounter one, and there are plenty of beings who would claim to be something they're not if they think they may get something out of it.

---

113. Ibid., 96–112, 120–156.

The following ritual reflects my belief that there are hierarchies among the elves. It can be somewhat controversial to go straight to the leader of a people, but it is the safest way that I can think of to eventually gain an introduction to the kind of elves that would be good to work with. By going to Freyr and building a relationship with him first, you hopefully mitigate this risk.

⇥o Freyr and the Álfar o⇤

You will need

A candle (a candle in a jar if working outside)

A large offering bowl (for liquid offerings)

Mugwort incense (if working outside, this can either be in stick form or loose)

An good handful of cornmeal and/or cup of milk/cream for offering to the local spirits

A small loaf of bread and/or bottle of beer for Freyr

A cup of milk and/or handful of coins for the elves

A representation of Freyr (you could use a homemade penis-shaped bread as both offering and representation)

The tools of whichever divination system you are most comfortable with

Charcoal discs and fireproof receptacle (if using loose incense)

Lighter or matches

Bottle opener (if offering beer)

Working the Ritual

1. The best place to work this ritual is outside in a place that feels welcoming, but it is not absolutely necessary. You may also perform this ritual at home if you need to for whatever reason. Begin by arranging your offering bowl, offerings, tools, and deity representation (if you have one) at the center of your intended ritual space.

2. If you are working outside, make a small offering of a cup of milk and/or handful of cornmeal to the local spirits and explain in your own words what you are doing. Once again, this offering is best poured or scattered directly onto the ground, and a short distance away from where you

intend to work. As you speak to them, don't forget to let them know where you intend to work and give them assurance that you will return the land to how it was when you are done.

3. If you are working the ritual inside, circumambulate your intended working area in a clockwise direction with mugwort incense to bless and purify your space.

4. Take three deep breaths, light the candle, and walk the boundaries clockwise while chanting the following hallowing charm:

> Fire I bear
> Bright it burns
> And ask for peace from all
> Fast flee the enemies
> Evil be gone
> This space is now safe from all harm
> This space is now hallowed and hæl.

5. Once you have hallowed your space, bring the candle to the center. Now it is time to invite Freyr and the álfar to the rite. Unlike the invitations in chapter 2 that were written in poetic meter, this invitation to Freyr relies heavily on kennings, descriptive titles given to deities in the poetic tradition. My group has found that speaking kennings is an effective way to connect with Freyr, hence their inclusion here. As always, feel free to substitute the invitations provided here with your own.

> I call to the son of Njǫrðr
> The brother of Freyja
> The shining Van
> To the harvest god
> Wealth-giver
> And god of the world
> Bright Freyr
> Lord of Álfheimr
> Mound elf
> I call to you and ask for your presence at this rite!

6. If you are offering beer, pour the beer into the offering bowl. If you are offering bread, hold it up before you in a gesture of offering and set it to the side of the bowl. Once you have made your offering, explain that you want to found a relationship with him and why. Be sure to explain that you would also like to get to know some of the álfar as well, and ask him as the lord of Álfheimr to enable that interaction. What you are hopefully looking to do here is ensure that you encounter hale and holy elves (as opposed to anything else) so that you might recognize how they "feel" in future encounters and hopefully eventually form a relationship with at least one of them.

After making this request, take a few moments to see how everything feels before proceeding. If everything feels positive and like you have the go-ahead, speak the following invitation to the elves:

> Álfar wise
> Kin to witches
> Skillful shapers of shot
> Shining beauty
> Bright and fair
> I weave my words that you might hear
> I weave my words and invite you here

7. Pour a cup of milk into the offering bowl as an offering to the álfar and speak to them in your own words. Express your desire to learn from them and begin building reciprocal relationships with them. Pay attention to any physical sensations you get as you speak. In my experience, the álfar are more readily perceived in physical sensation than psychically. For me, this sensation is experienced in my spine, but your mileage may vary. When you have said your piece(s), perform divination/look for omens.

8. Finally, thank the Holy Powers gathered and walk the boundaries counterclockwise to return the land to the spirits. Finally, make a small offering of thanks to the local spirits and be sure to pick up any trash before you leave.

Deepening Connections: Shrines

As with the ritual given in chapter 2, the ritual to Freyr and the álfar is intended to be both introductory as well as suitable for regular offering rites. Relationships with the Holy Powers are a key component of Heathen magic, and as we saw earlier in this chapter, the relationship with the álfar was especially important. Because of this importance, I encourage you to perform this offering at least once a month, but preferably once a week. If you seek a magical partnership with one of the álfar, you will discover that the witch-elf relationship is by necessity a close one; the time, effort, and offerings you make now are part of the foundation for it.

Outside of ritual offerings, there are a number of ways to connect with Freyr and the álfar. The most obvious way is to set up a shrine to Freyr or add a representation of him to an existing shrine. Most people don't have enough space to have separate shrines for each deity and end up grouping them by necessity. There are a number of Freyr statues and idols on the market. My preference is for reproductions of the Rällinge statuette, as it seems more "right" to me than more modern designs.

For the elves, you can set aside a small enclosure of space in your garden. This can be as simple as a cairn of rocks or a small mound at the end of the garden. Over time, you could also do as my family has, and build a collection of coin offerings that can then be used to make a treasure mound for them. Cairns, treasure mounds and symbolic mounds can all become places for ritual and a wellspring of luck. Keeping a garden is a great way to connect with Freyr and the elves in general. In a sense, this is a different kind of shrine-keeping that many Freyr cultists find to be a deeply satisfying endeavor. Some of my most Freyr-enamored friends run small farms, and the day-to-day work and muck forms a key part of their spirituality.

Fundamentals: Balance II

At the end of the last chapter, I discussed the importance of remaining balanced as a magic worker. As I explained, the practice of magic involves working with energies and emotions that, if allowed to go unchecked, can knock you off your center and eventually get you into trouble. I also presented a model based on the seventh century Irish text known as the *Cauldron of Poesy* for looking at how these deities and their areas of influence may be thought to map onto the body.

But the *Cauldron of Poesy* doesn't just give us the idea of three "cauldrons" located in three areas of the body through which inspiration (and by extension magic) is generated and moves. When used correctly, it can not only give us a possible roadmap for progression, but also warn us of some of the potential hazards ahead. Moreover, it can also be used as a method of checking in with yourself in order to hopefully spot imbalances before they become problematic. This was the focus of the body scan exercise provided at the end of chapter 2.

In this Fundamentals section, we're going to build on the work we began at the end of chapter 2, moving from diagnosis to restoring at least the energetic balance between the spheres.

These exercises aren't a complete fix, though—imbalance can exist at a number of different levels and one form of imbalance can affect other areas. For example, an emotional imbalance can affect the energetic, and the energetic can affect the emotional. You may also find that you yourself are putting more focus (and ergo more energy) into one sphere above the others. Maybe you are naturally drawn to that sphere or you have previously unrecognized fears or baggage surrounding working with the deities or practical elements associated with a particular sphere. Unfortunately, the exercises provided here do nothing to help untangle the knots of emotions or kind of personal baggage that can leave you stuck. For this kind of balance restoration, meditation remains the best tool by far.[114] There's a lot to be said for knowing yourself and having a practice during which you take the time to sort through and work with any emotions that arise.

Revisiting the Map

Before we can proceed to the balance exercise at the end of this chapter, we need to revisit the map. When I last described this map, we were yet to be properly introduced to Freyr and the álfar. Our map was mostly incomplete, suitable only for the surface-level work of a body scan. However, with the inclusion of Freyr and the elves, we can now complete our map.

---

114. See chapter 6 for full instructions on how to practice meditation.

As explained at the end of the last chapter, you will not find this map in the Norse or Germanic primary sources. But as you will see, the schema provided by the *Cauldron of Poesy* combines perfectly with the deities described in both this chapter and the previous, and the shape of the magic they are most associated with: seiðr.

1. Witches enter into partnerships with elves and practice a form of magic considered to be sexually deviant. In the schema taken from the *Cauldron of Poesy* as I use it, this is Freyr's sphere and is situated in the pelvis. Out of the three cauldrons, this is the only one that is upright at birth. It is what we bring into this world from our ancestors.

2. The goddess of witches (a goddess of passion and love who taught this art to Óðinn), spends much of her time in search of Óðr (a word often taken to refer to a personage but could just as easily refer to "mind" or "poetry").[115] In the *Cauldron of Poesy*, this cauldron is described as being half-upright but can be turned by the same kind of great passions that can also unbalance you. This, I believe, is the lesson that Freyja brings and also part of why seiðr was traditionally associated with sex and sexual promiscuity. This is the road of heart—the knife's edge of emotion upon which we must travel if we are to find the "good knowledge" of the final cauldron.

3. Óðinn sits at the top of the path as god of poetic inspiration and magic. His cauldron is completely tipped over and is the hardest one to turn. But once turned, it becomes the receptacle of the kind of inspiration that comes from outside the self. It is the perfect sphere to associate with a god known for being possessed.

It should be noted here that the model provided by the *Cauldron of Poesy*, while depicting an upward track, is not depicting a track that only goes upward. Freyr's sphere feeds those above it and is nourished by them in turn. No one cauldron is better than the others; without all of them, no progression or maintained wisdom is possible. In the following exercise, you will have the opportunity to not only visualize the spheres and the energetic flow between

---

115. Thor Ewing, *Gods and Worshippers*, 84–85.

them, but also learn to manipulate that flow in order to hopefully effect a restoration of balance.

→))o Restoring Balance o((←

You will need

10 to 15 minutes of undisturbed time

A place you can sit comfortably in an upright position

Practice

1. Begin by seating yourself comfortably in an upright position and take 9 deep breaths. If it is comfortable for you, try to inhale through your nose and exhale through your mouth. A good exercise to perform while you are doing this is to imagine yourself exhaling as much stress, tension, and distracting emotions as you possibly can. You can imagine these negative emotions as a black cloud that becomes harmless and dissipates as you breathe it out.

2. Now close your eyes and imagine your body as it is. Try to visualize yourself as clearly as you can, and in as much detail as you can. Really take the time to build this visualization up. Again, you want it to be as realistic as possible, so really lean into small details like how you would look to an observer.

3. Once you have this image clear in your mind, allow it to fall away to reveal your subtle body. I like to imagine this like a flipchart that is being pulled down to reveal a kind of ghostly outline of myself—intangible yet shimmering.

4. Using visualization, begin the process of adding three spheres in this subtle layer: one seated in your pelvis, one at the heart, and the final one in your head. At this point, you may already see them, or they may come into view organically and require no conscious effort to construct them. Either is perfectly fine.

   Although you are working with the non-physical body here, the process of constructing these spheres requires both visualization and physical sensation working in tandem. As you begin to visualize the spheres, try to attune yourself to any emotions and sensations in each of the areas occupied by the spheres and allow them to shape your spheres accordingly. Your spheres can be whichever color or colors you feel to be most appropriate, and vary in size and brightness depending on prominence.

5. When you feel you have your spheres right, take a few moments to contemplate them. How do they look? Are any of the spheres brighter, bigger, or stronger than the others? If so, which one/s? Why do you think that is? How has that manifested in your thoughts/emotions/health/behavior/life? What about your color choices? Make a mental note of what you see and the conclusions you come to at this point.

6. Now, focus on the sphere located within your pelvis, visualize Freyr, everything you associate with him, and the elves in as much detail as you can. When you are satisfied, see an iridescent, shining path of pure power reach up to the sphere at your heart, then begin building your visualization of Freyja there. Once you have completed your visualization of Freyja and all the things you associate with her, then allow that same iridescent path to continue its journey to the head/mind sphere. As with the other two spheres, build up your visualization of Óðinn and his associations in as much detail as you possibly can.

7. As you move from sphere to sphere, try to maintain the different levels of visualization spontaneously. This can be difficult, but don't worry if your visualizations are initially unclear or somewhat dim. The clarity will come with practice over time.

8. From Óðinn's sphere, visualize a second iridescent path emerge and head down toward the heart sphere, through the sphere, and then finally back down to Freyr's sphere in the pelvis. What you should have is three colorful, deity-filled spheres that are connected by two paths that run connecting the spheres in both directions. Take a few moments to observe the movement of energy and allow them to come into balance with one another again. Sometimes, the simple act of connecting them (or demonstrating to yourself that they're connected) can be enough to rebalance yourself energetically and recenter your practice. Other times, more concrete actions may need to be taken, such as making an extra effort to perform rituals and actions that are associated with the spheres that are weaker for you. For example, if you find yourself getting stuck

in Óðinn's sphere, you may want to make an effort to include more embodied practices like dance in your life.

9. Allow the visualization of yourself to crumble and fade into nothingness. Just let it fall, and return to your breath. When you feel ready, open your eyes and record what you saw in your journal.

The Path Forward

Like Freyr and the elves themselves, this chapter has been complex and nuanced. We've covered a lot of ground here and laid some deep foundations for the material to come. It's also at this point that if you do not already have a meditation practice, then you should start one. I have included full instructions in chapter 6 to help you get started. Additionally, there is a purification exercise in chapter 12 that you should also begin working on as well. These two practices, with the addition of the body scan given in this chapter, will help you build the solid foundation that you will need for mediating the emotional and mental pitfalls that potentially lie ahead.

Two of the greatest, yet underrated, abilities that any magical practitioner can have are the abilities to keep an even keel, and keep moving forward. These practices are far from exciting, but I promise you, they will stand you in good stead. In the next chapter, we move from our deities of Heathen magic and out into the cosmos they inhabit. We'll be taking a tour of Norse cosmology, looking at ways in which we can work creatively with cosmology in magical and religious ritual, and covering the fundamental skills of grounding and centering, as well as presenting a preliminary exercise for shielding.

Four
COSMOLOGY: CREATION, ENDINGS, AND GEOGRAPHY

How we describe the world around us and its origins has always been a matter of interest for humans. We've always wanted to know where we've come from and our place in the world/s, and the elder Heathens seem to have been no different.

Broadly speaking, there are two different types of cosmology: physical and religious. Physical cosmology (as the name suggests), seeks to describe the world around us and its theoretical origins. The idea that we exist within an ever-expanding universe that began with a big bang is an example of a commonly accepted modern physical cosmology. However, physical cosmologies often exist in tandem with religious cosmologies, and adherents often hold a mixture of views pertaining to both. For example, a Catholic may simultaneously believe in the heaven-and-hell cosmology of their religion while also subscribing to an empirically-based physical cosmology.

The most complete picture of possible Heathen-period cosmological ideas can be found in two collections of texts known as the *Eddas*, of which there are two: the *Poetic Edda* and the *Prose Edda*. But despite the cosmological information that can be gleaned from these sources, we cannot say what meaning (if any) this particular cosmological picture had for them. For us, the cosmology of the Eddas may seem obviously religious in nature. But for all we know, they may have considered it to have been no less physical than the big bang is to us. Moreover, it is possible that the cosmology of the Eddas was limited to a certain social milieu in medieval Iceland.

Strictly speaking, cosmology is concerned with both the birth and death of the universe, as well as its geography. During the course of this chapter, we'll be taking a look at the layout and creation of the Eddaic universe, but giving Ragnarök, the final, armageddon-like battle of Norse mythology, a wide berth. Instead, our eschatological focus will rest on the "final things" of the human soul and the various afterlife eschatologies suggested by textual and archaeological evidence. Along the way, we'll also examine the usefulness of cosmology, its function, and the reasons why you should tailor cosmology to fit your purpose.

In the Practical Exercises section, we'll be looking at ways in which you can work with the story of cosmology for creating ritual space as well as grounding and centering. Finally, I will give an example of a workable ritual framework based in the Heathen cosmology of the Eddas that is suitable for both offering rites and magical workings. But first, let us go back to where it all began.

Fire and Ice

If the Eddas are to be believed, the world of the elder Heathen began with a vast nothingness known as the *Ginnungagap* or "yawning gap." This void was bookended on either side by two opposing realms—*Múspellheimr*, a blazing inferno of a realm, and *Niflheimr*, a realm of ice.

The story of how these two primordial elements came together sounds a bit like something that might be settled upon during a fireside storytelling session late at night—somehow in this apparently empty yet elemental reality, there was also a spring by the name of *Hvergelmir* ("bubbling boiling spring") nestled in Niflheimr's ice and cold. The waters of Hvergelmir were venomous, flowing out into numerous streams toward unknown destinations. But the further they got from the boiling spring, the colder they got, and eventually their venomous waters turned to ice. Rain rose up from the ice and eventually became rime, and the rime eventually began to bridge the Ginnungagap until it met with the fires of Múspell.[116]

From there, I can only imagine that it was much like putting red-hot metal into a vat of water—only on a far greater scale. The sparks that rose up became the sun and moon, and somehow, in that primordial collision of opposing elements, the giant by the name of *Ymir* came into being.

Ymir's name has been translated variously as "twin" or "screamer." Some modern theories posit that he's a northern example of the Indo-European divine twin sacrifice myth in which one twin is a sacrificial priest and the other the victim. Regardless of the truth of the matter, Ymir is born of venomous waters and may himself therefore thought of as being venemous. The *Prose Edda* supplies the further detail of a primeval cow by the name of *Auðumbla* whose origins are as mysterious as those of Hvergelmir.[117]

Like Ymir, Auðumbla is also theorized by some to be a reflection of a wider Indo-European creation myth. But given her late addition to the storyline, it's hard to rule out the influence of external cultural influences on the story. Whatever her providence, it was from Auðumbla that Ymir gained sustenance, sucking at her udders like a newborn baby for three days.[118]

Around this time, two things seem to have happened: Ymir gave birth to male and female beings out of his armpits, and Auðumbla licked away enough salty rime to reveal *Búri*, the first male ancestor of the gods.[119]

Admittedly, there are a lot of details missing from this story; our next one concerns the newly-revealed Búri who somehow begat a son, *Borr*. Equally unexplained is how Borr encounters his wife *Bestla*, but he does, and together they have three sons: Óðinn, Vili, and Vé.

Together these brothers kill Ymir, dismembering him and shaping his remains to form the world from his venomous mass. His blood became the oceans, and his flesh the earth. His skull, we are told, is the sky itself, and his bones form the mountains.[120]

---

116. Rudolf Simek, *Dictionary of Northern Mythology* (Suffolk: Boydell & Brewer, 2007), 109.

117. Ibid., 377–378.

118. Ibid., 22.

119. Ibid., 47.

120. Ibid., 377–378.

This is one way of retelling this story. Like many stories of this nature, there are many points at which the story can differ depending on which textual clues are included or left out. And even when retold with the intent of creating a coherent narrative, it's still not easy to see the usefulness of the myth in magic and ritual.

We'll get to that, of course. But before that, we have a world tree to examine.

The Lay of the Worlds

The bloody creation described above is for a single world, the middle-world of humans also known as *Miðgarðr* (often referred to as Midgard by Anglophone Heathens). But the cosmological map provided by the Eddas was far more complex; it begins with a mighty ash tree called Yggdrasill, a tree so impossibly large that all nine worlds of Norse cosmology can apparently nestle within its roots and branches.

Over the years, these nine worlds have become a source of much confusion and discussion for modern Heathens, and especially for those who participate in trance-journeying activities. This is largely down to the fact that what information we have about the names of these nine worlds comes from the footnote speculation of the translator, Henry Adams Bellows.[121] In the primary sources themselves, the nine worlds are never specifically named; when they are, it is usually in conjunction with Niflheimr, that same icy realm from the beginning of our creation myth.[122; 123] And to further complicate matters, Old English source material speaks of there being seven worlds as opposed to nine.[124]

The name *Yggdrasill* has been translated as "Óðinn's horse," but there has been some debate about this; possible alternatives such as "yew pillar" have also been suggested.[125; 126] Yggdrasill is in many ways an impossible tree that

---

121. Henry Adams Bellows (trans.), *The Poetic Edda: The Mythological Poems* (Mineola, NY: Dover Publications, 2004), 3.

122. Carolyne Larrington (trans.), *The Poetic Edda*, 47.

123. Snorri Sturluson and Anthony Faulkes (trans.), *Edda*, 27.

124. Stephen Pollington, *Leechcraft*, 217.

125. *Yggr* ("terrible") is one of Óðinn's heiti.

126. Rudolf Simek, *Dictionary of Northern Mythology*, 375.

can be as difficult to pin down as the creation myth out of which it never came. It is somehow both an ash tree as well as an evergreen, surviving despite constantly being gnawed upon by a multitude of animals and serpents.[127]

Keeping the tree alive are the three maidens known as *Nornir*, who keep the tree nourished with the waters of *Urðarbrunnr* (or "Urðr's spring").[128] That's not their only role, but we'll get to their other functions in chapter 5 when we take a deeper look at ideas of fate and their relation to the mechanics of Heathen magic.

Urðarbrunnr is not the only spring to be found under the roots of Yggdrasill. We have already encountered the catalysing force of Hvergelmir in the creation myth related earlier in this chapter. In addition to these two is *Mímisbrunnr*, or "Mímir's spring," where Óðinn is said to have sacrificed an eye for wisdom and gained knowledge of the end.[129; 130]

The Final Things

When the end times come, we are told that Yggdrasill shakes and trembles, sending out warning to the worlds. The watchman of the gods, Heimdallr, sounds the Gjallarhorn ("loud sounding horn") and all Hel breaks loose.[131]

The dead return, the world is destroyed, and many of the gods meet with their final doom.[132] This is *Ragnarök*, the "final destiny of the gods," and the sources are unclear as to whether or not it has happened yet or is still yet to come. Some scholars theorize that the myth of Ragnarök is the product of Christian influence and possibly records the death of Heathenism to Christianity. Others, however, point out that myths of end times appear in other Indo-European pagan cultures as well. For my part, I don't concern myself with the Ragnarök myth; if anything, I find it to be the least useful myth pertaining to "final things." Eschatology is personal as well as universal. We all

---

127. Hilda Ellis Davidson, *Gods and Myths of Northern Europe*, 26–27, 191.

128. Ibid., 236–237.

129. Ibid., 216–217.

130. Carolyne Larrington (trans.), *The Poetic Edda*, 7.

131. Rudolf Simek, *Dictionary of Northern Mythology*, 110–111.

132. Ibid., 259.

must die and face our own "final things." The focus of this section is also a focus on a singular section of the wider cosmos: the road to Hel.

It's impossible to speak of a single Heathen-period eschatology—there seem to have been *many* roads to Hel. The primary sources speak of a road that slopes "downwards and northwards" and that takes the dead nine days to travel, possibly longer. This journey has been depicted as being both deep and dark as well as light and fragrant with the scent of helpful herbs. There is also usually some body of water that is crossed, but in the end, all end up in front of the *Helgrindr* ("hel-gate").

The Helgrindr is a mighty gate, the only entrance point into Hel's dead realm, and only scaleable with magical help. Only the dead are to pass beyond this point and into the halls of Hel. And it is there the dead are said to rest until Ragnarök, in the realm of Hel that may also be Niflheim.

This place isn't the only afterlife destination for the deceased; the textual sources also record the dead going to places like Valhalla or Freyja's hall, *Folk-vangr*. As mentioned above, there was no single eschatology in the textual sources, and this wide variety of eschatologies is also reflected in the archaeo-logical evidence.[133] Rather than a path to the land(s) of the dead set in stone, we find a malleable road shaped by practice and belief. If there is one thing that a cosmology must be—especially when it comes to the final things—it's *useful.*

The Usefulness of Cosmology

At this point, it would be easy to write off the information included so far in this chapter as being completely fantastical in nature. However, one thing that archaeologists are increasingly finding is that Heathen-period ritual sites often had cosmological elements. Finds of Heathen-period halls in Sweden, for example, have been shown to demonstrate remarkable similarities with descriptions of mythical halls such as *Valhǫll/Valhalla*. Similarly, human cul-

---

133. Cat Heath, "Waking the Dead: A Comparative Examination of Ancient Ritual Technologies for Modern Rites," in *Academia.edu*, June 2019, accessed October 31, 2019. https://www.academia.edu/39821235/Waking_the_Dead_A_Comparative_Examination_of_Ancient_Ritual_Technologies_for_Modern_Rites_Introduction.

tic activity centered around trees is well-attested in both textual sources and archaeology.[134]

As confusing and contradictory as some of these cosmological myths may seem, there seems to have been a usefulness to them in magical and ritual contexts. Cosmology can play a number of roles in ritual and magic. Woven throughout this book are multiple creation stories such as that of *Askr* and *Embla*. When read from the perspective of an interested party they are merely curious tales. But when these stories are read by a magical practitioner, they can become a guide for how to work certain types of magic. As we saw in chapter 2, the actions taken by the three gods, when enlivening the logs and making them people, mirror forms of human magic recorded in the primary sources.

Similarly, the killing of Ymir and creation of the world through what amounted to blood sacrifice can be seen as the first sacrifice upon which all human sacrificial activities were founded. From a certain perspective, participation in blood sacrifice might be thought to remake the world (or at least uphold that creation).

One of the most important ways in which creation cosmology can play a part in magic and ritual is in the creation or construction of sacred space. One doesn't have to look far to find historical examples of this kind of cosmological recreation. We have already mentioned the Swedish "Valhalla" hall, the various "cultic tree" finds, and how those archaeological sites reflect mythological places. In addition to these examples, we also have numerous other examples in some of the features found in Heathen-period grave-fields that we can also look to. For the elder Heathen, the idea of creating sacred space for ritual or magical practice that was reflective of cosmological ideas would probably not have been all that strange.

To (re)create a cosmos in ritual space can be considered as creating a setting for the ritual or magical story you wish to tell. It can be a way of locating you and your work in the most relevant part of the cosmos for what you are doing. And yet there seems to be a clunkiness about the textual sources

---

134. Olof Sundqvist, "The Temple, the Tree, and the Well," in *Old Norse Mythology—Comparative Perspectives*, ed. Pernille Hermann, Jens P. Schjødt, Amber J. Rose (Cambridge: Harvard University Press, 2017), 163–190.

that isn't present at the archaeological sites. So what are we as magical practitioners to do if we wish to work within this (and other) cosmologies?

The purpose of a religious cosmology is to explain the religious realities of the people who adhered to it. As previously mentioned in both chapters 2 and 3, there is evidence to suggest that the religion of the Eddas would have likely been somewhat foreign to all but a subset of medieval Icelandic society. Moreover, the wide variety of personal eschatologies, as evidenced by grave-field archaeology as well as the numerous additions to cosmological ideas over the years, demonstrates a malleability that we too can take advantage of.

The Necessity of Adapting or Changing Cosmologies

In my opinion, the best way of thinking about religious cosmology is as a *story* that can be edited until it makes sense. Pretty much every type of historical Heathen magic presented in this book is underpinned by story in some way. In my opinion, story and the adaptation of story is a key feature of Heathen magic.[135]

As stories go, the story of Norse cosmology has wide gaping plot holes that must either be simplified, filled, or rewritten in order for the story to be useful. As with all stories used in ritual and magic, they have to both make sense, and be meaningful for their target audiences, or the desired effects will not be achieved. If the story and ritual *performance* is useless, then ritual and magic both suffer. Moreover, there is the added factor of *audience* to take into account.

As best we can tell, religion was a localized thing for the elder Heathen. There were of course shared deities and ideas within the same overarching culture, but there were also a lot of local deities and cults too. The idea of *orthodoxy*, or the idea that everyone believes the same thing within a certain religious group or group of religions seems to have been foreign. Within this context, it's no surprise they had such a wide range of views on eschatology.

Our modern world is becoming quite similar in that respect. The days when it could be safely assumed that most people were of the same religious persuasion holding roughly the same beliefs are swiftly coming to an end. Instead,

---

135. See chapters 5 and 10 for more in-depth information on the use of story in magic.

we are entering into an increasingly diverse kind of society that is only further diversified by the various kinds of wihta that also inhabit our world.

As magical practitioners, the audiences we work with (whether human, dead, or *other*) need to be able to buy into what we are essentially selling them with our magic. In my experience, it's no good trying to sing some lingering nineteenth-century battleground dead to the afterlife using words like "Hel," because they're really not going to react well. In other words, it's the wrong *story* for that particular audience.

The same necessity for buy-in also applies to more personal forms of magic, too. A good example of this is modern trance journeying. One of the biggest issues I've encountered when attempting to work with or attend Hrafnar-based events is that I cannot buy into the cosmology as presented. As far as stories go, it's incongruous with what I feel and have experienced. That's not to say that what they do and experience is *wrong* or that it couldn't possibly work for them. It's just the wrong story for me.

At the end of the day, no cosmology—be it physical or religious—describes what is actually *real*. Because of the way our brains perceive and store bits of information, we only ever get a tiny snapshot of the whole. The rest is heavily edited out or distorted to fit with our existing perceptions and biases. In other words, what our brains store depends heavily on the consensus of our society.

From this perspective, cosmologies are not just a way of making sense of a reality that we can barely perceive, but a user interface too. We may as well make sure our interfaces are useful.

→)○ Experiential: Tailoring Cosmologies for Ritual ○(←

Have you ever read a book or watched something on TV that just didn't *work*? For example, maybe the characterization was off or the events didn't make sense within the context of the world. Whatever the issues, you probably had some ideas on how it could have been better. Most of us already do this to some degree. We consume media, critique, and think about how things could be improved all the time. Most of us never actually go to the extent of re-writing or producing alternate versions of these stories, but the majority of us have these foundational skills all the same.

Despite the ubiquity of these skills, it can be difficult to think about cosmology in such an interactive way. Adherents usually consider their religious cosmologies as sacred and untouchable. There is no editing in most religions, and if you are stuck on the idea of cosmology-as-a-sacralized thing, then it's very difficult to start taking it apart and moving the pieces around. So before you begin moving beyond the rituals given in chapter 13, it's worth taking some time to reflect on how you personally see cosmology and the model/s you grew up with.

When I engage in this kind of work, I have a series of questions I ask myself about the dramatis personae of the ritual. These cover any practitioners I'm working with, the numinous powers that are being invited, the tradition or traditions they're associated with, and where they're believed to live.

Finally, you'll need to consider your ability to "buy in" to the kind of cosmological set-up indicated by your answers. This bit of evaluation is one of the most important parts of the process, because there will be times when you are not a good fit for the kind of ritual that needs to be performed. There is nothing wrong with this; you just need to realize this so that appropriate steps can be taken. Please don't ever be afraid to say no to ritual participation or refer out to someone more appropriate if you find that you don't have the necessary level of buy-in. This is not so critical in acts of group worship, but it's quite another matter when you're running the proverbial (magical) show.

Example: A Cosmology for Elves

To give you a better idea of how this process might look, I'm going to walk you through the process of tailoring a cosmology to better fit your ritual needs.

For the purpose of this example, let's imagine that I want to create a ritual in honor of the álfar. In *Grímnismál*, we're told that the álfar reside in Álfheimr, literally "the land of elves." But we're not really told much more about Álfheimr, which would make it very difficult to represent through ritual action and speech. We must therefore find another cosmology or part of the cosmology to work with. This is when I ask myself the following questions:

1. Who am I working with?
2. What kind of beings/Who?
3. What tradition?

4. Where do they live?

5. Can I buy into that?

For my imaginary elf ritual, the answers I would give to those questions would probably look something like this:

1. Who am I working with? *Alone.*

2. What kind of beings/Who? *The elves as a collective group.*

3. What tradition? *Germanic/Norse.*

4. Where do they live? *In the textual sources, Álfheimr or the mound. In Icelandic folk tradition, in "elf churches" in the landscape.*

5. Can I buy into that? *The mound, yes. My primary association with elves is the mound. But Álfheimr and elf churches, not so much (at least outside of Iceland).*

From these answers, I might design my sacred space with the burial mound in mind. As burial mounds are circular and often moated, the sacred space will also be constructed in the form of a circle and its boundaries marked out with water. (This is not so dissimilar from the modern traditional practice of laying a compass.) Finally, the liturgy used will reinforce the idea of working within the mound, but that is where my concern for geography will end. In my experience, the more precise you try to be about where such a mound is located, the more convoluted your ritual will become. There can be such a thing as too much detail.[136]

Fundamentals: Cosmology in Personal Magical Practice (Grounding and Centering)

In a lot of ways, cosmology underpins much of what we do as magical practitioners. We look to creation stories for clues on magic, the lay of the worlds in our journeying practices, and the trees when grounding and centering ourselves.

Although not considered Heathen, grounding and centering are key magical skills. They're basic skills that never cease to be of use. The ungrounded

---

136. See chapter 13 for more examples of cosmological elements in ritual.

person can be filled with excess energy inadvertently taken on from people and places, or feel a sense of disconnect and lethargy. They can, as the saying goes, seem away with the fairies, not quite on this earth. Conversely, the uncentered person can be scattered, as though their thoughts and energies are spread out everywhere but where they actually are.

Most people ground and center after trance journeying or after noticing that something is amiss. I would advise you to ground and center at least once a day just as a matter of course. You may come to find that you choose different methods depending on why you are grounding and centering. For example, if you are recently returned from a trance journey, you may opt for more physical methods of grounding and centering such as movement and the consumption of salt. But if you are grounding and centering after noticing something is amiss or as a matter of course, you may decide to use more meditative means.

The most common meditation for grounding and centering is inherently cosmological in nature. In it, you imagine yourself a tree and root down deep before reaching up with your branches to touch the sky. For people whose religious cosmology is centered around a tree and whose forebears were perhaps believed to have been born of trees, the act of imagining oneself a tree can be powerful.

Although the most common, tree-based meditations are not the only kind of grounding and centering meditation you can do. Some people see grounding and centering as separate things and prefer to use two different meditations. Others will meditate as a tree to ground but verbally call their scattered pieces back. As with all things based in cosmology, it's the effectiveness of the story that's most important.

The following meditation is a tree-based one, but please feel free to substitute something you like better:

⤙ Tree People: Grounding and Centering Meditation ⤚

You will need

10 to 15 minutes of uninterrupted time to yourself

Somewhere comfortable to sit

Practice

1. Seat yourself comfortably in an upright position—you should ideally be in a straight-backed position for this exercise. Once you are comfortable and have taken a few moments to settle, then take nine deep breaths, breathing in through your nose and out through your mouth. As you breathe, imagine your stress and tension leaving with each breath and calm replacing it every time you breathe in.

2. Now become aware of your feet on the ground: feel them become roots that dig down deep into the rich, loamy soil of the earth. This isn't hard for you. In a sense, you are borne of trees, so lean into that connection. Feel your roots become more wooden and tree-like as they root down, digging deeper as you work. And when you feel you have gone as deeply as you need to, simply stop. Rest there and release any spare energy you are carrying into the earth where it may be grounded out. At this point you may also feel a sense of reconnection, so take a few moments to enjoy the feeling before moving on to the next step.

3. When you are ready, begin the process of imagining your arms becoming branches and reaching up to the sky. You do not need to physically reach up in order to do this, just imagine your arms becoming branches and imagine them reaching up as high as they possibly can. Some people find this part of the visualization harder than the first part, so take your time with it and really build in the details.

4. As you stretch your branches upward, imagine all your scattered and uncentered parts returning to you, unable to maintain their distance as you reach upward and snapping back like an elastic band. If that imagery doesn't work for you, you can also use your breath by imagining those parts of yourself that need to return being pulled in with each in-breath and tacked down so as not to be breathed out once more. Whichever you choose, keep doing this until you feel as though you have fully returned to yourself.

5. Try to maintain the visualization for as long as you can. When you are ready to finish, simply open your eyes and go about your day.

Fundamentals: The Mechanics of Shielding

The final basic skill covered in this chapter is shielding. Like grounding and centering, shielding isn't considered to be particularly Heathen (or at least there is no mention of it in any of the primary sources). Quite frankly, shielding has saved my behind more times than I can count over the years, so I'm going to stick with my shields and hope that you adopt this policy too.

It's hard to overstate the importance of good shielding practices. The world we live in isn't always kind, and when magic comes into the picture, it can become unkind in different ways. If you are a person with the right kind of talent, you become attractive to a multitude of different beings from the moment you work your first spell or ritual. They become drawn to you like moths to lamps. Moreover, other practitioners will be able to sense you too. They may not know what you do exactly, but nine times out of ten, they will figure you out without you saying a word. There's a saying that we can "smell" our own, and that has often proven to be the case in my experience. Without good shielding, all of this can become really messy and destructive really quickly.

Unlike with grounding and centering, I am not going to give you detailed instructions for shielding. The kind of shields you have and the form they take is best kept secret from other practitioners. Not everyone you meet will be for you, even if they claim to be so at first, so never tell anyone else the specifics of your shields. And along those lines, never use a shielding exercise from a book without adaptation. A form of shielding taken from a book in which you have a disco egg is a little bit like using "abc" or the word "password" as a password. If many people have it and use it, then it's far more likely that someone will figure out what you're using and how to crack it.

What follows are ideas on how to create your own shields and the underlying mechanics of that process. The main objective of any personal shield is to serve as a protective barrier between yourself and magical/non-physical threats. As magically created objects, shields are composed of three parts: visualization, will, and an energy source. Moreover, the more you practice your shields, the more effective and spontaneous they become. Because when you create shields for yourself, you're effectively adding something to your personal cosmology.

The visualization component is the area that provides the most opportunity for customization. This is where you really want to consider the imagery you use to shape and direct the energy and the potential ways in which that imagery could be destroyed. Moreover, whatever you choose for this has to be the right imagery for you. It's no good going with imagery if you find it hard to visualize or get a feel for it. So be sure to choose something that is meaningful and easy for you.

Following closely behind visualization for customizability is the energy source you choose. Some people choose to tack on energy-directing components to grounding and centering meditations in order to power their shields. Others prefer to use energy from the world around them or even design their shields so that anything flung at them magically sticks to and becomes a further source of power for their shields.

When creating a new shielding process, I prefer to begin with my chosen energy source and then shape it into the desired form using the visualization as a guide. A lot of people begin with the visualization and then add energy as they build the imagery. In my experience, it's better to focus on and develop the ability to manipulate energy first because when things are going wrong, it can be hard to concentrate on building a visualization. All too often, distractions such as psychic and/or sensory information about whatever you're dealing with, in addition to intense emotions, can make it very difficult to work in this way.

However, when you train to work with energy first, not only is the barrier almost instantaneous, with little-to-no conceptual thought, but it can be bolstered with the energy from emotions that are otherwise distracting. Visualizations can always be used to shape the energy into more long-term shields later.

As previously said, I am not a fan of giving specific shielding exercises, although there is one exception to this rule. What follows is a *preliminary* exercise. In other words, it's designed to help you practice the foundational skills of shielding such as energy manipulation and visualization. I recommend doing this several times before attempting to build your own shields; additionally, it is helpful to continue practicing it as an energy manipulation/visualization exercise whenever you think about it.

⟶⟩∘ Preliminary Shielding Skills Exercise ∘⟨⟵

You will need

10 to 15 minutes of uninterrupted time to yourself

Somewhere comfortable where you can sit in an upright position

Practice

1. Cup your palms and hold them so they are roughly three inches apart with the palms facing inward on each other. Now rest your focus on the area below your navel where your reproductive organs lie. Feel them as a constant and renewable source of energy, and as you do so, use your abdominal muscles to push the energy up to your heart and then down into your hands, where it takes the form of a small gray ball.

2. Continue to build the ball of energy, allowing your will to marshal the flow of energy from below the navel to between your palms. Try to visualize the ball as clearly as you can. When I do this kind of work, I feel energy as an electric tingle moving through my body that can be either hot or cold depending on the kind of energy being worked with. Energy can feel different for different people, so take note of any sensations you experience while working on this exercise. If you feel nothing, there are further energy sensing exercises in chapter 6 to help you recognize and develop your ability to feel energy in this way.

3. When you feel as though the ball is as real as you can make it, take a deep breath in and push it into your body through the solar plexus, pulling it into you as you inhale. Visualize the gray ball inside you as it enters. On your out breath, "see" and feel it expand beyond the limits of your body to create a bubble around you. The sensation you should feel as you expand the ball outward around you should feel like pushing—as though you somehow got into the center of the ball and then pushed it out around you to form the bubble. If you feel nothing, start over and try again. It may take you a few attempts to get the hang of coordinating the energy manipulation and visualization with your breath.

As always, the key is consistent and regular practice with these kinds of skills. When I was first taught this exercise it was around a campfire in the middle of nowhere, and didn't think much of it at the time. It seemed too limited to me and too overt for practical use, and so it fell from my rotation for a while. But over the years I've come to appreciate this exercise for the teaching tool it can be—not only does it help to train the coordination of energy, visualization, and will with the breath, it's also highly customizable. You can use it to experiment with pulling from different energy sources and augmenting their efficacy with emotional energy. You can also work on visualizing different things between the palms of your hands, and you can eventually move toward simply building the shield around you instead of pushing it into your body first.

In other words, it can be a helpful springboard toward developing your own shielding process—so why not build your personal fortress today?

The Path Forward

In this chapter, we've taken a deep dive into cosmology and the usefulness of cosmology for magic and ritual practice. And as we have seen, the ability to work with and within one or multiple cosmologies is one of the foundational skills of working magic within an inspirited world. It can underpin everything from ritual design to personal magical practices such as grounding and centering. This approach is not so different from the use of magical paradigms in chaos magic.

In the next chapter, we're going to be taking a look at some more foundations of the magical Heathen's world and concepts such as fate, luck, and wholeness. Well would ye know yet more?

Five

FOUNDATIONAL IDEAS IN HEATHEN MAGIC

I've found over the years that there are a number of reasons people get into researching and experimenting with historical magic. For me, it was that initial draw to the word *seiðr* and a deep sense of recognition experienced upon first seeing the word. After encountering modern seiðr traditions both online and in the workshop format, however, I came to feel a sense of disconnect between those modern traditions, and the hints of Heathen-period worldview I was uncovering in textual sources. It did not seem logical to me that the magical traditions of a culture would be rooted in anything other than the worldview of the culture itself. This may seem like a basic realization nowadays, but the conversations at the time about magical practices as belonging to culture were yet to be had. And with this realization came a change of approach. Instead of simply trying to recreate actions and activities, I also began the process of working to uncover as much as I could about concepts like "fate," "soul," and "luck"... in other words, the kind of concepts that might pertain to magic. My working theory at the time was that if I could understand how the elder or historical Heathen understood these concepts, I might not only gain a better understanding of Heathen-period magic but also be able to create new magic from within the framework of that *system*.

The word *system* is a good one to use here when discussing magical traditions. Systems have procedures, and function in accordance with certain foundational ideas or (more accurately) *principles*. In this chapter, we're going to take a look at some of the concepts I believe to be foundational principles of Heathen magic, as well as examples of how you might see them playing out in your life and practice. Finally, we'll end the chapter with a set of exercises to help you get started working with the material presented here in a more intentional way.

Foundational Principle I: Hæl/Heill

I first encountered this concept in the Old English magico-medical manuscripts, but it exists in almost exactly the same way in the Old Norse sources as well.[137]

Ostensibly, the Old English word *hæl* and its Old Norse cognate *heill* describe physical health. However, unlike our modern word, the Old English and Old Norse words for "health" encompassed a range of ideas that stretched far beyond the physical and into the holy. To be *hæl* or *heill* was to have physical health, but it was also luck, wholeness, and whole-making, as well as well-being, prosperity, mental or spiritual health, and auspicious omens. Grammatically speaking, both *hæl* and *heill* can be used as nouns and adjectives. However, as a speaker of modern English, I find it strange to use *hæl* as a noun when using the Old English term for this concept. I'm far too accustomed to thinking of the modern derivation of hæl ("hale," as in to be "hale and hearty") as an adjective, and so I tend to use *hælu* (a word with the same meanings) when using the word as a noun.[138]

Additionally, hæl/heill are not just words—the way in which a culture conceives of health also informs the way in which sickness is viewed and treated. For example, in our modern world where the word "health" almost always refers to physical health, sickness almost always has a physical cause, and healing must therefore be focused on the physical body. The idea of healing as a magical skill would probably be quite foreign to most people in the

---

137. Geir T. Zoëga, *A Concise Dictionary of Old Icelandic* (Oxford: Clarendon Press, 1910), 190.

138. Joseph Bosworth and T. Northcote Toller, *An Anglo-Saxon Dictionary, Based on the Manuscript Collections of the Late Joseph Bosworth (Supplement)* (London: Oxford University Press, 1955), 497.

US and UK today. However, as we have seen, health (and sickness) were not considered to be purely physical to the early English and Norse cultures; as you might expect, the view found here is more holistic regarding sickness, health, and healing.

To the early English and Norse, sickness was often conceived of as being the product of an invading force that either detracted from the hæl/heill of a person or introduced an unhæl element (the opposite hæl) to the patient's body. For the early English, at least, these invading forces could be everything from curses to attacks by elves (a belief also shared by the Norse), the product of "worms," or any one of the other creatures they believed capable of attacking a human.[139; 140]

In order to make the person well again, a battle had to be fought between the leech (an old word for "healer") and whichever invading or attacking force was making the patient unwell. It was an inherently magical and animistic form of healing that cursed and banished the illness while working to restore the patient to a hæl/heill state once more.[141]

It is here we get into the usefulness of this concept for modern practitioners of magic. As stated before, hælu/heill isn't just health; it is often the very quality that we manipulate in our magic and underpins interactions between humans, the unseen, and the land.

Hæl/Heill in Magic and Life

When I discovered this more expansive concept of health, I began to gain a new understanding of some of the experiences I'd had in both magic and life. But most importantly, I began to assess people, places, and circumstances through this framework too.

For example, when deciding if I want to participate in a magical group or practice, I take some time to consider the people involved and how their lives look. Some practices are inherently hæl/heill and are a source of strength and healing to those who participate in them. Generally speaking, even where

139. Stephen Pollington, *Leechcraft*, 453–468.

140. Thomas A. DuBois, *Nordic Religions in the Viking Age* (Philadelphia: University of Pennsylvania Press, 1999), 102.

141. Stephen Pollington, *Leechcraft*, 453–468.

chronic illness and financial difficulties are present, you'll find that the people who are involved in those groups and/or practices do better than people in comparable situations outside of those groups and practices. Conversely, you may find that the people within a group or practice do worse in both life and health after becoming involved. In these cases, the practices are clearly unhæl and negatively affecting the group members. A variant on this I have also seen is when the leader of a group or teacher of a specific practice shows no signs of sickness or ill luck, but their group members are plagued with issues. These are all examples of how unhælu might look in real-world terms.

Along similar lines, if you are ever called upon to deal with curses, or are unfortunately the recipient of a curse yourself, one of the first things you will likely notice is that your health suffers with your luck. This is because health and at least some kinds of luck are inseparable—they are both hælu—and if you negatively manipulate the luck of a person, their physical health is sure to reflect that.

However, "luck" didn't mean the same thing we now understand it to mean as modern English speakers. There are some nuances present in the older view that need to be understood if we are to gain a fuller picture of what it is to be hæl/heill and the subtle qualities we manipulate when we practice magic.

Foundational Principle II: Luck

In the modern world, "luck" is a phenomenon sometimes used to explain events that would otherwise be considered improbable. We may say that somebody is lucky when they survive a deadly situation seemingly against the odds; a person may be said to have been born with a certain kind of luck that only operates in limited situations. For example, my mother has incredible success when it comes to winning competitions for completely weird and useless prizes, but I cannot think of a single time when she won something actually good.

For the elder Heathen, luck was less of a phenomenon for explaining away improbable outcomes. It could be something that was both intrinsic and extrinsic to a person, as well as a quality that could be personified externally. Moreover, depending on circumstances and ancestry, a person could have multiple types of luck. In this section, we're going to take a look at these various types of luck before looking at a few examples of how these types of luck may manifest in your life and magic.

Intrinsic Luck (Gæfa, Gipta, and Heill)

The first kind of luck is what we might call "intrinsic luck," or luck as an inherent quality that a person is born with in much the same way as they might be born with brown eyes or curly hair. This kind of internal luck was often referred to as *gæfa* or *gipta* in the primary sources, both words that are derived from "gift." You could also use the word *heill* to refer to intrinsic luck, but (and this is where things become a little confusing), *heill* also carried a connotation of omen when used in these contexts.[142]

Heill could be intrinsic to a person, but it also seems to have been a form of luck that could also be extrinsic to a person, or at the very least affected by external circumstances. For example, the word *heill* appears in phrases pertaining to ideas such as being "forsaken by luck," having a "turn of luck," or even to refer to runic talismans.[143]

Extrinsic Luck (Fylgjur and Hamingja)

But there were other sources of luck for the elder Heathen. These might be seen as existing independently of humans, yet functioning as bringers of luck for those whom they kept watch over. One such type of luck-bringing was a class referred to as *fylgjur*, or "accompanying beings." There are two different types of fylgjur in Old Norse sources, but only one is associated with luck: the *fylgjukona* ("accompanying woman"), a female spirit who acts and speaks as a guardian goddess for the family line with which she is associated.[144]

But not all forms of extrinsic luck or luck-related beings existed independently of a person. Bridging the gap between independently-existing and intrinsic forms of luck is the *hamingja*. The word *hamingja* is believed to derive from *hamr-gengja*, and the hamingja itself was considered to have form and personality in much the same way as a *fylgja* (the singular form of *fylgjur*). The

---

142. Bettina Sejbjerg Sommer, "The Norse Concept of Luck," *Scandinavian Studies* 79, no. 3 (2007): 279.

143. Richard Cleasby and Gudbrand Vigfusson, *An Icelandic-English Dictionary* (London: Clarendon Press, 1874), 248.

144. Sommer, "The Norse Concept of Luck," 279–280.

hamr compound is discussed in greater depth in the section on the soul; for now, we just need to know that the word *hamr* refers to the embodied expression of a thought or mind, and *gengja* to "luck," "help," and "success."[145] As far as we can tell, the original hamingja seems to have been the personified luck of a person, but as time went on became more like gæfa/gipta.[146]

In this section, you've been introduced to a lot of new terminology. But please do not worry if you cannot remember it all. As we saw with hamingja, these concepts were not static, but rather changed over time. The bare minimum takeaway from this section is an understanding that luck is both intrinsic and extrinsic, that it may be brought from outside sources by externally existing beings, and that it may also be personified and exist externally.

Luck in Magic and Life

There are several key ways in which the various kinds of luck play out in magic and life. As mentioned at the beginning of this section, most people are lucky to some degree, and a lot of people (like my mother) are lucky in some ways but not others. Rarely you may encounter a person who is someone the elder Heathen may have referred to as a "person of luck," or someone who was more or less equally lucky in all areas. For such a person, luck was thought to be both the cause and expression of success, manifesting itself in beauty and desired skills. There is an almost magical quality to this luck too. Things always seem to work out for the lucky person, and events fall into place in accordance with their desires.[147]

It's easy to see the relevance of luck to a magic worker here. Luck is useful for everyone, but for magic workers who actively seek to shape events and circumstances, it takes on an added importance—because when it comes to creating physical change in the world, the magical practitioner who is lucky is always going to be more effective than someone who is "luck-less."

But it's important to keep in mind here that not all forms of Heathen magic are focused on creating tangible changes in life and circumstances. Seiðr, for example, can enable a practitioner to ensnare and manipulate every-

---

145. Richard Cleasby and Gudbrand Vigfusson, *An Icelandic-English Dictionary*, 196, 236.

146. Bettina Sejbjerg Sommer, "The Norse Concept of Luck," 281–282.

147. Ibid, 275.

thing from the perceptions and luck of others to various types of numinous beings. So even unlucky practitioners can have visions and launch effective psychic attacks with seiðr.

Generally speaking, as a practitioner, it's almost never bad to have luck. We all have what we are born with, and the person with more intrinsic luck is always going to fare better if attacked than the person who has less. I can think of at least one case in the Old Norse sagas in which a magical practitioner not only ceased her attacks against a family but committed suicide because she realized that the luck of her enemies was greater.[148] Some forms of luck (such as hæl/heill) may be increased through magic and offerings to the Holy Powers as well as fylgjukonur, and growing one's luck in this way can be an effective defense against magical attacks.

A Word of Caution About Hamingja

Before moving onto the next concept, I would like to make a point regarding some modern practices involving the hamingja. Over the years, I've come across people who talk about sending out their hamingja to either perform tasks while other "soul parts" are off doing something else, or to retrieve the luck of others. In my opinion this is not only a bad idea, but it is potentially dangerous too. As a personified expression of your luck, the hamingja is not something that should be sent away from you under any circumstances. In my experience, the hamingja of a person can become damaged just like any other "spirit" being, and when this happens, it can make it very difficult to gain any forward traction in life even when other issues of luck (such as curses) are addressed. Over the years, I have found it necessary to develop a process for healing the hamingja (included at the end of this chapter). That said, prevention is always better than cure, and as we will see in the next section, there are far better options for faring forth.

Foundational Principle III: The Shape of the Soul

To Christians, the soul is singular and eternal. You are born ensouled, you live, and when you die you either go to heaven or hell, or await judgement day in your grave (depending on which "flavor" of Christian you are).

---

148. Jane Smiley, *The Sagas of the Icelanders: A Selection* (New York: Viking Penguin, 2000), 247.

By comparison, the elder Heathen's soul (if we can truly call it that) seems to have been dynamic and composed of multiple parts, both internal and external to the individual. In this way, it is not so dissimilar from what we have already seen with luck. The primary sources concerning the specifics of the Heathen "soul" can be confusing, and a number of theories have sprung up throughout the years that try to make sense of them. The model I present is yet another model in a sea of theories, but it has been of great use to me over the years.

Once again, I will divide the various component parts by location and examine each in turn before discussing the different "soul" parts and how they feature in magic.

The Internal "Soul"

As I understand them, the internal soul parts are the mind/"free-soul" or *hugr* to the Norse and *hyge* to the early English; the "body soul," which was known to the early English as *mōdsefa/sefa*; and the "breath-soul," which was *önd* to the Norse.[149]

For me, each of these parts had their roots in the life-giving gifts bestowed by the gods when they first enlivened the trees that would become people in the *Poetic Edda* poem *Völuspá*. In the poem, three gods, Óðinn, Hœnir, and Lóðurr, encounter two logs on the beach. One log is of ash and the other elm, but through the gifts of the three gods become the first humans.

We are told that Óðinn gave *önd* to the logs. This the breath-soul that is also inspiration. It is that which connects us to the winds, the thing we share with every other being that breathes, and it will return to the winds when we breathe our last. Next came Hœnir, who gave *óðr* or "sense." This is not so different from hugr/hyge. Both *óðr* and *hugr* carry the meaning of "mind," and I equate them with the "free soul."[150] Finally, there's Lóðurr's gift of *lá*; and *litr*. *Litr* may be translated as "hue" or "color," but the meaning of *lá* remains uncertain though it is often translated as "warmth" (and sometimes as "blood"). Unlike the gifts of Óðinn and Hœnir, Lóðurr's gifts are overwhelmingly phys-

---

149. Richard North, *Pagan Words and Christian Meanings* (Amsterdam: Rodopi, 1991), 97.

150. Richard Cleasby and Gudbrand Vigfusson, *An Icelandic-English Dictionary* (Oxford: Clarendon Press, 1874), 471.

ical in nature, and although *lá* remains ambiguous, I still find these gifts to be a good match for the "body-soul" or *mōdsefa*.

You may have noticed that some of my "soul parts" are only listed in Old English and others only in Old Norse. This is because some pieces of lore survived better in one set of sources than in others. So for example, there's evidence to suggest that a similar term to *mōdsefa* also originally existed in Old Norse but was subsumed by *hugr* as time went on. The names of Óðinn's ravens, *Huginn* and *Munin*, are believed to be a survival of that original conception.[151]

In the Old English sources, hyge was conceived of as being an active, "masculine" principle, whereas mōdsefa (or simply sefa) was the passive "feminine" principle. Where hyge (like its Old Norse counterpart *hugr*) could go wandering and be seen by other people, sefa was confined to the body and served as a store of memory that could be accessed by the hyge even at distance.[152] The two are inseparable, even after death, and there is evidence to suggest that the "free soul" hyge was forced to return to the physical body until it rotted into the earth.[153]

The External "Soul"

In addition to the internal "soul" parts, the Old Norse sources also mention an external being known as the animal fylgja.[154] The animal fylgja exists as an expression of a person's self, taking the animal form that most reflects the personality of the individual. It is a part of the soul that only exists for as long as a person is alive and, despite the popular misconception among modern Heathens, cannot be worked with or sent forth intentionally (although it can apparently wander). Unfortunately, if you or someone else sees your animal fylgja, it's generally an omen of death.[155]

---

151. Ibid., 92–93.

152. Joseph N. Bosworth and T. Toller, *An Anglo-Saxon Dictionary: Based on the Manuscript Collections of the Late Joseph Bosworth* (London: Oxford University Press, 1954), 695.

153. Alexandra Sanmark, "Living On: Ancestors and the Soul," in *Signals of Belief in Early England: Anglo-Saxon Paganism Revisited*, eds. Martin Carver, Alex Sanmark, Sarah Semple (Oxford and Oakville, Oxbow Books, 2010): 158–180.

154. Bettina Sejbjerg Sommer, "The Norse Concept of Luck," 279–280.

155. Ibid.

A lot of the confusion surrounding the animal fylgja seems to come from the fact that it is often conflated with shapeshifting practices. But while shapeshifting *was* a part of Heathen-period magic, we can be reasonably certain that it had absolutely nothing to do with the animal fylgja.

The "Soul" Parts in Magic and Life

As modern people trying to figure out a historical form of magic with no instruction manuals, we often have to rely on models in order to build the frameworks we need for practice. The models we use are important: not only do they shape the way that we see the thing that we're modeling, they also provide the frameworks for the practices we build. Some models are relatively minor and limited in scope. However, others are far greater in both scope and importance.

The way in which we see the "soul" is one of those greater models that underpins many different kinds of Heathen magic. We know that, historically, the elder Heathen practitioners worked magic in trance, that they were believed capable of sending forth parts of themselves, and that they also engaged in necromantic rites. These are all skills that may seem unconnected at first glance but share the common skill set of being able to manipulate the various "soul" parts, which is part of why we find a lot of variation in modern recreations of historical Heathen magic. As mentioned at the beginning of this section, there are multiple models for that intangible faculty we call the "soul" in modern Heathenry. So what kind of a framework does the model provided here give us?

From the perspective of practical magic, what we have is essentially a tripartite soul. Because while we also have an animal fylgja, it's not a piece we can work with (nor should wish to). This leaves us with the internal parts: the hugr/hyge or mind/"free-soul," *mōdsefa*, or the "body soul," and *önd*, or "breath soul."

The hugr/hyge can be worked with in a number of ways—some are inner practices in which the hugr stays within the body of the practitioner, and others involve faring forth. I'm going to begin by talking about the inner practices that can be done with the hugr.

Of the two main inner practices involving the hugr that I work with, meditation is the most common (and I would argue important). There is no definitive evidence of a Nordic meditation tradition that I have been able to find, but terms like *hugsi* and *hugrenning*, which seem to have meant "meditative" in Old Norse, suggest that it may not have been entirely alien to the Norse. There will be a full discussion and instructions for meditation in chapter 6.

The second inner practice can be summed up with the terms *hugsjón* and *hugspæi* ("mind sight" and "mind-spaeing/seership"). These seem to have hinted at more prophetic or vision-based practices involving the mind that were distinct from outer practices involving faring forth.[156] In my experience, there are two ways in which this may be performed. The first is through attaining a meditative state that is deep enough to allow access to a kind of hidden layer of reality and have visions.[157] The second is the practice of trance-journeying in search of answers. Despite the common belief among many modern practitioners that their journeys take place externally, I believe that they are predominantly internal, and that this practice would more rightly qualify as a form of *hugspæi*. I have included full instructions for embarking on your own trance journeys in chapter 8.

In the model that I present here, there is only one external practice that may be done with the hugr, and that is faring forth. However, as with the hamingja, the hugr could not go alone or as it was. As an intangible faculty, it required a vehicle or form in which to travel.

Magical practices involving (what we assume to be) the mind faring forth or shifting shapes seem to have involved the *hamr*, a word that translates to "shape" or "skin."[158] To change shape was *hamramr* and faring forth was *hamfarir*.[159] Given that the *hamr* in *hamingja* refers to an intangible part of the self, it's easy to assume that all Heathen shape-changing practices were purely non-physical in nature. However, there was a physicality to these accounts that cannot easily be dismissed, and there are multiple stories of shape-changing in which the shape is not only witnessed by outside observers, but also actively

---

156. Richard Cleasby and Gudbrand Vigfusson, *An Icelandic-English Dictionary*, 291.

157. See chapter 6 for discussion on how meditation can lead to visionary experiences.

158. Ibid., 236.

159. Ibid., 236–237.

participating in activities such as battle.[160] Unfortunately, I believe we are a long way from being able to manifest as large animals and cause physical damage (if indeed it was ever truly possible and not merely fantastical elements added to make a better story), but I have included instructions at the end of this chapter to help you get started with moving your hugr outside the body.

Before we get to the experiential component of this chapter, there is one final foundation of Heathen magic we've yet to explore: fate.

Foundational Principle IV: Fate

Our final concept is the weightiest and most complicated of all. However, as you will see, the way in which a culture views fate is usually central to the foundations upon which that culture's magical traditions are built. As with the other three concepts presented in this chapter, we find ourselves once more wading in a sea of theories. Both scholars and Heathens alike have debated Old Norse and Germanic ideas of the force we refer to as "fate" for years. As always, all we can do is fish out the pieces, put them to test, then keep what works. The information and ideas presented here are the parts I have tested and found to be useful.

The Importance of Beginnings

Beginnings seem to have been important to the elder Heathen, and as we have seen in previous chapters, beginnings in myth may often be connected to and even potentially explain later ritual and magical practices. When it comes to the Old Norse conception of fate and the origins of fate, we find the origins of spoken and spun magic and the principles by which they work.

In the Old Norse world, "fate" and her agents were inherently female, and the most prominent of these were the *Nornir*. We have already had brief encounters with the three Nornir who reside at the foot of Yggdrasil in chapters 2 and 4, but these are not the only Nornir to be found in the primary sources.

The thirteenth-century Icelandic historian and poet Snorri Sturluson records that there were also other Norns who came to individual children at birth, and

---

160. Claude LeCouteux, *Witches, Werewolves, and Fairies: Shapeshifters and Astral Doubles in the Middle Ages* (Vermont: Inner Traditions, 2003), 120–121.

that some were good while others were bad. Those who were visited by a good Norn at birth were believed to have good lives. But woe betide the child visited by the bad Norn! The Nornir of Snorri were also a diverse bunch, and were thought to hail from different races; some were said to be of divine origin, while others were thought to be of elvish or dwarven parentage.[161]

By far, the most famous Nornir are the three we have already met. In *Völuspá*, their names are given as *Urðr, Verðandi,* and *Skuld,* but these names are believed to have been a relatively late addition, with Verðandi the youngest of the three. Although they are often interpreted as being "past," "present," and "future," there is no evidence that they represented the procession of time in this way.[162]

Instead, the names *Urðr, Verðandi, and Skuld* may be thought of as representing cause and effect. *Urðr* (a cognate of the Old English word *wyrd*) may be translated as "fate" or "death"; *Verðandi* is the easiest of the Norn names to translate and may be understood to mean "happening" or "taking place" (right now); and *Skuld* may be translated as "debt" or "something owed," but also has a possible extended range of meanings including "shall," "must," "duty," "need," and "obligation".[163; 164; 165]

As a collective term, etymologies connect the word *Nornir* with ideas of "twisting" and "winding," as well as "secretly communicating."[166] Initially, these ideas may appear to be strange bedfellows, as two of the meanings relate to fiber and textiles, and the other to speech. However, as we will see, both of these ideas play a part not only in Norse ideas of fate, but also the forms of magic that developed.

161. Rudolf Simek, *Dictionary of Northern Mythology,* 236–237.

162. Karen Bek-Pedersen, "Nornir in Old Norse Mythology," *Core,* University of Edinburgh, 2008, accessed November 5, 2019. https://core.ac.uk/download/pdf/153530959.pdf, 74.

163. Ibid., 69–70.

164. Ibid., 70.

165. Ibid.

166. Ibid., 208–209

Spoken Law and Spoken Fate

When we first meet the Nornir in *Völuspá*, aside from being given their names and dwelling place, we're told that they "carve on slips of wood," "lay down laws," and choose "the fate of men."[167] However, it's clear that the kind of law laid down by the Nornir is not the law of men. It is *ørlög* "fate," a word literally translated as "primal-law," or "that which is set down before birth."[168] *Lög* or "law" was itself a thing of layers for the elder Heathen. It was "that which has been laid down, decided, determined," and speech was key to bringing it into being. Whether human law or the primal-law that formed the basis of human life, law was a thing that had to be spoken in order to become "real."[169]

The Nornir were not the only dealers of fate; völur also fulfilled a similar role with their prophecies, and just as with ørlög and law, a prophecy was not "real" until it was spoken out loud. There was a sense that prophecies were mutable, and that the speaking of them was not so much a proclamation as casting a spell. A völva could be *blamed* for the disasters she prophesied or even *bribed* for a better fate.[170]

For the modern völva, the idea of changing what you see in order to please people or avoid trouble may be considered somewhat unethical. After all, you see what you see, right? But there is an element of choice suggested on the part of both Norn and the seeress in the primary sources, suggesting that rather than simply seeing one singular possible fate, often there were a number of possible fates that the Norn or seeress could choose from. More importantly, it was the words of the Norn or seeress that set down or shaped a particular fate. This is the root of the belief in the shaping power of words—without it, spoken forms of magic would not have existed.

Fate and Fiber

So far in this book, we've found mythological roots for both magical practitioners and types of magic. But the mythological roots (and accompanying principles) of fiber-based forms of magic prove difficult to find. In chapter 2, we

---

167. Ibid., 67.

168. Ibid., 189.

169. Ibid., 189–191.

170. Ibid., 199–202.

made some headway in uncovering the mythological roots of spun seiðr during our investigation of the "Spinning Goddess." But what of the other forms of fiber magic that we find attested in law, textual sources, and the archaeological record? What of the inspiring stories of Valkyries weaving the final doom of their enemies, the tablet-weaving tablets marked with spells and spindle whorls inscribed with prayers?[171]

Here again we must look to the Nornir (though not in the way that one might think). At first glance, the Nornir are not the most obvious roots for the various kinds of fiber magic we find in the sources. Contrary to popular belief among Heathens and scholars alike, the Norns themselves (unlike their Greek counterparts), are arguably never depicted spinning. In fact, they are only ever shown engaging in fiber arts once in the entire Old Norse Corpus. In the poem *Helgakviða Hundingsbana I*, they are described as "twisting" (as opposed to "spinning") the örlögþátto, or "fate threads" of a young prince in order to secure for him an auspicious future.[172] Despite this minor foray into the fiber arts, the Norns remain overwhelmingly concerned with the choosing and laying-down of fates.

Norns and Humans

In order to understand why it is the Norns lay down law/fate with words rather than fiber, it is necessary to first understand something of Viking Age gender roles.

Compared with our own society, Old Norse society was heavily divided along gender lines, with men and women inhabiting different and often opposing spheres. For men, the world was outside the home, but for women, life was eternally focused on home and hearth.[173] Men were considered active agents in the world and in the eyes of the law, whereas women were expected to be passive and, in Viking Age Iceland, denied the ability to legal redress without the intervention of male relatives.[174] Where men spoke their words openly, women

---

171. Ibid., 153.

172. Ibid., 91.

173. Ibid., 158.

174. Jenny Jochens, *Women in Old Norse Society* (Ithaca: Cornell University Press, 1998), 113–114.

wove stories in cloth in the half-sunken weaving rooms known as *dyngjur* and recounted deeds in tapestries.[175]

The Norns here represent an inversion of this social order, mirroring the roles and actions of human men in mythic time. Like the human men of Middle-Earth, they are active agents who "lay down the law" and speak it into being. But because of who they are and where they "reside," that law is greater than any human law. It is none other than ørlög, the "primal law." They are not relegated to weaving silent stories or stitching epics on cloth.

Words and Textiles

But the Norns do not just speak fates into being. We are also told that they carve them on slips of wood, or in other words, they create a piece of text that accompanies the spoken word.[176]

What exactly is written on those slips of wood is a matter of debate, but what is important is that a *text* of some kind is created, and that brings us to the relationship between text and textile.[177] When you get down to it, *text* and *textile* are not so different in the historical sources. They both derive from the Latin *textere*, a word meaning "to weave," and both may be used to recount deeds and tell stories.[178] Although they are both silent methods of communication, only text reflects the spoken word. By necessity, stories related via textile rely on the interpretation of imagery and symbolism in order to be "read."[179] This makes textile a kind of secret language in a sense, a way of silently communicating messages hidden in plain sight.

We find a similar demarcation between "male" and "female" spheres here as well, with the written word of text primarily associated with men, and the woven or embroidered textile image with women. Where men recounted deeds overtly with words, women seem to have done so silently with woolen threads, producing finely detailed tapestries and embroideries that could be "read" by those with the requisite knowledge to do so. Although we do not know exactly what the Nornir carve onto their slips of wood, they seem to fall into the male

---

175. Karen Bek-Pedersen, "Nornir in Old Norse Society," 109–111.

176. Ibid., 67.

177. Ibid., 89.

178. Ibid., 154.

179. Ibid., 156–158

sphere of activity by carving something that may *overtly* be read, as opposed to inferred and interpreted.

This is where I believe we find the mythological root for woven and stitched forms of magic albeit through an inverted lens. Where (once again) the Nornir mirror the actions of human men in mythic time, producing text in the form of carved slips of wood, the human women of Middle-Earth produce textile. This is what we do when we embroider or weave. We produce our text-in-textile, laying down our designs and intent layer by layer. But where the völva could simply speak a new fate into being, textile magic seems to have also required the spoken word in order to work. Here is where we hit up against two mythological roots. The first is, as we have seen, the carved "texts" of the Nornir. But the second returns us to the windswept beach where two logs lay until three gods breathed, colored, and spoke "sense" into them. Textile magic isn't just a silent way of communicating intent; it is *also* the birth of a magical item, and, as such, requires its breath, color, and sense.

Fate in Magic and Life

As we have seen in this section, "fate" seems to have been viewed as a form of law—the "primal-law" that shapes life. For the elder Heathen, law seems to have been a *layered* thing, that grew and gained weight every time it was added to or reinforced. But fate was never just about law (primal or otherwise).

When we enter this world, we have ørlög, or "primal-law." This is what is the Norns give us. And as time goes on, our actions, the relationships we build, and the choices we make all set down new layers of action. Over time, if we make the same kinds of choices, and continue to act in a certain way, we may find that our life seems to have recurring themes that crop up again and again.

On a magical level, I've found it useful to view magical workings in a similar way. Some forms of magic (like spun magic) seem to have only been temporary, performed only until a desired effect was obtained. For example, in chapter 20 of the *Eyrbyggja Saga*, a woman called Katla works spun seiðr that ensnares the perceptions of her son's enemies so that instead of seeing her son, they see only a distaff. When Katla stops spinning, the illusion ends and her son's enemies realize that they've been tricked.[180] This is a powerful but

---

180. Hermann Pálsson (trans.), and Paul Edwards (trans.), *Eyrbyggja Saga* (London: Penguin Books, 1989), 60–63.

temporary effect. Conversely, other magic—such as the spell found carved on a tablet-weaving tablet to transfer the weaver's ill luck to an enemy—would have probably been much longer lasting. Not only was the action worked over and over again (setting down layers of magical action), but the weaver would also have a magical item imbued with that purpose by the end of her weaving.[181] This tells us that if we wish to create permanent magical change, that change must be worked repeatedly and over a period of time. In other words, we must set down enough layers of magical action for the desired result to become one of those recurring themes in life.

Regardless of the type of magic we practice, we need to remember that none of us experience our lives completely separate from others; that whatever we do will always probably also have unintended additional effects because of that interconnectedness. Remember that for the elder Heathen, this was also a *shared* world, one that was inhabited by Hiddenfolk and humans alike. We are also subject to the consequences of the decisions and actions of others (both human and non-human), something that we should always be mindful of, both in magic as well as our daily lives.

Throughout the course of this chapter, we've wrestled with some pretty weighty concepts and ideas. In my experience when teaching these concepts, people either get them right away or need some time to come to terms with them and test them out for themselves. Once again it bears repeating that my ideas on these concepts are just some of the many out there. To give a quick summary of those ideas before moving on:

1. Fate is a layered thing that behaves much in the same way as law. There is the "primal law" that you are born with (the fate chosen by the Norns). But every action (magical or otherwise) that you take sets down further layers of "real" that in turn may become recurring themes in life.

2. Fiber arts and the spoken word represent two of the most powerful fate-altering tools in Heathen magic, the first because it mirrors the magical speech of the Nornir, and the second because it combines magical speech with the creation and birthing of a magical textile.

---

181. Mindy MacLeod and Bernard Mees, *Runic Amulets and Magic Objects* (Woodbridge, Suffolk: Boydell Press, 2006), 61–62.

3. Old Norse society had very definite ideas about gender and gender roles, with men occupying "active" roles, and the women "passive." The actions of the Norns may be seen as an inversion of the actions of human women, putting them more in alignment with human male roles.

4. When setting the fates of people, the Norns are depicted both speaking and producing a "text" by carving on slips of wood. This may be viewed as the inverse of the actions of human women producing "texts" in the form of textiles that may be read.

5. Magical textile production was also a form of birthing magic not unlike the creation of a magical tool. As such, magical textiles required spoken or muttered incantations in much the same way as the creation of the first people required incantation or "sense" in order to work.

Though weighty, each of the concepts explored in this chapter are of practical use: they don't just inform ways of working but provide the all-important foundations for them as well. If used correctly, this knowledge of (even theorized) foundations can enable us to not only understand how our magic might work, but also create new forms of magic that are congruent with the Heathen worldview.

⟿ Experiential: Assessing Hæl/Heill ⟾

The ability to assess hæl/heill is one of the most important and protective tools in the "medicine chest" of magic. It's not a skill that comes automatically (at least not at first), but with enough practice, you'll find yourself performing this assessment without even really thinking about it. Once mastered, this can be a useful method for assessing places, magical practices, groups, teachers, and potential partners. Over time, you can even adapt the criteria to reflect and assess physical places too.

In the diagram that follows, you will be prompted to answer a range of questions pertaining to the different ways in which hælu/heill may manifest in a person's life. If you do not currently have anyone in your life whom you would be well-advised to assess in this way, you can still practice this skill by substituting characters from your favorite books, TV shows, or movies.

You will need

A piece of paper

Pencil/pen

Method

1. Draw the following chart on your paper and answer the questions to the best of your ability. Once you have filled in as many areas as fully as you can, take some time to think about your answers. How hæl does this person appear to be? How do your answers affect your planned level of involvement with this person? Please remember that you are not looking for perfection here, but red flags.

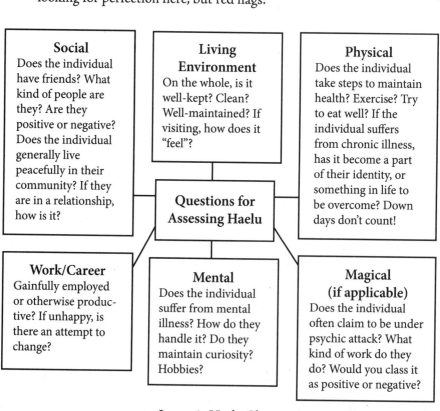

Social
Does the individual have friends? What kind of people are they? Are they positive or negative? Does the individual generally live peacefully in their community? If they are in a relationship, how is it?

Living Environment
On the whole, is it well-kept? Clean? Well-maintained? If visiting, how does it "feel"?

Physical
Does the individual take steps to maintain health? Exercise? Try to eat well? If the individual suffers from chronic illness, has it become a part of their identity, or something in life to be overcome? Down days don't count!

Questions for Assessing Haelu

Work/Career
Gainfully employed or otherwise productive? If unhappy, is there an attempt to change?

Mental
Does the individual suffer from mental illness? How do they handle it? Do they maintain curiosity? Hobbies?

**Magical
(if applicable)**
Does the individual often claim to be under psychic attack? What kind of work do they do? Would you class it as positive or negative?

Image 1: Haelu Chart

⤛ Experiential: Hamingja Repair ⤜

One of the practices that I've felt the need to develop over the years is that of hamingja repair. Although not attested in any way, shape, or form in the primary sources, I've found a need for it and have had great success with it, regardless.

We don't really discuss the aftermath of attack or traumatic situations in Heathenry. But I have found that even when the source of that trauma is spiritual, there is still a process of recovery that differs from person to person. In my experience, it is essentially a process of rebuilding, reclaiming, and rediscovering who you are. One of the ways in which you can aid that rebuilding and reclaiming is by engaging in hamingja repair.

While I typically recommend this for a damaged hamingja, this is actually something I do on a semi-regular basis as a preventative measure in the same way that I might choose to go to the doctor for a regular checkup. The biggest sign of an actual problem is luck that remains unusually and abnormally bad despite an absence of external factors such as attacks.

When I engage in hamingja repair, I enter a relaxed state and begin by visualizing a horse. As far as I know, no hamingja have been recorded in the form of a horse, but hamir are changeable and the image of a horse works better in my head because of the charm.[182] Then I begin to chant the healing incantation from the *Second Merseburg Charm* as I visualize the horse becoming whole again.

This will likely take more than one or even a couple of practices to complete, but those who have done this have noticed some pretty powerful effects stemming from this working. Luck has improved and, with it, their lot in life.

You will need

Somewhere quiet where to sit

The charm memorized or written down somewhere you can easily see it

Practice

1. Make yourself comfortable and begin by taking nine deep breaths. As you breathe, imagine the stress from your day leaving your body with

---

182. *Hamir* is the indefinite plural form of *hamr*.

every out-breath. When you have breathed your nine, close your eyes and allow your awareness to rest with your breath for a few minutes.

2. Once you are sufficiently relaxed, begin to build the image of your hamingja in your mind's eye. When you start this work, you may find that you have definite ideas about how it looks, but the more you tune in, the more spontaneous details pop up. Some of these details will be physical features like what the ears (if they have ears) look like, or the size of your hamingja. But others will concern the damage taken.

3. When you have built up this picture in as much detail as you can, approach your hamingja and lay your hands upon it as you repeat the following chant:

Bone to bone
Blood to blood
Limb to limb
So they may be glued[183]

4. As you chant, imagine a healing light gold coming from your hands and passing into the body of your hamingja. See the hamingja progressively taking on that golden glow and injuries slowly knitting themselves back together. Keep going until you feel that you are done for the day, and when you are ready, thank your hamingja and allow the vision to fall away.

5. Once more, return to your breath and rest in that calm until you feel ready to open your eyes. Sometimes you may feel something as soon as the hamingja disappears or even as you are healing the hamingja. Other times it can take a few days to settle in, so be patient.

6. Finally, remember that this isn't "once and done" kind of work. It is something that you will likely have to return to over and over again.

—))o Fundamentals: Digestion Diary o((—

In the Old English magico-medical journals, attacks from magical sources were generally associated with ailments of the mind or torso. In the mind,

---

183. Adapted from the Second Merseburg Charm.

these ailments could manifest as hallucinations or even epileptic seizures. But in the torso, it was digestive issues that were indicative of being subject to magical attacks.

For the early English, these attacks could come from a range of magical and otherworldly sources. Sometimes the symptoms were specific enough to narrow down to a specific kind of being, but a lot of the time, the treatments given were sufficiently broad so as to target many possible causes.[184]

As the "passive" part of the soul, mōdsefa and her importance are often underestimated. We tend to work more actively with the hugr/hyge and its hamr, and aside from being a source of miht and memory, mōdsefa tends to go ignored.

However, without mōdsefa the hyge/hugr cannot perform its function; when unhealthy, that function can become impaired. As the seat of the mōdsefa, the torso makes sense as a target for magical attack because if you attack the source of memory and power, health and function become impaired as well. This is why I recommend paying attention to digestion and any stomach issues you may have.

One of the best ways to get a picture of how your digestive system (and possibly your mōdsefa) reacts to your magical practices is to keep a diary for at least a month. You don't need to be too detailed, but be sure to note any abnormalities that occur after working magic or encountering the otherworldly. Be especially observant of changes that coincide with runs of bad luck. Over time, you'll learn to recognize the patterns of your digestive system, early signs of potential problems, and the times when you need some extra care. As always, if you are experiencing persistent problems, please go see a medical professional to rule out physical causes before leaning wholly into magical explanations.

Fundamentals: Hamfarir (Preliminary Exercise)

The art of moving and manipulating one's moving (soul) parts can be difficult to learn, but without it, a whole range of practices remains outside the realm of possibility. I have included exercises for working with the hugr/hyge (mind or "free soul") internally in chapters 6 and 8. In chapter 6 are full instructions

---

184. Alaric Hall, *Elves in Anglo-Saxon England*, 96-119.

for meditation that if followed may eventually enable you to attain a state in which you may experience visions—a possible way of practicing *hugspæi* or "mind seership." And in chapter 8 you will find instructions on how to go on a trance journey (another possible way of practicing *hugspæi*). In this section, we are going to practice the preliminary skills that will hopefully eventually allow us to fare forth outside of the body. As always, do not forget to record your experiences, even with these preliminary practices.

⤚⟩ᵒ Before You Begin ᵒ⟨⤛

Out of the various "soul arts," the skill of faring forth is probably the hardest to master. It can take a lot of work to even begin to move outside of the body, and it's exhausting in a way that trance journey simply is not. The first time I fared forth in the form of an animal, I only made it up the road before exhaustion forced me back to my body. It is also somewhat riskier than embarking on a trance journey within, and generally, what is experienced by the hamr (the shape the hugr takes while outside the body) translates to the physical body too. This is something primary sources are clear on, and in my experience, you may come back with muscles aching in ways you have never felt before (especially if taking the form of something other than human).

Depending on your personal aptitude, the process of learning to leave one's body in this way can be a journey of many stages. First you begin by relaxing your physical body before attempting to flex the subtle. At this stage, most people are still thinking in terms of human bodies and progressively test the degrees of separation from the physical body with a range of activities focused on moving the subtle body equivalent of the physical. For example, they begin by lifting their subtle fingers and when they have mastered that, move the hand, then arm, et cetera.

By thinking of your subtle and physical bodies in this way, you are already giving shape to your hamr. It's important to realize that the "skin" your hugr is wearing in this case is that of a human. When you first slip free of your body, it's best to stay close. As I said, this is an exhausting practice at first. Start slowly and build from there. Although you cannot really get separated from the body (hyge and mōdsefa remain together even after death if the body is kept whole), going so far that you're too exhausted to get back leaves you open to all kinds of issues. As always, it's better to walk before you run.

Finally, you may notice that you're not just exhausted when you get back, but all the next day too. From talking to others, this seems to be a common side effect of faring forth. You can build your capacity for it, but once you can do it, you can also find yourself spontaneously going or being pulled away while in sleep. No matter the capacity you manage to build up for yourself and your own activities, I guarantee these spontaneous jaunts will return you sore and exhausted in barely believable ways.

Aftercare is required here, so be good to yourself. This is a time to eat well and rest as much as you can.

As previously mentioned, the exercise provided here is preliminary, meant to help you begin the process of separating the hugr from the physical body. The end goal of this exercise is to end up positioned outside of your body, looking at yourself. If you would like to continue to build on what appears here, I recommend moving on to changing your shape before going any further.

You will need

Somewhere comfortable and quiet to lie down where you won't be disturbed.

A blanket (in my experience, the physical body can get quite cold during this practice)

Practice

1. Although I normally recommend a seated position for trance work, I've found it better to lie down for this exercise. The more you can forget your physical body in these early stages, the better. Begin by lying down with your eyes closed. Concentrate on your breath, center your awareness on the gentle filling and emptying of your lungs as you breathe in and out. And as you breathe, allow your body to relax. You want your body to become as relaxed as possible for this, so really take the time to get yourself to the point where you feel boneless.

2. When you feel relaxed to the point where you can no longer feel your body, then allow the lines of your physical body to "fall" away in your mind's eye to reveal your "subtle body." Remember that this is merely the "skin" your hugr is "wearing" and that it's your "active mind" you see. Try to see this as clearly as you can, and when you are ready, begin by slowly lifting a finger of your hamr.

3. The aim here is to lift a single finger without also lifting any physical fingers. If your physical fingers move even involuntarily, then you are instantly reminded of your physical body and will need to start over. Remember, this takes *practice*.

4. When you master the finger, then it's time to begin work on lifting more parts of the body. Keep the increments small. Going from "finger" to "whole arm" is not a good idea. If you work at this diligently, you will eventually get to the point where you can separate your entire hamr from your physical body. If you get to this point, then take the time to practice moving in this form, but stay near your body!

5. Before you become too tired, you need to begin the process of getting back to your body. The easiest way is to lie upon yourself and then allow yourself to pull your focus to your breath again and try to move your physical limbs. Moving the physical is an excellent way of snapping you out of the mentality required for separation. Finally, if you're worried about getting back in, you can have someone "spot" you. One of the most common themes we see repeated about people who fare forth in this way is that no one is to call their names while they're under. So don't be afraid to ask someone you trust to sit with you and call your name after a certain period of time if you need the extra help returning.

6. Once back, be sure to ground and center properly, and record as much as you can remember in your journal.[185]

Final Words: Fate and Divination

The final topic I'd like to discuss in this chapter is divination, and some of the implications of ørlög for our divinatory practices. When most people read the runes or whatever preferred form of divination they have, they are either reading for the future or receiving messages and advice from the Holy Powers. The idea of performing divination to ascertain the will or obtain the wisdom of the gods is quite ancient. However, the idea of reading for the future is quite strange from a Heathen perspective, because even when we read for the future, what we are really reading is the past!

---

185. See chapter 4 for instructions.

If we are to believe that ørlög is set before we are born and that our lives are composed of countless layers of interactions, choices, and actions, past and future are not so different after all. Even Skuld boomerangs between the two, bringing the weight of debt and obligation from the past to weigh on the present and future. Like the mistake in a woven pattern, it is what was set down in the past that informs and shapes the work performed in the now and the work yet to come. In a sense, the past is the only thing that is truly "real" while the future (with the exception of our final doom) is yet to take shape. We can read for a potential future, but often we're far better served asking about past events and events yet unseen in the present.

As fatalistic as this system may sound, it's also a system in which it is possible to magically "edit" circumstances and outcomes, and almost everything is left to play for until we meet our final doom.

Part II
THE PRACTICE
OF HEATHEN MAGIC

Six

BASIC SKILLS

When I was a child, we were told this story in school: two men each built a house. The first man built his house on sand because it was easier. But the second man took one look at that, envisioned the potential issues, and built his house on much firmer foundations. One day when the inevitable storm came, the house that was built on sand was destroyed and its owner made homeless. The house that was built on those firmer foundations would stand for generations to come. It's important to have good foundations.

But the importance of good foundations doesn't just apply to houses. The basic skills required for magic are the foundations upon which you build your practice. If you take the easy path and build on metaphorical sand, then you're going to run into issues down the line. But if you take the time to develop and hone those skills, then they'll stand you in good stead for when the storms hit (because they will).

Another story now. Years ago, a good friend of mine bought a new book on witchcraft. She'd been feeling limited in what she could do magically, and she wasn't wrong. She *was* limited. The so-called monkey mind—that part of us that chases distractions—was most unkind to her and she found it hard to muster the motivation to practice. She got the book with the intention of doing the exercises in it and developing her hefty natural talent. But when I asked her how it was going a few weeks later, the only thing she had done was try out the cookie recipe in the back of the book.

There are two points I want to make here. The first is that no book is ever going to somehow magically provide an easy way around the need to develop these skills or a way of circumventing the work. Unfortunately, there is no substitute for the work, and to attempt to build a practice without doing this work is the same as building a house on sand. The second point is that my friend already knew what was in the book—she'd encountered the same types of exercises in all the other books she'd read. You see, the thing about these basic skills is that they're actually quite universal, and for good reason—they have been found to work by magic workers in multiple traditions. I can't claim that any of this is what elder Heathen witches did, but I do know the importance of these skills on a practical level and so I include them here.

Now I'm not going to lie to you, this is *boring* stuff. It's also really hard to keep up at times, and you can even end up dreading practice! But for all the boredom and difficulties, there are definite returns. For example, in meditation you will gain not only an anchor in the world and a way to know your own mind, but also a way to develop psychic faculties. These are all invaluable tools for a practitioner of magic! So, as cliché as it may sound, try to think of these practices as ways of "showing up for yourself" because that's absolutely what you're doing.

Before we get into the actual practices, I'd just like to deconstruct the concept of boredom a little bit. Because it is something that a lot of us struggle with. But boredom is not necessarily a *bad* thing, and, if used right, can become a tool in and of itself.

Boredom

Boredom is probably one of the biggest (if not *the* biggest) obstacles to practice. It's certainly the number one reason that people give me when explaining why they stopped working on basic skills. Nobody likes to be bored, and we tend to do whatever we can to avoid it, because at times boredom isn't just unpleasant; it can be a burden.

But incredibly, boredom is actually really good for sparking deep thought and creativity. This is something that has been backed up by psychological studies too.[186] Boredom, it would seem, is more of a blessing than a curse. So lean into it, and know that even when you're bored, you're still doing something that is inherently good for you and your practice. The sessions where all you feel is boredom are not failures or a waste of time. None of this is a waste of time.

Meditation

The first boring (yet incredibly important) basic skill that all practitioners should learn is meditation. This is a key skill that not only makes up a good chunk of your foundations, but also ironically provides the foundations for other foundational skills.

There are many excellent reasons why magic workers should learn how to meditate, but I will stick with the two most important ones here. The first is that it is a way of getting to know yourself, and the second is that it can allow you to reach different stages of consciousness. But what do I mean by "getting to know yourself" here?

People are complex beings. We're a mass of thoughts and emotions piloting meat-suits powered by mundane and subtle energies. To know yourself is to not only know how busy your mind is or the kinds of things that scare you. It is to know the *shape* of your thoughts so you can tell what is of you and what is not. It's being able to recognize *why* you feel a certain way, deconstruct that "why," and make a deliberate choice rather than simply reacting. It's also being able to sense the subtle energies of your body, recognize emotions for the energy they are, and then direct that energy appropriately. To know yourself is to have control over yourself and be firmly anchored in this world.

The second main reason meditation is so important is that it can allow you to reach different states of consciousness. As well as being a foundational practice for trance journeying, meditation can also enable you to enter into a *blissful* state in which you can perceive the interconnectedness of reality and access greater knowing. There is a term in Old Norse, *hugspæi*, that translates as "mind-spæing," "mind-seeing," or "prophecy."[187] I cannot prove that this kind

---

186. Sandi Mann and Rebekah Cadman, "Does Being Bored Make Us More Creative?" in *Creativity Research Journal* 26, no. 2 (2014): 165–173.

187. Cleasby and Vigfusson, *Icelandic-English Dictionary*, 291.

of meditational wisdom was what was originally meant by this term, but I do not think it would be inappropriate to use it here.

All of this probably sounds quite lofty and maybe even impossible. But in my experience, these skills tend to develop by degrees. For example, you might start getting the sense that someone already came home about twenty minutes before they actually do. In other words, you sense the part of them that precedes the rest of the person before that person actually arrives. Or you might start to get a sense that something is off with your luck even before anything happens, only to discover through divination that you've inadvertently offended some of your local wîhta. These skills almost always start small. So, while you may not ever achieve enlightenment with your practice, there is a good chance that you will develop a deeper awareness of the subtle energies both within yourself and the world around you.

Meditation as Mind-Training

As mentioned before, meditation can be both hard and boring. But take comfort, because meditation is not what most people think it is. It's hard, yes, that's a given. But it's not as impossible as trying to keep your mind completely clear of thoughts for prolonged periods of time from the very first time you take to the cushion. That *does* eventually come with practice, but there is no failing here, and it's not disastrous if it doesn't. You are where you are, and as long as you are putting in the practice hours, you are still somewhere better than where you were before. Meditation is often compared with stringing a bow. If you string it too tightly because you're stressed and worried about not failing then the string will snap and the bow become useless. Another comparison that's often made is that training the mind is like training a puppy. What happens when you're too harsh with the puppy? The puppy will become afraid of you and you will feel terrible about your behavior toward the puppy. So, try not to stress out about it too much. Because if you do, all you'll be left with is a useless bow, a fearful puppy, and negative feelings toward stringing bows and training puppies.

Meditation is a skill that requires moderation; you cannot solve the problem of stringing the bow by stringing it too loosely, nor can you solve the problem of training a puppy by being too lenient. You may as well have done nothing at all! You need to find a balance here, and the first step in finding that balance is developing an appreciation for the nature of your mind.

The puppy analogy is very apt for the mind, because a puppy generally doesn't misbehave out of a sense of malice. It's just being a puppy and has not yet learned the control required to live in human homes. Your mind is not so different. Your mind is a ridiculously powerful computer that processes something like 11 million bits of sensory information per second. Being the "monkey mind" that jumps from thought to thought is simply in its nature.

So how do you train a puppy without getting angry or upset? You remain gentle, patient and loving, and keep a good sense of humor about you. Training your mind is no different. This is a skill that takes time to develop, which makes patience a necessity. But most importantly, don't judge yourself too harshly when you have a bad session. Because not only can you put yourself off practicing, you can also become locked into a mindset of failure. As your abilities grow this can even become dangerous, because stray thoughts can easily become curses when had by a person with power. Being kind to yourself—as well as keeping a good sense of humor—is how you avoid falling into this trap, so don't be afraid to laugh and be a little playful in your approach.

Every time you sit down to meditate, you are effectively training a muscle. Again, like the puppy, this muscle is a form of self-control, and forms the basis for your magical *will*. Every time your thoughts wander and you regain your focus in a meditation session, you are strengthening your self-control and your will. This is why you cannot fail at meditation. All the ways in which we typically envision failure in this skill are actually things that are beneficial to us!

—)}o Foundations: Meditation I o{(—

The form of meditation taught here is a simple breath awareness meditation that can be expanded into other forms of practice. In this form of meditation, the breath is what is called a "support" to the meditation. In other words, by focusing on the breath, you are using it as a support for training your mind in much the same way as a person training a puppy might hold up a ball to get the puppy's attention long enough for it to sit.

Before you begin, we'll cover two very important points: how you sit for this exercise and how you breathe.

When most people think about sitting for meditation, it's the *Vairocana posture* that comes to mind. This is the straight-backed, lotus-crossed legs posture with hands folded in the lap, and it's probably the most common depiction of meditation and enlightened people out there. But not everyone can get into that posture, let alone sit comfortably in it for any period of time.

Again, this is a matter of "stringing the bow." For people like myself who have joint issues, sitting in the Vairocana posture is stringing the bow too tight. It's impossible to meditate (especially at the beginning) if the posture you are in causes you pain. But you also don't want to be so comfortable that you are encouraged to fall asleep. A good compromise here is to sit somewhere or in some way that is comfortable for you and where you can ideally maintain a straight back.

Similarly, you may also need to adapt how you breathe for this exercise. There are a lot of people who find it difficult to focus solely on the breath, and find it easier to count breaths in the beginning rather than simply staying with the breath. If this is you, and you need the extra support of counting, then there are a couple of options for you to choose from at this stage.

The first is that you can count the length of each breath and aim to make each breath the same length. A good example of this kind of practice is the fourfold breath. As the name suggests, each stage of the breathing cycle lasts for a count of four. So, you breathe in for a count of four, hold your breath for a count of four, breathe out for a count of four, and hold your breath again for a count of four. For some people with previous trauma or breathing issues, the fourfold breath can be difficult and even produce sensations of panic. Those who have this difficulty may find it easier to breathe to a count of three, or simply hold the breath between inhalation and exhalation for less time.

The second option is to *just* count how many breaths you take. This is a great option for people with trauma or breathing issues who really can't deal with counting the length of each breath. It is also entirely acceptable to move between different ways of breathing depending on the day, or how your session is going. For example, if you are particularly distracted when you first come to sit down, you may need the extra support of counting the length of your breaths. But as you calm, then you may move into counting the breaths before simply focusing your awareness on the breath without counting. As an asthmatic, I tend toward just counting my breaths on my bad breathing days, and counting the length on good days. I almost always have some stress when I first sit, but then as it loosens, I drop the counting. You can be flexible depending on your needs. Remember: focusing on the breath is a *support* for training your mind. It cannot be a support if it does not actually support your practice. So don't be afraid to use whichever form of breathing works best for you.

You will need

A place where you may sit in a straight-backed posture

An alarm or meditation timer (there are excellent free apps for this)

Ten to fifteen minutes of undisturbed time

Practice

1. Before you begin, set your alarm or meditation app timer for at least five minutes. Do not hit "start" until you are in position and ready to begin meditating. When you first begin a meditation practice, it's best to start with short, regular sessions and then progressively move to longer ones as you become more experienced. If you find that your meditation sessions feel comfortable (i.e., you're not constantly thinking about how many minutes are left on the clock), or even a little too short, then you may want to consider increasing them by five-minute increments.

2. Once your alarm or timer is set and you are sitting comfortably (again, preferably in a straight-backed posture), start your timer and, if you wish to do so, close your eyes. You do not have to close your eyes at this point. There are many different types of meditation, some practiced with closed eyes, and some with eyes open but gently focused on the tip of the nose.

3. Allow yourself to become aware of your breath. Stay with it as it moves in and out of your lungs and airways. Really lean into the sensations of breath and breathing, and allow yourself to become curious about those sensations.

4. At this point, it can be really easy to get caught up in mentally narrating your breath and thinking about how the sensation of breath-experienced-mindfully makes you feel. But try not to conceptualize anything.

Just stay in the moment, and if you notice your awareness wandering from your breath, gently bring it back.

5. Continue in this way until your alarm or timer goes off. Record your session in your journal. You do not have to be detailed here. A simple note that you meditated, how it felt, any particularly strong memories or emotions that surfaced, and a description of any visual or auditory effects you experienced is good enough.

Moving Beyond the Breath

Once you have a few sessions under your belt, you may wish to experiment with other forms of meditational support. Remember, the support is like the ball used to distract the puppy while getting it to do what you want! If breath doesn't work for you, then there is nothing wrong with finding another support to focus on.

There are a number of possible alternative supports, and they can be physical or non-physical. An example of a physical support would be focusing your attention on a candle flame or, in other words, using the flame as a ball for distracting the puppy. But you do not need a physical object to focus for meditation; you can also use non-physical or *visualized* objects for the same purpose. This is one of those areas in which meditation overlaps with visualization, and can be a good way to cross-train both meditation and visualization skills at the same time. This is especially helpful if you practice with your eyes open and visualize the object on the ground roughly five feet in front of you. When I do this, I allow my eyes to become relaxed and work on visualizing a silver ball in the middle of my floor where I can then rest my focus. It can be an interesting experience to meld the visualized with the physical world in such an intentional way.

Common Mind Tricks in Meditation

Regardless of the form of support you use, thoughts are going to arise when you meditate. At first it can feel like every single possible thought in your head has just set up a parade for your benefit! But the goal here is not to break up the parade and send it home. The goal is to observe the tomfoolery from a distance and just let it do its thing without judgement or interacting with it. One of the most helpful analogies that I've ever heard for describing the right way to approach thoughts in meditation is to view them like cars on a road. When you're standing at the side of the road, it's easy to just watch the cars go by without paying particular attention to any of them. You can see that they are cars and that they're doing their own thing, but you have no need to pay them any more attention than that. This is exactly how you should try to see your thoughts.

That said, beware of the monkey mind—it will try to *trick* you even when things are going well. You may get to a point where you realize that no thoughts have drifted by to tempt you away from your focus on breath (for example). But then you start to think about how *well* you're doing *not* thinking about anything other than your breath, and boom! Just like that you're getting caught up in thoughts about how good you are meditating (but no longer focusing on the support). See what I mean? Even when you have no thoughts floating through, the mind will try to generate some to get you back to giving it more distracting things to do. The lesson here, for the good and bad of it, is to never underestimate your mind.

Meditation and Shadow Work

A lot of the time, the thoughts that arise are completely random. Sometimes you'll see memories, theories, shopping lists, or just that cheeky little monkey mind running an ironic narrative about "not thinking." Sometimes (depending on your history), the thoughts that arise can be horribly distressful and reflect and include things like memories of awful past experiences, negative self-talk, reruns of nightmares, or your worst fears. This is one of the ways in which meditation bumps up against *shadow work*, a term used to refer to the process of digging up, confronting, and reintegrating the parts of yourself that are normally suppressed.

The image of a meditator is always one of a blissfully calm person (usually in the red or saffron robes of a monk). But meditation can be a hard, shadow-filled process too. In our society we spend an inordinate amount of time trying to fill the gaps in our lives with some form of distraction. Part of this is to avoid the dreaded boredom, but for a lot of people, this is also about a sense of comfort. Silence can be disconcerting. Being alone with your thoughts can be terrifying even if you haven't had anything particularly bad happen to you before. But when you have a difficult history, this can be even worse. The goal of meditation is not to suppress what arises. It is to observe (and sometimes deconstruct) what it is you are experiencing, and eventually reintegrate those newly re-encountered shadow parts of yourself.

You have two options when you encounter these bad thoughts. The first is to simply allow them to make their way through your mind without clinging to them. Like all thoughts, if you don't cling to them or engage with them, they will simply go and you will have rendered them inert by being able to avoid clinging to or engaging with them. The second option is to lean into the thought/memory/fear and to deconstruct what you are seeing in as logical a way as possible.

To give you an example of how this might look, about a decade ago I went through a very rough patch after a miscarriage. Without going into too many details, it had been quite a horrible experience and I was no longer sleeping because of it. Worse still, I was getting flashes of what I'd experienced every time I closed my eyes. It was affecting my ability to function, so I decided to spend a week in complete silence, meditating and working through everything that came up. Whenever I got the flashes, I would stop them and deconstruct the scene. But I could not do this from my own perspective as it was at the time. In order to do this work, I had to adopt the (imagined) perspective of a compassionate stranger. I began talking myself through what I was seeing and forcing myself to question the impressions I'd already put on my memories and the ways in which they were already being enshrined. During the course of the week, I wore through these memories again and again until eventually the flashes stopped coming and I was left with a sense of peace. I have done this with other issues many times since, but this method is not safe for everyone.[188]

Meditating Safely

For the vast majority of people who practice meditation, meditation is an incredibly rewarding practice. But for some people it can be quite dangerous, especially without the guidance of an experienced and trusted teacher. So there are a few things that all would-be meditators need to be aware of with regards to safety and staying well as a meditator.

---

188. See Tsultrim Allione, *Feeding Your Demons* (New York, Little, Brown and Company, 2008) for a guided and much safer process for working with complex shadow issues.

The first is that meditation is best practiced little and often until you build up the capacity to engage in more intensive practice. You don't need to worry about devoting an hour a day to the practice when ten to twenty minutes will suffice. Just make sure that you *do* make the effort to meditate every day. It's far better to build a regular and consistent practice than one in which you meditate for long periods of time but infrequently. Trust me, I've been meditating in various ways for over twenty years now, I know all about that. There have been times when my practice has dropped and then I've tried to "make up for it" by meditating too much. But unlike sleep, meditation is not accumulative. Putting in eight hours on the cushion over the space of a week does not somehow "make up" for the three-week lapse; if anything, you'll just end up making yourself feel unwell.

The second thing to be aware of is that there have been cases where people have been negatively affected by meditation practice. In some cases, intensive meditation practice has led to a minority of people having frightful hallucinations and eventually, sadly, taking their own lives. Generally speaking, these were people with pre-existing mental health conditions who then practiced too intensely for their capacity, had inadequate support, and frankly needed someone to step in and gently remove them from whichever class or retreat they were in. Intensive meditation retreats can be challenging for people without significant mental health issues, but when there are underlying conditions present, there is an increased risk factor. Most people—even those who live with mental health and/or trauma issues—are fine with a short daily practice. But if you begin to find yourself in distress because of your practice, please stop and seek help. We all need help sometimes.

Visualization

In the previous section, I discussed the use of visualized objects as meditational supports. In this section, we're going to dive into the practice of creating visualized images for magical use.

Most of us already have the ability to visualize to some degree, and many of us even do it unconsciously while reading books. But there is a difference between allowing the mind to spontaneously generate images in accordance with external stimuli, and willfully visualizing a reproduction of an object/person/scene/iconography of a spirit in as much detail as possible for as long as needed in order to complete magical acts.

Like meditation, visualization is an important skill; without it, we struggle when directing our will and energy. Imagine trying to work magic to bring about a certain scenario without being able to represent that scenario in some way. Imagine trying to shield yourself magically. I mean, sure, you can create physical representations of a scenario or the shields you wish to create. After all, that's what sympathetic magic is about. But the best and most effective magic doesn't *just* rely on words, actions, or physical representations. Those are just the *outer* expressions (and, to some degree, supports) of your magic. Magic must also have *inner* expression, and this is where visualization comes in.

So, you need to be able to "see" in order to bring something to pass, but that is not the only way in which visualization should play a role in ritual or magic. There is a concept in Tibetan Tantric Buddhism expressed in the Tibetan word *jendren* (spyan 'dren), or "conjuration," "invitation," and more directly, "to pull the eye." The deities and spirits are visualized, and physical offerings are augmented by visualized offerings. To see is to call; the iconography allows the introduction, and the visualized offerings the enticement.[189]

→}∘ Foundations: Visualization I ∘{←

You will need

Somewhere comfortable to sit

Ten to fifteen minutes of undisturbed time

An alarm or meditation timer

An object to study for visualization

Practice

1. Begin by setting your alarm or timer for five minutes and place your chosen object where you can easily see and touch it. Seat yourself comfortably and start the timer.

2. In these first five minutes, study the object in as much detail as you can. Familiarize yourself with the shapes, textures, colors, weight, and any images

---

189. Ben Joffe, "To See Is to Call: Tantric Visualization, Summoning Spirits and the Mind as a Petting Zoo," in *A Perfumed Skull: Anthropology, Esotericism, and Notes on the Numinous*, May 7, 2017, accessed October 19, 2019. https://perfumedskull.com/2017/05/07/to-see-is-to-call-tantric-visualization-summoning-spirits-and-the-mind-as-a-petting-zoo.

or words on the object. This may feel like a long time to spend studying a single object, but the ability to observe an object in detail and commit as many of those details to memory is a crucial part of practicing visualization. In my experience, the better you get at observation and remembering your observations, the clearer your visualizations will become.

3. Once the first five minutes are up, set your timer for another five minutes. This time when you start the timer, close your eyes and try to imagine the object in as much detail as you can. You can begin by viewing it head-on, reproducing it in your mind's eye as faithfully as you can. Once you can do this and hold that image consistently, then you can work on moving the object and manipulating it in other ways. Change the color, flip it, make it bigger, make it smaller, change the texture—whatever you can think of to manipulate it, do it. When this becomes easy, then it's time to move on to visualizing entire scenarios.

⟶⟩○ Foundations: Visualization II ○⟨⟵

While training to visualize a single object can help you develop and hone your visualization skills, the vast majority of the visualization you will use in magic will involve the visualization of entire scenarios as well as the appropriate accompanying emotions.

If you have ever fantasized about getting the perfect job, meeting the perfect person, or (perhaps more commonly) experiencing a certain kind of sexual scenario, then you have already used this faculty (albeit unintentionally). The only real difference here is that fantasies involve the highly improbable and are good for nothing more than providing a small escape from the daily grind. A better way of describing this kind of visualization is *intentional daydreaming*. Unlike fantasies, dreams can be ambitious, but not so ambitious that they are impossible to build.

One of my favorite ways of training to daydream in this way is to conjure up scenarios and put myself in them—to see them in as much detail as I can, and follow them through, allowing them to sweep me away on the tides of emotion. Another way I like to train is by watching an episode of a favorite show, picking a scene, and then recreating it in visualization (again with the appropriate emotions). I've recreated entire episodes in this way before now, but a single scene is plenty of practice.

As a rule, I prefer to train with unlikely scenarios rather than realistic ones. This is because I feel I have a responsibility to keep a handle on my thoughts as much as possible, especially where emotions are also involved. Experience has taught me over the years that even people who have never so much as cast a spell can unintentionally cause harm with their thoughts when emotional. Without that control, the possibility of that happening only increases as a person develops their magical abilities. So, I prefer to stick to the mostly fantastical in order to build in a layer of protection for the people around me.

In the following exercise, we're going to recreate a scene from a movie or TV show in as much detail as possible. Do not worry about replicating the script beyond the key messages and intent of any characters in the scene. But do try to think about the appropriate emotions attached to the situation being depicted and try to generate those emotions within yourself as you visualize.

You will need

Somewhere comfortable to sit

Ten to fifteen minutes of undisturbed time

A scene memorized from a favorite show or movie

Practice

1. Seat yourself comfortably in a place where you may do so undisturbed, and begin by taking three deep breaths.

2. Now, close your eyes and bring to mind your chosen scene. Try to remember in as much detail how it began. How did the set look? Which characters were on screen? How did they look? What event was being depicted? What emotions do you think the characters experience in this scene? Try to visualize all of these elements as you remember them, allowing the various elements to come into being in your vision until you have as complete a picture as possible.

3. Once you have the start of your scene, then try to play it through. This kind of visualization involves a lot of moving parts and so can be difficult at first. However, the level of investment you have in your chosen show or movie can help make it easier. Try to feel the appropriate emotions for the situation depicted in the scene. As you play it through, do not be afraid to stop the scene when you feel as though your visualization is fading to recreate any missing parts.

4. Try to make it to the end of the scene, and when you do so, allow the entire scene to fade or crumble away. End by meditating for a few minutes. This will help you to fully ground out any emotions you felt while interacting with the scene.

5. When you are comfortable performing this exercise, you can increase the difficulty by choosing one thing to change about your chosen scene and playing it through to its natural conclusion.

Pitfalls of Visualization

The quality of visualization can make or break a magical working, and distractions that may seem insignificant, like wandering thoughts or uncontrolled emotions, can lead to a lot of trouble for a sufficiently talented practitioner.

In the section on meditation I described emotions as being energy, and the realization of this as being one of the benefits of meditation. As energy of various "flavors," emotions are incredibly powerful things, and working with them magically when you are not in control of those emotions is one of the biggest pitfalls of working with visualization.

In the end, it all boils down to control. Consciously cultivating and adding the appropriately "flavored" emotions to a visualization for magical purposes is effective. But working while emotions are in control of you rarely turns out to be a good idea; whether you realize it or not, you are grasping the proverbial tiger by the tail. It's really difficult to see a situation for what it is when a powerful emotion is driving you, and that alone will have a knock-on effect down the line. Depending on the emotion, the average person is capable of making some really bad decisions while "under the influence." Add magic into the mix and things get a whole lot worse.

To tackle a problem with magic, you need to be able to formulate an end goal as well as how you will achieve it. But in order to do that, you *have* to be able to see the situation for what it is. The visualizations that you will create in your magic are like bridges from point A to point B. They connect the *what is* with the *how you want things to be* and act as a vehicle for your intent. But if emotions are in charge, your chances of building a bad bridge are increased because you're not even starting in the right place, and worse, the mistakes you make will have a whole lot of power from the added emotions.

To further complicate matters, you may not even be able to conceptualize where point B needs to go. There are a lot of reasons why this may be the case.

For example, a lot of people point to the abject poverty of historical witches as "proof" that they either weren't witches or weren't very good at what they did. But few people consider the role of generational poverty on not only framing expectations, but also the ability to even dream of better in order to make it happen. You cannot work magic for something if you can't even dream of it in the first place. The ability to dream and to set helpful goals is critical in this work—without those skills, there is no way to see how best to build your proverbial bridge.

It is important to point out here that visualization is not just about the ability to dream on command. You also have to have good goals. If you aim too high and become too specific, any energy you generate through your magical work can get stuck, like a bottleneck with too much trying to get out through too small a space. Eventually this energy becomes stagnant and can actually add to any problems you have. Likewise, if you aim too low very little will change in your world and instead of creating long-term fixes with your magic, you essentially end up trying to find magical bandages for problems that occur over and over again.

There is an art to setting good magical goals, but that art is unfortunately beyond the scope of this chapter. Instead, here are two rules that should keep you out of a lot of unnecessary trouble when setting goals and coming up with the visualizations for working on those goals. The first is to ensure that they include provisions centered on continuing to fulfill your basic needs. It's all well and good to have lofty goals, but magic always tends to take the most direct path unless otherwise instructed. For example, the simple goal of moving house when you need a whole lot more money to do so is far more easily fulfilled by you losing your current house and then taking whatever comes up. You still moved house, but in the worst way possible. So, always include provisions for things like continued income, housing, good health, and so on.

The second rule relates to the way in which you visualize any movement of energy or luck (if you visualize them). It can seem intuitive to visualize these things as staying in place and growing, especially when you're being ridden by fear. But energy and luck need to move and be shared in order to bring the most benefit. For example, if you create a visualization in which you visualize luck entering into your home as golden energy, it's a really bad idea to just imagine the energy sitting there. If you must visualize energy entering the home, keep it dynamic, moving in and out in a constant flow.

Dreamwork

From the pitfalls of intentional daydreaming, we now come to the kind of dreams we have at night. For most people in our culture, dreams and the act of dreaming are largely unimportant. They're trivial, oft-forgotten things that happen at night and scatter like cicadas with the dawn. But in the Heathen period, dreams were taken extremely seriously, and those who were unable to dream were considered disabled in some way.

Before Christianity, dream was one way in which we could enter and experience the Other. We could incubate dreams for healing or in order to receive messages from the dead. But then came Christianity, and temples became churches, Pagan feasts were coopted, and some of the older deities found themselves dressed in the brilliant golden gleam of icons. Most troublesome for the church fathers was the fact that too many people still toyed with the idea that the waking wasn't real. This sounds like a half-baked conspiracy theory, but as academics such as Lisa Bitel have demonstrated, the effort to effectively colonize dream and purge it of its Pagan elements is well-recorded.

The first step was designating who could have "true dreams." Previously, any person was capable of dreaming true, but Christianity saw to it that only the "right" had the capacity and everyone else was said to be experiencing "devilish illusion." Eventually, all dreams were unimportant, and we lost one of our most important ways of connecting with and learning from the numinous powers of our world.[190]

Developing the ability to dream lucidly (let alone dreaming true) is some of the most important work that a practitioner can take on. It's not easy; it takes discipline. The world we live in is hard for dreamers because it's all too easy to fill our minds with the thoughts and opinions of other people instead of having thoughts and opinions of our own. This kind of "content overload" fills our short-term memories, overloading our ability to process and shaping our own thoughts and dreams.[191] The first step of learning dreamwork is taking control of the content we consume in our daily lives.

---

190. Lisa M. Bitel, "'In Visu Noctis'": Dreams in European Hagiography and Histories, 450–900," *History of Religions* 31, no. 1, 1991: 39–59.

191. Peter Grey, *Apocalyptic Witchcraft* (n.p: Scarlet Imprint/ Bibliothèque Rouge, 2016), 43.

Naturally, the best way to regulate the flood of content would be to cut yourself off from all media, which is just not possible for many of us. Social media has become so central to our lives that it's now the most common way to organize in-person events, keep in touch with distant relatives, and some of us even work online. So what can we do? How can we stem the tide?

In *Pharmako: Poeia*, Dale Pendell describes habit as being the true poison.[192] Although he's talking about tobacco, his advice is just as useful for regulating the content we consume. The problem for Pendell is doing things without intention, as a side activity, or out of boredom. His advice is to consume deliberately and see the significance of your actions. You are not simply mindlessly surfing the internet—you are filling your mind. Moreover, you are robbing yourself of productive boredom and the chance to consume and produce original content.

Once you have a handle on content consumption, you go to sleep with the intention of dreaming and sleep for long enough periods during the night to dream. Some people find it helpful to fast, ingest helpful herbs, or wake themselves up intermittently during the night (as counterintuitive as that may seem). There are also rituals you can perform to help open yourself up even more to dream (the *Headless Rite* from the Greek Magical Papyri is good for this). Whatever you choose, don't forget to write everything down in your journal. Record your experiments and every dream you remember, no matter how weird or useless it seems at the time. But do it quickly, before you talk to anyone else, and most definitely before you open that first-cigarette-of-the-day-Facebook page.

Recording dreams is always best done in verse or song. You'll be surprised at how easily it all comes out and comes back when written in verse. Things you thought you'd forgotten will come back clearly as you write because there's always been something about poetry that is particularly good for enticing and recording the otherworldly. Later, when you read them back again, you will be surprised how much more tangible your dream poems are, despite the far less "solid" nature of poetry itself. The best part is that you don't even need to be a great poet to do this; you just need to be able to let it flow.

---

192. Dale Pendell, *Pharmako Poeia: Plant Powers, Poisons, and Herbcraft* (Berkeley, CA: North Atlantic Books, 2010), 50.

But this process doesn't end with writing the dreams down. If we see another reality in dream, then why wouldn't we reconnect it with our waking one? Dreams can be doorways, leading you to new spirit relationships, knowledge, and practices. It's important to integrate and work with the gifts you are given while in that state. For example, I have a friend who, on being shown a recipe for cakes to offer to the Fair Folk in dream, went and tried the recipe out (it worked), and now has a regular offering cake recipe. Along similar lines, I was once shown a situation in which a lot of people were getting possessed by otherworldly spirits and came up with a depossession oil shortly afterward that I've had to use a surprising number of times since receiving the dream. Once you integrate the knowledge that it is possible to interact with spirits and a whole other reality through dream, the idea of not completing the circle between waking and dream makes no sense.

When you get to the point where you're making regular forays into the world of dream, you need to begin work on your lucid dreaming skills. If you're going to see and interact with the Other in dream, then it is important that you are able to interact as opposed to simply watch yourself playing a part (sometimes very poorly). Dream is a place of lessons and secrets, and you may find yourself returning with symbols, rituals, and magic that no one you know has seen before, but that works. This is one of the biggest reasons why we go, and why we must.

⟶⟩∘ Preliminary Exercise:
The "Am I Dreaming?" Game ∘⟨⟵

One of the easiest ways to start preparing your mind for lucid dreaming, by far, is by playing the "Am I Dreaming?" game. The idea of this exercise is to build a strong enough habit that the habit carries over into dream. As the name of the game suggests, you play this "game" by asking yourself a simple question. If you do this enough, you will eventually probably find the question popping up while in dream.

Begin by asking yourself the following question: "Am I dreaming?"

1. This game can be played anywhere and at any time, but should be played at least whenever you remember it. All you need to do to play is to simply ask yourself the question: "Am I dreaming?"

2. Every time you ask the question, take a few moments to *feel* waking reality around you and make a mental note of how it feels. If you're in a

place to do so, end the exercise by verbally telling yourself, "No, I am not dreaming."

3. Try to remember to ask yourself this question as often as you can. The more pervasive it becomes in your life, the more chance you have of it becoming pervasive in dream too and that question triggering lucidity.

If you manage to trigger lucid dreaming with this question, some practitioners advise not focusing too intently on things and just allowing a soft focus, lest the lucidity becomes lost or you startle yourself awake.

One thing I experience that may also prove useful is that as you begin to dream more lucidly, you may find that you get a certain sequence of images or events occurring in dream that signals a move from the simple to more significant dreams. This sequence, when viewed, triggers lucidity in the dreamer, allowing them to interact with the Other. One such sequence for me begins in a store that is never the same but always has far more departments than is reasonable for a store in the waking world. At some point during this sequence, I will be required to move toward the back of the store. On my way, I will pass by a series of bearded men of varying ages, eras, and races all staring at me intently. If I am not already lucid by then, then the parade of faces snaps me into lucidity … and quickly.

This sequence has been, and is, a savior to me. The thing about the otherworld and the kinds of beings that you might encounter there is that they don't much care whether you're lucid or just along for the ride: Fairy-tale rules *always* apply.

To that end, always remember that manners are imperative, so be respectful, because it's often the rude who are punished in fairy tales. Never pledge what you cannot fulfill (or at all if you can avoid it), because the Good Folk are experts at finding loopholes that often turn out to be detrimental to humans. Never forget that the beautiful are not always good and safe either. Ice can also be beautiful, but that doesn't make it less treacherous to cross! Finally, try not to eat the food. It almost always looks good (and suspiciously a little too perfect), but it's rarely a good idea to eat it—one of the most important fairy-tale rules I can think of. There are of course plenty more (and I'll be recommending some books in the Recommended Reading section), but those are good to start.

Working with Energy

As a practitioner of magic, you need to know about energy and how to sense it. Energy is at the heart of what we do—we bend it, manipulate it, and shape it, herding it with our will toward our visualized goal. Without the ability to sense energy, there is no raising and shaping, nor is there any way to know whether our magical engine has gas or not, so to speak.

Different practitioners may sense energy in different ways too. For me, it's mostly a tingling sensation, or in other words, it feels how I imagine electricity feels. But depending on what I'm doing, I also experience it as heat or cold on occasion (usually accompanied by the tingling). Maybe you've felt these sensations yourself but have never really paid attention or known what they really were? But if you haven't, don't worry—this is a faculty that can be developed with practice—I have a friend who is proof of that.

Some people can also *see* energy. For most people, this occurs in an altered state of consciousness. But some people are able to visually perceive it without requiring a change of consciousness in order to do so. This can manifest in different ways for different people. For me, the world appears pixelated—kind of like how images appear on a television when you sit too closely. I've always seen the world in this way, and it's no different when I wear my glasses. The only things that are solid in appearance to me are those things that are alive or ensouled in some way. The pixels are more noticeable in the dark, but they're there all the time and become more noticeable in places with more energy. When a place is really active, it can look almost like the "snow" on an old TV that isn't tuned in. Sometimes those pixels even move in a uniform direction in an isolated area. Unfortunately, I'm not entirely sure if this can be taught, so I will focus on teaching how to sense energy in a more general way.

⟶⟩○ Fundamentals: Energy I ○⟨⟵

For a lot of people, a good way of introducing them to energy in this way is through the use of a seated exercise during which a person focuses on the sensation of where the body makes contact with the chair/floor/whatever they are seated upon. This is what you will be doing in the following exercise.

You will need

Somewhere comfortable to sit or lie down outside

A blanket that is big enough to lie down on

Ten minutes of undisturbed time

Practice

1. Find somewhere to lie down outside. Ideally you want to be on earth rather than manmade materials like concrete. When you have found your spot, spread out your blanket and lie down on your back. Take a few moments to relax, and allow yourself to settle in place.

2. When you are comfortable and feel settled, begin to focus on your body and the sensation of it against the surface of the ground beneath you. Try to feel the weightiness of your body pushing downward into the earth.

3. Now set your focus on the areas of your body that are in contact with the ground. Try to home in on those physical sensations. What do you feel?

4. If you are successful, you will feel a kind of tingling sensation begin in these contact areas—focus on this sensation, and allow it to grow within you until it fills your body.

5. Finally, make a mental note of this sensation, because this is what you're looking for in any objects or places you try to "read" for energy. Once you have a good handle on the seated exercise, then you can practice with objects using the same technique of hyperfocusing on the parts where your body makes contact with the object. Over time, you will be amazed by how well your perceptions of energy in an object aligns with those of other people.

Taking it Further

Next, you will need to start going for walks so you can practice this skill while out and about. Heathen magic is often a wild form of magic that meets with the numinous Other in the between-places away from the warm glow of houses. Going out to the lonely places without the ability to sense energy can make these practices a lot more dangerous. So, begin by trying to sense the energy in trees, rocks, plants—anything you come across that draws you. You may find that you begin to experience certain feelings, see colors in your mind's eye, or even hear snippets of information in your mind during these experiments. This is all quite normal and helps you to build up a multilayered picture of your local environment.

—)}o Fundamentals: Energy II o{(—

Another form of energy sensing you should work on is of the more ambient kind—in other words, what you can discern about the environment you're in on the whole. Most people already have some experience with this kind of ambient energy of place; it is part of what people are referring to when they talk about places having vibes. This exercise may be done indoors or out, but if done outdoors, please be sure to go to a place that feels friendly to begin with.

You will need (if working outside)
Offerings (handful of cornmeal/pinch of tobacco/small creamer pot of milk/prepackaged pat of butter)

Practice

1. You may stand or sit for this exercise. If working outside, begin by addressing any local Hiddenfolk. Explain what you intend to do and give them assurances that no harm is meant on your part. Make an offering. If the place still feels friendly, then continue to the next step.

2. As with the seated exercise, begin with an awareness of the outer boundaries of your skin. Take note of where you make contact with any other surfaces, and allow yourself to acknowledge the energy before letting it fall away to focus on the parts of yourself that aren't in contact with anything else.

3. Now take a deep breath in, and on the exhale, expand your awareness outward and past the outer boundaries of your skin. Repeat that last step, until you feel your awareness bump up against something "solid." This "solid" may be wards (either your own or those of your neighbors (if they have them). It could also represent the edge of whatever energy is in the space you occupy, and the nebulous border between that and another "front" of energy. It could honestly be any number of things, but whenever you reach it, stop and think about the space encompassed by your bubble of awareness. How does it feel? What impressions do you get? Do any areas in particular stand out? Sometimes when doing this,

you can come across non-human persons that inhabit the space. What impressions do you have of them? Do they seem amenable to forming reciprocal relationships with you?

4. When you have explored this expanded energetic awareness to its fullest extent, simply allow that awareness to fall away. Some people prefer to imagine themselves retracting their awareness with each inhale. However, I find it just as effective to visualize that awareness fading as a dream fades upon waking.

5. If you are performing this exercise outside, be sure to leave a small offering for the local Hiddenfolk.

Energetic Etiquette

Once you gain an awareness of the energy in the world around you (if you do not have that awareness already), you will notice that there is a certain etiquette to manipulating and interacting with energy. For example, especially at magical events, you may encounter people who seem to wear energy like a cloak—in my experience, this is usually a form of showing off and trying to impress. Generally speaking, you're going to want to keep any energy you have to yourself and mind other people's energetic business unless asked.

A similar principle operates when performing exercises such as the previous exercise. If you are outside, that kind of expansion of scope and pushing up against other energies, even in a nonaggressive, way can easily be taken as rude. Not all beings like to be seen, sensed, or energetically felt by humans, nor do they always appreciate us wandering into places they consider theirs. It's thus generally a good idea to get into the habit of always carrying small offerings when out and about. Since I moved to the United States, cornmeal and tobacco have been recommended to me as offerings to the local unseen. Readers in Europe can make excellent use of small butter and cream packets for the same. I carry a mixture of both sets of offerings in the hope that the spirits I encounter will like at least one of my offerings.

However, while we generally want to leave a place on good terms, it's always a good idea to carry salt too. This is because salt is one of the most easily accessible and portable apotropaic (protective) substances there is, and it is always good to be prepared in case things go wrong. For more information on how you can stay safe and troubleshoot any potential problems, refer to chapter 12.

Seven

MAGICAL TOOLS

W hen compared with practitioners of other modern magical traditions, practitioners of Heathen magic tend to have fewer tools on average. Moreover, outside of Heathen occult groups such as the Rune Gild, there is no standard or basic set of tools that all völur, seiðrworkers, haliarunnae, or galdra-maður must have. The tools often vary from practitioner to practitioner and depend on the type of magic the practitioner most commonly does. However, despite this high degree of variety among Heathen magic workers, there are some items that are more common than others, and most seem to have some kind of knife, runes, and a staff. The tools included in this chapter are the kinds of tools that I work with and are not intended to be representative of all practitioners of Heathen magic.

In this chapter, we're going to take a look at some of the ways in which tools were possibly viewed by elder Heathens and some of the implications of those views for modern practice. Then we'll be moving on to ideas of "storied tools" and how they fit in with the model of fate presented in chapter 5. Finally, there will be an overview of the five main tools that I use in my magical practice as well as suggested processes for creating your own.

Til Death Do Us Part

First, let me ask you a question. What will happen to your tools when you die? This is a question I think a lot of us currently struggle to answer. A good percentage of the people I have spoken to about this plan to gift them to friends or be buried with the most important ones. Others are setting up exchanges where people can send their tools after death so they can be rehomed with people who will respect them. This is an aspect of end-of-life planning that is becoming increasingly important as more people die Heathen.

The concerns reflected in these questions are nothing new. If anything, this anxiety over the continued or final fate of magical tools is one that the elder Heathens seem to have also shared.

For the elder Heathen, tools (or at least staffs) seem to have been considered living and treated accordingly at death, an idea that's attested in archaeological sources. For the elder Heathen, this postmortem treatment was a curious mix of respectful yet apotropaic practices. The magic worker could have been well-liked in life and gifted accordingly in death but then have their body smashed by heavy rocks. Where found, the theorized "staffs of sorcery" seem to have been intentionally broken before being subjected to the same fate under heavy rocks as their owners.[193]

There are some interesting cultural anxieties reflected in these practices. To crush the dead under heavy rocks suggests a belief that dead magic workers are more likely to become revenants.[194] Far more interesting is the ritual breaking and crushing of the staff, because not only do these actions suggest that the staff also represented a similar potential danger to the living, but that it, in some way, was considered *alive*.

But not all tools are created equally or carry the same dangers. In the Viking Age, it only seems to have been the staffs that were subjected to this treatment, or in other words, the tools that may have originally been considered to *live* or possess life in the first place.

---

193. Leszek Gardeła, "A Biography of the Seiðr-Staffs. Towards an Archaeology of Emotions," in *Between Paganism and Christianity in the North*, ed. Leszek P. Słupecki and Jakub Morawiec (Rzeszów: Rzeszów University, 2009): 207–209.

194. Karen Bek-Pedersen, "Nornir in Old Norse Mythology," 192.

The implications of this evidence are incredibly useful for modern practice. Because it implies that some tools could, in a very real sense, be considered living beings with enough agency to merit destruction in the grave. And where there is life, you will always find *story*.

Tools and Story

Story, and the idea of storied tools, plays an important role in the kind of magic I practice. Heathen magic is inherently animistic and founded in story, and so too are the tools of the craft. Within the context of tools, tool-making, or tool acquisition, "being storied" is essentially having layers of ritual words and actions built into either the creation process or acquisition process of the tool that link that tool to a story of purpose in some way. These stories of purpose can either be the primal law (ørlög) given during the act of creation, or with bought tools, added as layers of story during the acquisition process in order to better align the tool with your desired purpose.

Tool Creation and Myth

There's a long-held convention in various magical traditions that it's always better to make your own tools, and modern Heathens (myself included) have also tended toward this. It is undeniably the best option for building those layers of story into a tool. When we create tools for ourselves, we play both mother and Norn, giving them a kind of ørlög in a sense as we birth them into the world to serve the purpose given to them. This process is quite different from the layers of story that are built into an already-created item in the hopes of aligning it with our purpose.

Mythologically speaking, there is something very reminiscent of the creation myth of *Askr and Embla* in tools and the process of making your own tools. Because as Óðinn, Loðurr, and Hœnir transformed the raw materials of the ash log (Askr) and the elm log (Embla) into the first humans, we transform the raw materials of our tools into something more. And as the gods gave ørlög to logs without ørlög, so too with us and the tools we make—when it comes to tools, the intended purpose of a tool *is* its ørlög.

But the creation of Askr and Embla is not the only example of this process; elements of it are found littered throughout accounts of magical tool creation. In *Hávamál*, for example, is mention of carving and staining the runes, or in other words, giving them shape and color (the "sense" is already contained within the symbols themselves and the associations they hold).[195] Another example may be found in the short story "Þorleifs þáttr jarlsskálds," in which a tree-man is created with the intent of sending him to assassinate someone in Iceland. Here the tree-man is enlivened with prayers, breath, warmth, and color in the form of the sacrificed man's heart. He is then dressed as a man and sent on his way.[196] Similar ideas can also be found in old English magico-medical manuscripts. In charm 66 of the *Lacnunga* manuscript, prayer (likely conceived of as a form of spellcraft to early Germanic Christians) is sung over a healing drink in such a way that the *breath goes wholly in* as one chants.[197]

The idea that tools are something that should be essentially enlivened or given life and ørlög of a sort has become central to my approach to tool-making. When I make a tool, I am engaging in an act of creation by emulating the actions of the gods on that mythical beach in a time that never existed. I give my breath like Óðinn, and "sense" in the form of incantation like Hœnir. Then finally, I give warmth and hue like Lóðurr, staining and passing over/through flames as necessary. By doing this, I not only give life, but by creating with an intended purpose in mind, I also set the ørlög of my tools.

Tool Acquisition and "Smaller Stories"

Not everyone makes their own tools and, depending on the tool in question, may not have the skills to do so. For example, there is no way I could forge my own iron staff, because I lack not only the skills and access to a forge, but also the time to acquire the necessary level of skill to forge such an item. Sometimes, it's just a necessity to buy tools.

Unfortunately, there is no way to set the ørlög of tools already wrought then bought. That window of opportunity is simply gone by the time you come into possession of the tool. However, that does not mean that your bought tools have to be completely utilitarian or lacking in any way. There are still plenty of opportunities to add layers of ritual actions and words to imbue a new tool with stories that best align with an intended purpose.

---

195. Carolyne Larrington (trans.), *Poetic Edda*, 34–35.

196. North, *Heathen Gods*, 95.

197. Pollington, *Leechcraft*, 205.

In a way, ørlög and story inhabit a similar field of experience because as previously mentioned, there is no ørlög without story; orlög is both a product and generating force of story. The story you are born with (ørlög) shapes the choices and opportunities you have. It also provides the framework (law) within which you work, and every choice and action (as well as what happens to you) combine to build the story of you. Over time, your choices and actions will create their own frameworks within your life, either constraining or broadening what you have to work with in the future depending on the choices you and those around you make. Tools are not so different from people in this way.

In the beginning, tools are created with a purpose in mind. For a magic worker, that purpose will be inherently magical. For someone who is making the tool for more practical reasons, that purpose will be mundane. For example, the magic worker who forges a knife will forge it with the intent that it can perform all the various tasks expected of a magical blade. The blacksmith churning out blades for sale will forge that blade with a completely different intent. Your bought items may not have the ørlög of your choosing, but you can ensure that they at least have a kind of "story" (or series of ritual actions and words) that align them more closely with your purpose before use.

When buying tools, the process of imbuing a tool with the right kind of story begins before and at acquisition. Sometimes, you may find that the circumstances in which you get your tools are eerily appropriate for the purpose you have in mind without any effort on your part—this is another way in which tools may be said to be storied. In other words, the tale of how you came by them is uncannily appropriate for the tool in question and the purpose you had in mind. Sometimes you may even find that these tales of acquisition have uncanny parallels to the bigger stories of mythology, and to a degree that makes you wonder if some kind of external force had a hand in it all along. Rarely, you may even find yourself the recipient of magical tools gifted by numinous powers. However, not all tool acquisition is as exciting; in many cases, magic workers need to rely on the smaller stories of magical correspondences through the processes of acquisition and hallowing tools in order to build in those important stories of purpose.

The "Smaller Stories" of Magical Correspondences

Although story is an important part of the Heathen magic that I practice, ideas such as magical correspondences are absent from the Heathen-period sources (or at least I have yet to find them). However, despite this absence, I find magical correspondences to be incredibly useful when acquiring and preparing bought tools for magical work, and over the years, I've come to look at magical correspondences as the barest remnants of stories pertaining to planets, days, plants, stones, and trees. When tapped into appropriately, these smaller stories of correspondences can help us to ritualistically set down layers of the right kind of story for our tools.

Working with Planetary and Lunar Correspondences

Despite the fact that they are not of Heathen origin, I find planetary day correspondences and lunar phases to be useful additions to my magical toolkit for building story into everything from tools to the timing of rituals.

In my practice, magical correspondences function as a series of "smaller stories" that may be added to the "metaplot" (or here, the ørlög of a tool) in order to better align a tool to your purpose. My primary use for these smaller stories is in magical timing. So for example, I will use a combination of planetary and lunar correspondences in order to figure out the best time for working a certain kind of magic or creating a certain kind of tool. When using correspondences during the process of creating a tool or even hallowing a purchased tool, I sit with it for a while and think about my intended purpose for it before looking for the best correspondence. For example, if I have a set of old railroad spikes I intend to use for home protection, my purpose would be protection/defense. From there, I can look at the planetary correspondence table and choose the most appropriate day for ritually imbuing those spikes with that purpose.

As you will see from the following correspondence tables, Tuesday and Saturday would both be appropriate day choices for our hypothetical working. However, my personal preference would be for Tuesday because of its connection with the god Tyr/Tiw. Tyr, as he was known to the early English, was a god of war who sacrificed his hand to keep his community safe. It is from his Old English name form, *Tiw*, that we derive the word "Tuesday," literally "day of Tiw."

Once I have made a decision on the day, then I would take the moon phase into consideration. As our hypothetical example is defensive, I would probably perform the magic as needed rather than waiting until a chosen moon phase.

If the use of these tables does not yet make sense, do not worry. There will be plenty of opportunities to practice this way of thinking throughout the course of this chapter.

Planetary Days

Day	Associations
Monday	Visions, psychism, journeying, divination, the moon.
Tuesday	War, attack, defense, summoning the battle dead . Associated with Mars and the Norse war god Tyr (Tiw in Old English).
Wednesday	Divination, necromancy, communication. Associated with Mercury and Óðinn.
Thursday	Health, wealth, good fortune, happiness, and success. Associated with Jupiter and Þórr (Thor).
Friday	Love, binding.[198] Associated with Venus and Freyja.
Saturday	Control, protection, necromancy, defense, containment. Associated with Saturn.
Sunday	Purification, healing, divination, exorcism, growth; the day of the sun.

---

198. Due to associations between Freyja/Frigga/Frige and Friday, I consider Friday to be a good day for seiðr and binding magic in general.

Lunar Phases

Phase	Associations
Waxing	Healing (strengthening), growth, increase, and improvement.
Full	Reinforcement or culmination magic, stability, psychism, necromancy.[199]
Waning	Banishment, healing (of growths), getting rid of situations that no longer serve.
Dark moon	Dissolution and endings; liminality.

→}o Tools: The Censer o{←

The first tool is the censer, as this is the one tool that will feature in the instructions for every other tool included in this chapter. The censer is a fireproof receptacle in which loose incense can be safely burned. In the Old English magico-medical manuscripts, the healer would use a chafing dish for this purpose. Then as now, chafing dishes were used to keep food warm. This was not a dedicated magical tool by any means, and was likely just what the healer had to hand. Because of this, I consider a separate ritual censer to be an optional tool. In my personal practice, I do not have a dedicated censer and instead tend to use whatever I have to hand that is heatproof enough that the charcoal disk will not burn through. In the past, this has been everything from an actual censer purchased from an occult store, to my cast iron "cauldron," to a flat, medium-sized rock that I keep around. You could even use a plant pot filled with sand if needed! Regardless of what you use, I have included a hallowing charm to be spoken over the censer in each set of instructions given.

→}o Tools: Hallowing the Censer (Optional) o{←

For those of you who want to have a dedicated censer hallowed for the purpose of creating sacred smoke, I provide the following instructions.

---

199. The full moon may have been associated with necromancy in Norse sources; see Hilda Ellis Davidson, *The Road to Hel*, 91.

You will need

The receptacle you wish to use as a censer

A bowl of water big enough to contain your intended censer

Three teaspoons of salt in a small bowl or ramekin

A good handful of mugwort (fresh if possible)

A clean towel

Procedure

1. The best places to hallow your censer is either on a table, or outside on relatively flat ground. Before you begin, you should have all your required items to hand. If working inside, I recommend laying out the towel on your table so as to help prevent everything getting wet.

2. Begin by taking three deep breaths. Although we do not necessarily need to create sacred space for making our tools, it is always good to begin any tool-making sessions in the right mental space. As you breathe out, imagine yourself exhaling all the distractions and stresses of the day. If three breaths are not enough, then take nine breaths instead. You may also wish to take the time to ground and center at this point.[200]

3. Now bring the bowl of water and bowl or ramekin of salt toward you, and pour the salt into the water. Stir the salt water clockwise with your right hand three times. As you do so, know that you are moving your hand with the course of the sun to stir in blessings and holiness. Let this be your intent as you stir.

4. Next, either lean over the bowl or lift it to you so that your breath goes wholly into the water, then speak the following charm. As you do so, imagine the intent of the words you speak leaving your mouth, riding out upon your breath and filling the salt water with golden light:

> Over water and salt
> A galdor I speak
> With wise words I will it

---

200. See chapter 4 for full instructions on grounding and centering.

> And my breath goes wholly in
> Making clean waters holy
> Fast flee the evil from it!
> Fast flee evil magic from it!

5. Now take up your mugwort. Once more holding it so that your breath goes onto the herb, awaken your mugwort with the following words. Again, "see" the words flowing from your mouth as gold light that moves over the herb and awakening her as you speak:

> Remember, Mugwort, what you revealed
> what you set out in mighty revelation.
> "Una" you are called, oldest of plants
> You have might against three and against thirty.
> You have might against poison and infection
> You have might against the evil that travels around the land.[201]

6. Finally, take your censer and wash it in the salt water, using the mugwort to scrub the surface of the receptacle as you do so. While you wash the censer chant the following charm at least nine times, visualizing the gold of the waters and the force of the awakened herb neutralizing any impurities as you work:

> With holy herb
> And holy waters
> I scrub this censer clean
> Hallowed it is
> A holy dish
> Þūnor/Þórr make holy this dish!
> Þūnor/Þórr keep holy this dish!

Once you are done washing and chanting, simply place your censer somewhere where it can air-dry without being disturbed.

---

201. Taken from the Nine Herbs Charm, in Stephen Pollington, *Leechcraft*, 215.

Tools: The Spindle

The Spindle as a Magical Tool

When most people think of magical tools, very few would ever think of spindles. They're just not typically associated with magic. However, as we saw in chapters 1 and 2, the spindle is, both symbolically and practically, at the very heart of the kind of magic I practice.

Although there are different types of practice recorded in the lore as *seiðr*, the oldest threads of this magic seem to reach back into wider Indo-European ideas of fate. As discussed in chapter 2, there are a number of Indo-European deities of childbirth and death who are also deities of magic and spinning who seem to hint at there being something inherently fate-bound about spinning. The sense of spinning as a fateful activity is also reinforced by ideas of spun fate at birth and the ensnarement of the deceased at death. But as we have seen with the Norse sources, these associations are nowhere near as explicit as in other Indo-European cultures.

Regardless of its origins, seiðr remained primarily a form of magic that was inextricably bound up in the work of pulling and binding, of enticement and ensnarement, even when spinning was not involved. Unlike other forms of magic, spun seiðr required no special tools over than what the witch herself would have already possessed. Spindles were ubiquitous to the home in the Heathen period, and I suspect that that ubiquity was part of the reason why seiðr seems to have been so feared.

In order to do this kind of seiðr you have to be able to spin, and not just a little, either. You need to be able to spin well enough that you can rely on muscle memory to carry the spinning while you work magically.

Practitioners in the Viking Age would likely have just used whatever spindles were to hand. However, there is at least one example of a spindle whorl that was marked for (Heathen) magical or prayerful purpose which suggests that some may have also worked with dedicated spindles too.[202] Although I do not believe in the necessity of having a dedicated spindle for this kind

---

202. Dr. Adam Daubney, "Spindle Whorl: Unique ID: LIN-D92A22," *Portable Antiquities Scheme*, 2010, accessed November 6, 2019. https://finds.org.uk/database/artefacts/record/id/409249.

of work, I do think that the idea of a dedicated spindle is something we can adopt today.

Planning Your Magical Spindle

If the idea of having a dedicated magical spindle is something that interests you, there are three factors you need to take into account when planning your magical spindle: the purpose (ørlög) of your spindle, the materials you use, and ritual timing.

The first and most important factor is purpose. This is something that you really need to be clear on: Why do you want a dedicated spindle? What specifically would you want to use it for magically? Remember, seiðr was a magic of binding and pulling. So do you want to pull something to you or pull to take from someone else?

Once you have decided the purpose of your spindle, you can begin to think about the kinds of materials you might want to use when constructing it or look for when buying. Here we come to another area of magical correspondences that, once again, is not found in Heathen-period sources. That's not to say that certain trees, plants, and stones didn't have specific associations; there is quite a lot of material in the Old English magico-medical manuscript tradition that clearly associates different types of tree, herb, and stone with different healing actions that can be used as a basis for extrapolating sets of correspondences that can be used magically. As always, we need to bear in mind that this material (while wonderful and full of probable remnants of Heathen-period material) is the child (children?) of a later, syncretic worldview. I make no claims to old Heathen tradition here.

However, despite this lack of definitive historical foundation, I have found wood correspondences to be useful in various types of magic, so what follows are the ones I use. Please be advised: this is an eclectic mix. Some of the following correspondences are from natural magic sources, some are pulled from folklore, and others are pulled from the tree information found in traditional sources on the Irish Ogham writing system.

Wood Correspondence Table

Tree	Correspondences
Apple	Long life, youth, love, Iðunn (Norse goddess of youth and renewal), the otherworld/passage between the human world and the otherworld.[203; 204]
Ash	Protection against witchcraft, the tree Yggdrasil and the first man in Old Norse myth, healing, protection against fire.[205] Spears and weaving looms were usually made of ash.[206] Considered a masculine tree and associated with the sun in natural magic.[207]
Birch	Protection, cleansing, healing, purification, love, fertility.[208; 209] Considered a feminine tree and associated with Venus in Natural Magic.[210; 211] I personally associate birch with the Spinning Goddess.
Blackthorn	Both protective and malefic; cursing and protection against spirits.[212]

---

203. Corinne Boyer, *Under the Witching Tree* (London: Troy Books Publishing, 2017), 60–64.

204. Erynn Rowan Laurie, *Ogam: Weaving Word Wisdom* (Stafford, UK: Immanion Press, 2007), 94.

205. Corrine Boyer, *Under the Witching Tree*, 209–218.

206. Erynn Rowan Laurie, *Ogam*, 75.

207. John Michael Greer, *Encyclopedia of Natural Magic* (St. Paul, MN: Llewelyn Publications, 2005), 57.

208. Corrine Boyer, *Under the Witching Tree*, 125–132.

209. Erynn Rowan Laurie, *Ogam*, 60–62.

210. Stephen Pollington, *Leechcraft*, 501.

211. John Michael Greer, *Encyclopedia*, 67.

212. Corrine Boyer, *Under the Witching Tree*, 161–163.

Tree	Correspondences
Elder	Strong protection, Frau Holle, often believed to be possessed of a spirit, spirit summoning, considered unlucky or even evil in folk tradition.[213] Associated with the planet Mercury.[214] (Hollow wood, generally unsuitable for making spindles.)
Hazel	Wisdom, divination, weather magic, protection, luck, prosperity.[215] Also associated with the planet Mercury.[216]
Oak	Healing, protection, lightning and storms, fertility, boundaries, thresholds, sacred to Þórr/Thor/Þūnor.[217] Associated with Jupiter.[218]
Rowan	Protection against hostile spirits, magic, and nightmares. Also may be used for curse-breaking. Associated with the sun.[219]
Willow	Divination, heartbreak, grief, death.[220; 221]
Yew	Funerary tree, associated with death, ancestors, the dead, underworld, and Saturn. Protective against evil spirits.[222]

---

213. Ibid., 19–23.

214. John Michael Greer, *Encyclopedia*, 99.

215. Corrine Boyer, *Under the Witching Tree*, 33–42.

216. John Michael Greer, *Encyclopedia*, 116.

217. Corrine Boyer, *Under the Witching Tree*, 197-204.

218. John Michael Greer, *Encyclopedia*, 166-167.

219. Ibid., 181–182.

220. Boyer, *Under the Witching Tree*, 137–142.

221. Erynn Rowan Laurie, *Ogam*, 72.

222. Boyer, *Under the Witching Tree*, 79–84.

Once you have decided on your spindle's purpose and chosen the materials accordingly, you may wish to incorporate magical timing into your planned tool creation rite using the tables provided earlier in this chapter.

To give you an example of how this planning process might work, let's imagine that I am planning a spindle for necromantic work. Because I want to pull the dead to me, a good choice of wood for my spindle would be yew. As you can see from the *Wood Correspondence Table* that I have given, yew has long been associated with the dead and would therefore be the most obvious choice for my hypothetical necromantic spindle.

Depending on where you live, you may find it growing in churchyards or as a shrub at the side of the road. The earliest spindles were little more than sticks, but your spindle can be as simple or as complicated as time, tools, and skills allow. Alternatively, you could simply buy a yew spindle from any number of online vendors on sites such as Etsy.

As I like to observe planetary days, I would construct or buy my yew spindle on a Saturday. As the day of plodding, old Saturn, Saturday can be a good day for necromantic rites as well as reaffirming boundaries (important in necromancy). I would probably also want to begin the construction of the spindle (or buy it) on a Saturday when the moon is waxing, and then wait for a Saturday on a full moon to finally bring it into being as a tool.

Whatever choices you make when planning your magical spindle, you will want to hallow your spindle and give it purpose before use.

⇥ Spindle-Setting Rite ⇤

When making tools, I do not normally create sacred space. However, because I recommend calling upon the Spinning Goddess during this rite, I have included a simple process for creating sacred space using water or wet yarn. From a practical perspective, this rite is best done inside, but depending on the kind of floor you have in your home, it may not be a good idea to sprinkle water directly onto the floor. For this reason, I give an alternative option using wet yarn that I have used in my own home for years. If wrung out properly before laying on the floor, the wet yarn not only clearly delineates the boundaries of your sacred space, but holds the potency of the hallowed water within its fibers without making the floor too wet. The suggested amount of ten yards should be enough to give you a nine-foot diameter circle. Ideally, your sacred space should encompass a table where you can work, with all the necessary items laid out in your workspace before you begin. Set your deity representation up so that it will face where you are sitting, but so that you will still have room to work.

Before beginning your rite, you will need to prepare a charm or set of notes laying out the "sense" or purpose of your new tool. The charm you use should not only set down the purpose of the tool, but your expectations for it as well. You can find more information on creating your own charms in chapters 9 and 10.

If you are making your own spindle, I recommend that you construct the component parts and put them together before this rite. Additionally, I would also advise you to varnish or otherwise seal your new magical spindle. You want it to stand up to the work you put it through and varnish will help to protect it—especially if you do a lot of work outside. This can be done whenever the paint is dry or you have time.

You will need

The spindle you intend to hallow and/or parts for constructing it

Bowl of water with three teaspoons of salt

A paintbrush

Censer

Charcoal disc

A small bowl of dried mugwort

An offering of a small cup of mead and/or homemade bread roll

Candle

Knife or permanent pen (optional)

Around ten yards of woolen yarn of any color (optional)

Lighter or matches

A previously prepared charm for giving "sense" (or purpose) to your tool

Spinning Goddess representation (either a statue or noose used for the ritual in chapter 2 will suffice)

Procedure

1. Begin by taking three deep breaths. With each breath, allow the stress and distractions of the day to fade away, and feel yourself moving into a state of mind that is more conducive to ritual. If you find after those three breaths that you need more time to transition into ritual space, then take nine breaths instead. Light your charcoal disc and place it in the censer.

2. Now, speak the following charm over the salt water mixture. Be sure to make sure that your breath goes wholly into the water as you do so. As you speak, imagine your words taking form as golden light that moves into the water with your breath, purifying it and imbuing it with purpose:

> Over water and salt
> A galdor I speak
> With wise words I will it
> And my breath goes wholly in
> Making clean waters holy
> Fast flee the evil from it!
> Fast flee evil magic from it!

3. Then take roughly half of the mugwort from the small bowl. Cup it in your hands and bring it to your lips before awakening the herb with the following words. Once again, "see" the words flowing from your mouth as golden light that moves over the surface of the herb and awakens it as you speak:

> Remember, Mugwort, what you revealed
> What you set out in mighty revelation.
> "Una" you are called, oldest of plants
> You have might against three and against thirty.
> You have might against poison and infection
> You have might against the evil that travels around the land.[223]

---

223. Taken from the Nine Herbs Charm, in Pollington, *Leechcraft*, 215.

Speak the charm three times, then sprinkle the mugwort into the salt water before stirring clockwise with your right hand three times. Again, your intent here is that you are stirring with the course of the sun and, in doing so, aligning yourself with the blessings and holiness conferred by the sun.

4. If you have a dedicated censer, simply burn a small amount of mugwort in order to purify your working space. If you are like me and tend to use whatever you have to hand, then you may wish to use the following hallowing charm before burning the mugwort.

> Over fire and smoke
> I speak my spell
> To twisting tendrils of cleansing heat
> Ravenous beast of fire I command you
> Reeking spirit of smoke I conjure you
> Wherever you burn, chase away the ill-wights!
> Wherever you burn, cleanse away all blights! [224]

5. Now you have prepared the waters and purified the space with mugwort smoke, it's time to create your sacred space. If you have no concerns about your floor getting particularly wet, then simply take up the bowl of salt water and mugwort, and beginning in the east, circumambulate your space three times sunwise while speaking the following charm. If, however, you do have concerns about your floor, then take your yarn and soak it in the salt water and mugwort mixture. As you do so, see the yarn becoming increasingly imbued with that same holy energy as the water mixture in the bowl. Generally speaking, it's easier if the yarn is loosely tied in a small bundle when doing this; wet yarn easily becomes knotted. In addition, be sure to carefully unknot your bundle before wringing the yarn out and removing it from the bowl. Instead of sprinkling water, lay the yarn in a circle in the space around your work area while chanting the space-hallowing charm:

---

224. The charms for the water and censer can also be used for general purification and space clearing.

> With waters clean I wind my way
> Around this sacred space
> Sained within, yet wild without
> Þórr make sacred this space
> Þórr keep sacred this space.

6. The next step is to invite the presence of the Spinning Goddess to the rite. If you wish to use different words to the ones that are included here, please feel free to do so:

> High Lady
> Life-giving one
> Shaper of luck with spindle in hand
> Slayer of death
> Desirous of wisdom
> Far-faring Freyja propitious and fair.
> Far-faring Freyja come hear my prayer.

7. Once you have spoken your invitation, offer the mead and/or bread to the Spinning Goddess, setting it aside or placing it before whichever representation you have (if you have one). Then, in your own words, address the Spinning Goddess and explain to her what you're doing and why you asked for her to come. Ask her to guide and bless your work as you make a tool worthy of her magic.

8. Here we come to the work proper of giving our spindle a "life" of its own. This is where you will give the three gifts of life to your new tool. Take up your spindle and breathe onto it three times, saying:

> Önd I give you, Óðinn's gift
> That you might breathe and know life.

At this point you may feel the energy begin to awaken within the spindle with each breath. To me, this feels like a crackling heat that works its way from my mouth and through the material of the tool.

Now, bring the spindle close to your mouth and say:

> Óðr I give you, the gift of Hœnir
> Hear my words and be shaped by them.

Speak the charm you prepared over the spindle and repeat as many times as you feel is necessary. As a rule, I repeat three times as a reflection of the three life-giving gifts of Óðinn, Hœnir, and Loðurr.

Then, pass the spindle over the candle and say:

> Lá and Litr I give you, the gift of Lóðurr
> That you might gain color and warmth.

At this point, you may also wish to mark your spindle with appropriate symbols or runes. In the case of my fictitious necromantic spindle, I would mark it with the nauðiz rune, as there is evidence that rune was associated in some way with necromancy.[225]

9. Now, sprinkle the spindle with some of the salt and mugwort water you used to create your space (if not soaking it entirely). If you marked the spindle with symbols using a permanent marker, be careful of your work as you do so. Here, the salt water mixture serves as a symbolic stand-in for the hue of paint or blood.

10. Finally, present your new spindle to the Spinning Goddess, holding it up in a gesture of offering and ask her to hallow and bless your new tool for use. You may also perform divination at this point to see if she has anything she wishes to communicate to you at this time. When you feel as though this part of the rite is over, thank her for her help and burn some more mugwort in her honor as a final offering.

11. If you used yarn to delineate your space, take up the yarn once more, beginning in the east and moving counterclockwise, winding it into a small ball as you do so. This will help keep it tidy until you can dry it out and eventually burn it. If you have one, move your offerings to your Spinning Goddess shrine for three days before disposing outside or in

---

225. There is some evidence that suggests a connection between the nauðiz rune and necromancy. For more information, see Pollington, *Runes, Literacy in the Germanic Iron Age* (Little Downham, UK: Anglo-Saxon Books, 2016), 304–305.

the most ecologically responsible method for your area. If you do not have a shrine, leave the representation and offerings out for three hours before disposing in the same way. Tidy up your space and store your new spindle.

After nine days of "life," you may wish to give your spindle a name. There's an entire tradition of naming special items (usually weapons), so why not your tools?

➳ Tools: The Cauldron ⟆

While common to many witchcraft traditions, cauldrons are not particularly well-represented in Heathen magical traditions. Nevertheless, my cauldron has become an important part of my magical work. It is a multipurpose tool that can be used for everything from representing the watery passage between the living and dead in necromantic rites, to burning offerings and holding incense.

There are two main ways in which you can acquire a cauldron. The first (and easiest) is to buy one from either your local witch/occult store (if you have one) or one of the many online retailers. The second is to make a habit of checking out your local antiques stores for cast iron or copper receptacles. If you have never gone in search of magical implements in antiques stores before, you may find yourself surprised by the amount of yesteryear items that lend themselves to magical uses. For example, I picked up a cast-iron dutch oven that now serves as my cauldron.

As a secondhand acquisition, my biggest priority was purifying the cauldron of any unhæl influences. First I washed out my cauldron with a mixture of salt water and mugwort while chanting the charm to awaken the mugwort and remind her of her abilities.[226] After that, I lit a charcoal disk for incense; spoke a charm over it; then burned a mixture of rosemary, vervain, and juniper incense, passing my cauldron through the smoke as I did so.

Finally, I rubbed hyssop oil into the inside of the cauldron. The biggest "story" for me with my cauldron was keeping it clear. As a cosmological prop, receptacle for burning, tool for healing, and occasional source of ashes and scrapings for making black salt, this was the only story that made sense.

---

226. You can find this charm in step two of the *Spindle-Setting Rite* given earlier in this chapter.

Tools: The Knife

Knives can be used a number of ways in Heathen magic, for everything from carving runes and cutting materials, to marking out space. As a (usually) steel implement, there is also an apotropaic element to knives that can be useful for dealing with the dead and otherworldly, which makes it a useful addition to any magical go-bag.[227]

However, the knife is one tool I prefer to consecrate in the style of a witch. This is because experience has taught me that there are a lot of beings that don't recognize Heathen deities and rituals, and so it's good to have tools with diverse layers built in.

As always, it is better to make your own knife; however, this simply isn't an option for the vast majority of us who use knives in our magical practice. It takes time and resources to learn how to forge knives, and most of us lack the access. The second-best option would be to commission a blacksmith to make one for you, and there are a couple of blacksmiths who are currently vending online who make their blades in a ritual fashion. These are generally very expensive (and rightfully so—there's a lot of work and skill that goes into making those blades). But not everybody has the ability or desire to pay for such a blade. If this is you, then a simple black-handled, double-edged blade will suffice. You can generally buy these in occult or witch stores.

Ideally, you're looking for a sturdy knife, with a steel blade that's about five to six inches long. If you are making or commissioning your knife, you may wish to make the haft out of a specific kind of wood such as ash or oak and then paint or stain it black. But if you are buying a knife from a regular occult store, you probably won't have a choice on the haft beyond black, which is fine, because the blade is the most important part of this tool anyway.

In terms of magical timing, if this is something you wish to observe when building the "story" of your knife, then the usual recommendation is to buy or make your knife on a Thursday, or Jupiter's day, a day of prosperity and success. The knife is supposed to be both protective and commanding as well as *magnetizing* and able to bring things to you. When I followed this recommendation while making my own knife, I found the daily energies of Thursday/

---

227. See chapter 12 for more about magical go-bags.

Jupiter a good balance to the otherwise very martial/Mars energies in the rest of the rite.

The following procedure is based on one given by Paul Huson in *Mastering Witchcraft*. It's incredibly effective. And as someone who connects with the idea of elves as smiths, I find the act of ritually tempering and quenching a blade while speaking charms appealing from the perspective of birth and setting ørlög too. By tempering and quenching the blade, you effectively put yourself at the point of creation/birth, enabling you to effectively have a do-over and birth the blade as you would like.

Before I go any further, I must warn you that this rite does involve the use of blood. This can either be your own blood or, if you cannot do that for whatever reason, from a packet of meat bought at your local supermarket. If using your own blood, *please* use sterile lancets instead of a knife to draw that blood. Lancets can easily be bought in pharmacies and are far less likely to leave you with an infection. Along similar lines, it's also a good idea to prepare the area you will draw the blood from with alcohol wipes before pricking yourself and covering it with a bandage when finished.

⟶⟩o Blade Rite o⟨⟵

You will need

Martial herbs[228] such as pepper, blackthorn leaves, ginger, ground chilis (don't worry if you don't have all of these; use whatever you have)

A bowl of boiling water

Sterile lancets or blood from a butcher/meat packet

Alcohol wipes and a bandage (if using your own blood)

Salt water and mugwort hallowing water (see *Spindle-Setting Rite* for instructions on how to make this)

Censer

Charcoal disc

Lighter or matches

Lodestone

---

228. Martial herbs are herbs that correspond with the planet Mars.

Pestle and mortar (or one large flat rock and a smaller stone that you can use in a similar way)

Paint or permanent marker (optional)

Procedure

1. Begin by making an infusion of water and martial herbs. Retain some of the herb/spice mixture, and powder it using a pestle and mortar to create incense for later use. If you are comfortable doing so, you can add a few drops of your own blood to the mix. If this makes you uncomfortable for any reason, you can also use blood from meat bought from the supermarket.

2. Now, light a charcoal disc and place it in your censer before speaking the following hallowing charm over it:

> Over fire and smoke I speak my spell
> To twisting tendrils of cleansing heat
> Ravenous beast of fire I command you
> Ravenous spirit of smoke I conjure you
> Wherever you burn, chase away ill-wights
> Wherever you burn, cleanse away all blights.

3. For the next step, you need to allow the censer to get as hot as you can get it before burning some of the martial incense you created in step one. A lot of the recommended herbs from step one are irritants or just plain smell bad, so make sure you do this in a well-ventilated area.

4. Hold the blade of your knife against the charcoal and allow it to get hot. When you feel it is hot enough, plunge it into the infusion while visualizing it glowing with power after each immersion. Chant the following words as you work:

> Blade of steel
> Beast of battle
> Work of Wayland's wise kin
> I conjure thee
> I command thee

Banish all banes as I name them!
Banish all banes as I declare them!

You will need to repeat this step three times.

5. The next step is to magnetize your blade so that it can also help draw good things to you. Take a lodestone, and, holding your knife by the handle in your left hand, rub the lodestone from hilt to tip for about five minutes while chanting:

Blade of steel
To you I sing
Son of Wayland's work
Magnetism I gift you
Mighty shall it be
Attract to me that which I name!
Attract to me what I desire!

Keep the same direction as you rub the lodestone down your blade. At this point, you may wish to paint symbols upon your blade and your name. I chose not to do so, but if you wish, you can mix some of the infusion in with the paint. Lastly, bury the knife point-down in the earth for three days and three nights. Do not forget to mark where you buried your knife or you could easily lose it to the earth. After the time has passed, dig up the knife and put it away for use.

Tools: The Cord

The cord is usually only something that is acquired upon initiation in more formal traditions, but that doesn't mean only initiated witches can have them or that they are the only ones with uses for them. The cord as I use it is a measuring tool for circle casting with further applications in binding spells and necromancy.

When it comes to making your cord, there really is no way to buy one ready-made, because the act of making the cord is what makes the cord. In terms of materials, you can use fingering weight yarn. You will likely not find those weights in the colors you will need for this rite in big box stores like

Michael's, but the online store Knitpicks has a large selection of well-priced fingering weight yarn that works well for making a cord. You will need to buy three balls of yarn: one white or natural, one red, and one black. These colors are the most common colors in the form of folk magic that I practice; I take them to represent birth, life, and death.

I personally found it important to spin and dye the flax for the cord myself. If you are able to do this, you need to spin roughly one hundred inches per length in order for it to still be long enough after braiding and knotting. Mine is also made up of nine strands as opposed to the usual three; I didn't want it to be too delicate, so that would be nine hundred inches in total. However many strands you use, you need a third of them to be white or natural, a third to be red, and the final third to be black. Flax dyes well with Rit brand dye from a craft store. As this is an act of creation involving textiles, my preference for timing for this ritual is on a Friday when the moon is waxing.

Because of the close connection with flax and thread-based magic, once again I recommend creating sacred space and invite the Spinning Goddess to the rite.

Begin by constructing your sacred space in a way of your choosing, and invite the Spinning Goddess to the rite using either your own words or one of the invitations from chapter 13.

In order to make things easier, I've included the charms and bare bones instructions from the Spindle-Setting Rite. Full instructions resume at step five.

⇥ Cord Construction Rite ⇤

You will need

Fingering weight yarn in white/natural, red, and black (one ball each) *or* corresponding flax lengths as previously described if making your own

A bowl of water with three teaspoons of salt and three teaspoons of mugwort stirred in

Censer

Charcoal disks

Lighter and matches

A pair of scissors

Procedure

1. Take three or nine deep breaths. With each breath, allow the stress and distractions of the day to fade away. Feel yourself moving into a state of mind more conducive to ritual. Light your charcoal disk and place it in the censer.

2. Speak the following charm over the salt water mixture. As you speak, imagine your words taking form as golden light and moving into the water with your breath, purifying it and imbuing it with purpose:

> Over water and salt,
> A galdor I speak
> With wise words I will it
> And my breath goes wholly in
> Making clean waters holy
> Fast flee the evil from it!
> Fast flee evil magic from it!

3. Take roughly half of the mugwort from the small bowl. Cup it in your hands and bring it to your lips before awakening the herb with the following words:

> Remember, Mugwort, what you revealed
> What you set out in mighty revelation.
> "Una" you are called, oldest of plants
> You have might against three and against thirty.
> You have might against poison and infection
> You have might against the evil that travels around the land.[229]

Speak the charm three times, then sprinkle the mugwort into the salt water before stirring clockwise with your right hand three times.

4. If you have a dedicated censer, simply burn a small amount of mugwort to purify your working space. If you do not, you may wish to use the following hallowing charm before burning the mugwort.

---

229. Taken from the Nine Herbs Charm, in Pollington, *Leechcraft*, 215.

> Over fire and smoke
> I speak my spell
> To twisting tendrils of cleansing heat
> Ravenous beast of fire I command you
> Reeking spirit of smoke I conjure you
> Wherever you burn, chase away the ill-wights!
> Wherever you burn, cleanse away all blights! [230]

5. Now that you have prepared the waters and purified the space with mugwort smoke, it's time to create your sacred space. If you have no concerns about your floor getting wet, take up the bowl of salt water and mugwort. Beginning in the east, circumambulate your space three times sunwise while speaking the following charm. If you do have concerns about your floor, take your yarn and soak it in the salt water and mugwort mixture. Instead of sprinkling water, you will lay the yarn in a circle in the space around your work area while chanting the space-hallowing charm:

> With waters clean I wind my way
> Around this sacred space
> Sained within, yet wild without
> Þórr make sacred this space
> Þórr keep sacred this space.

6. The next step is to invite the presence of the Spinning Goddess to the rite. Feel free to use different words to the ones that are included here:

> High Lady
> Life-giving one
> Shaper of luck with spindle in hand
> Slayer of death
> Desirous of wisdom

---

230. The charms for the water and censer can also be used for general purification and space clearing.

Far-faring Freyja propitious and fair
Far-faring Freyja come hear my prayer.

7. Once you have spoken your invitation, offer the mead and/or bread to the Spinning Goddess. Then, in your own words, address the Spinning Goddess and explain to her what you're doing and why you asked for her to come. Ask her to guide and bless your work as you make a tool worthy of her magic.

8. Take up your threads and put a knot in the top. Divide the colors so that you have three strands of white/natural, three of red, and three of black. When you have done this, begin your braid. Visualize white light being braided into the cord itself and chant something along these lines:

A bridge to the underworld I make
A ladder to the above world I create
A circle measure and wrought to bind
Blessed be this cord entwined.

When you come to the end of your braid, tie a knot in the end to prevent it from unraveling, and sprinkle it with the water mixture before passing it through mugwort smoke and presenting it to the Spinning Goddess. Ask her to hallow it for you and bless it for your work.

9. Thank the Spinning Goddess for her presence and aid with the rite. Gift her a final offering of mugwort smoke and then take up the yarn around your space if you used it. Once again, begin in the east and walk counterclockwise. Dispose of offerings in the same way as you did at the end of the Spindle-Setting Rite.

Distaff/Staff/Stang

Staffs have been a part of the magical tool inventory in a number of traditions for a long time, but they were especially important in Heathen-period magical traditions where the völva or seiðrworker seems to have been considered almost inseparable from the staff.

There are two types of staff found in the Norse textual sources and archae-ological record: the first type was made of iron, and the second of wood.[231]

Remarkably, given the associations between seiðr and spinning, the iron staffs resemble distaffs from the period. For spinners, distaffs are a kind of stick, usually with a cage configuration at one end that can be used to hold unspun wool. But these staffs were quite different from those everyday dis-taffs—as anyone who spends any amount of time spinning with a distaff soon discovers, the distaff has to be quite light or it cannot be spun with for very long. Your arms simply grow too tired from trying to hold it in place. The iron staffs were both heavy and cold, impossible to spin with, and uncomfortable, to boot.[232]

The wooden staffs would have been more serviceable as distaffs, but they too have their potential issues as practical tools. It is possible that some of those wooden staffs were "crooked" in a similar way to the divinely crooked staffs of the Baltic priests, and, in the case of one wooden staff found in the Oseberg ship burial, it was actually hollow in the center.[233; 234] Speaking as a spinner, I would not want to spin with either staff. Wool on the crooked staff would probably get caught in the twists as I draft, and the hollow one might break too easily with use.

There was also the matter of length to consider. Historical staffs of sorcery were somewhat shorter than the ones carried by modern practitioners. For example, the Oseberg staff measures 107 cm, a far cry from the usual image of the seer/ess with a staff that comes up to at least shoulder length.[235]

There are other peculiarities too, and this is where things get really inter-esting...when you get down to it, these iron staffs are really quite curious. They were in all likelihood far more difficult to make than swords, which means that not every blacksmith was capable of producing them. Moreover, they may have even been carbonized with human or animal remains; after all, iron production itself was sometimes located in cemeteries and the dead

---

231. Leszek Gardeła, "A Biography of the Seiðr-Staffs," 197.

232. Eldar Heide, "Spinning Seiðr," 167.

233. Gardeła, "A Biography of the Seiðr-Staffs," 203.

234. Ibid., 194.

235. Ibid.

a ready source of carbon.[236] This would have symbolically (if not magically) created a link to the ancestral or animal world.

Why Staffs?

The ritual and magical role of these staffs in seiðr has long been debated. It's not uncommon for these staffs to be interpreted from within a shamanic framework and taken as a representation of the world tree. However, there are two other possible interpretations that I would like to offer here.

One interpretation is that these staffs possibly served as symbols of authority, both to those around the staff-carrier and as a symbol of authority wielded on behalf of whichever deity patronized her art. This may not be so far-fetched either, as some scholars have noted that some of the staffs of sorcery resemble spears. If this interpretation is correct, this would create a correspondence of tools between both the Spinning Goddess and Spear God.[237]

While this is tempting, there are some issues with this interpretation, the biggest of which being that the usefulness of the staff seems to have been limited. Beyond denoting authority, it's not entirely clear how the staff would have functioned in ritual, or why it would have been considered such a key part of the völva's work that her title would reference it.[238; 239] Most importantly, as a theory, it does little to explain why anyone would consider these staffs to be a risk to the living after death.

In my opinion, there is only one interpretation of these staffs that fits the available evidence: the staffs themselves were *inhabited* in much the same way as idols were believed to be.[240] Thinking of staffs as houses for the numinous opens up a whole continuum of spirit-based ritual practices. Moreover, it recentralizes the staff at the center of the völva's art. It's difficult to make much of the wooden seiðr-staffs as so few have been preserved. While it is impossible to definitively prove the connection, their hollowness is reminiscent of later Danish folk belief that spirits live in the hollow branches of elder

---

236. Ibid., 204.

237. Ibid., 200.

238. *Völva* means "staff-bearer."

239. Rudolf Simek, *Dictionary of Northern Mythology*, 367.

240. Richard North, *Heathen Gods in Old English Literature*, 94–96.

bushes.[241] And when we come to the iron staffs with their potential origins in grave-fields and possible added cremains, we find ourselves pushing up against a model first seen in chapter 3, of seiðwitch and elf.

It's impossible to say for certain that the staffs were considered to be inhabited, let alone that their inhabitant was an elf. But given the associations with the dead in addition to the pattern of partnership already demonstrated in chapter 3, I believe elves to be the best candidates for our possible staff inhabitants.

Obtaining a Staff of Sorcery

Because of the potential elven component to these staffs of sorcery, there are no rituals or suggestions I would give you here for creating your own staff. That would be a little bit like putting the cart before the horse. In my experience of working with staff-elves, you either first come across an already inhabited staff that seems to have made it its business to encounter you, or you first encounter the elf and then *together* find a suitable staff.

This is not a connection that can be forced, however. If you have aspirations to work with an elf in this way, the best thing you could do is to continue growing your gifting relationship with Freyr as ruler of Álfheimr. When that relationship is sufficiently strong, make a ritual and ask him to pair you with an elf. I would advise you not to rush into this—as exciting as it may sound to work with elves on this level, it also comes with a lot of commitments and challenges.

It's also worth keeping in mind that not all practitioners of Heathen magic had staffs (nor presumably inhabiting elves). You do not need a staff in order to practice magic—I was several years into my craft before I encountered my first staff elf and suffered no disadvantages for it. So be patient. Take the time to build and deepen your core relationships before attempting to add someone as viscerally present as an elf to your life.

Final Words on Tools

As I mentioned at the beginning of this chapter, the tools used in Heathen magic vary from practitioner to practitioner and often depend on the kinds

---

241. Corrinne Boyer, *Under the Witching Tree*, 20–23.

of magic a person practices. The tools discussed in this chapter are the tools I find the most useful in Heathen magic as I practice it, but they are not the only tools I have, nor the only tools you will see in Heathen magical groups by far. Other common tools you might see are drums and runes.

Regardless of which tools you use, the way in which you "birth" them into practice is an important part of magical work. It is not just some onerous task to be gotten out of the way—it is imitation of the gods themselves.

As we have seen, a magical tool may be thought of as having a birth date and can be addressed directly as a living person. Through incantation, something akin to ørlög in the form of purpose can be bestowed upon it too. But there is also a great responsibility that comes with this kind of creation. Because when you create in this way, you eventually make yourself responsible for a group of non-human beings, and depending on the power involved in those items, some may even gain something like sentience.

The matter of how to retire, discard, or put our tools to rest is important for modern practitioners; frankly, it's not a matter we collectively wrestle with enough. The most obvious solution in some cases is clearly gifting to friends who are well-suited to take the tool in question.

However, as mentioned at the beginning of this chapter, there is evidence that some tools were ritually killed after the death of the practitioner. The tools in question in this case were staffs—the most alive/inhabited tool of all. This idea that a tool can be ritually killed is one that we can potentially adapt for modern use, although I prefer to only do this when a practitioner has died or a tool becomes troublesome. In order to kill such a tool, burning or crushing under heavy rocks seem to have been the most common ways in which tools were killed historically; fire has always worked for me.

Unfortunately, I have yet to discover a kinder way of dealing with tools that are no longer needed. So please be careful what you create, and breathe your stories responsibly into your creations. Out of everything you will ever do magically, it's the tools you birth that will remain the most connected to you and for which you will ultimately be responsible.

Eight
THE PATHWAYS BETWEEN

In chapters previous, I have mostly discussed ritual with deities and the process of creating sacred space. In these rituals, sacred space may be thought of as a way of separating our ritual space from the mundane world and entering into what might be called *sacred time*. In very simple terms, this is a religious studies term that refers to a kind of time beyond time in which the Holy Powers exist.

However, this place *beyond*, this sacred time, is not the only place in which we work as magical practitioners. Nor are the Holy Powers and their aligned beings the only beings we work with. If anything, it's more common for witches to work with the dead and otherworldly than the gods, at least on a day-to-day basis.

With some (mostly elf-shaped) exceptions, you will generally not find the dead or Other in that place beyond, and many of the things we do to create sacred space cause them to flee. So how can we encounter and work with the dead and otherworldly if not through creating that kind of sacred space?

We do so by seeking the liminal spaces *between* the realms of the dead and the otherworld. We find a place to meet them halfway.

This chapter will focus on those halfway points, the forms they may take in the natural world, and ways in which we can create our own ways between for ritual. We'll begin by taking a look at the different kinds of liminality, the concept of "the veil," and how it pertains to the idea of liminality. Then from there, we'll move into a discussion on the practice of going under the cloak and the possible liminality of "inspiration." Finally, we'll return to the active world of embodied ritual and the use of intermediary spaces for both ancestor veneration and necromancy.

Types of Liminality

There have always been what might be termed *liminal* places in the world. These are the places that are neither here nor there, but instead exist on a threshold between.

Sometimes, as with the birches and the bridge from the story at the beginning of this chapter, liminal space can serve as a passage to a different layer of reality or level of perception. Other times, they simply exist as they are, in a constant state of betweenness.

Most, if not all of us, have encountered places that feel strange or even uncanny…places where reality feels a little *thin* and the otherworld (whatever that is) feels closer than usual. These are the places in which that oft-unsettling sense of liminality is a feature rather than a fluke. In other words, they're the kinds of places where one might actively choose to work magic. But there are other, more *mobile* kinds of liminality too.

The best-known example of mobile liminality is the eerie silence that suddenly descends when you're out walking in the woods. If you've ever experienced this phenomenon, then you will know firsthand how unsettling it can be to have the entire forest fall silent around you. But it's never just silence when this happens; it's not just a case of the birds becoming suddenly silent for seemingly no reason. In my experience this silence is accompanied by a feeling of tension in the air, as though something has become impossibly stretched but bursts as soon as you ring a bell or a rattle a bundle of keys.

Another kind of liminality concerns liminal times. We saw a good example of this kind of liminality in the story at the beginning of this chapter. This is the kind of liminality in which certain times of the day, month, or year can also be liminal (such as the acronychal rising of the Pleiades). Times like the transitions from day to night, month to month, year to year, and season to season all have inherently liminal qualities. Here, liminality is tied to calendar and consensus rather than places in the land (as are the limits of what is believed possible during those times).

The final type of liminality—and the focus of the practical work in this chapter—is the created kind, or the internal and external spaces we enter or create in order to work our magic. But before we can dig further into some of the ways in which we can create liminal space, there is a veil to rend.

Perception versus Veil?

Growing up in a largely spiritualist family, I had the belief in a "veil" that separates this world from the next (whatever that is). Particularly haunted places were always explained to me as being places where the veil was "thinner" in some way, and Halloween was always a time when the veil was thin. Like many children facing numerous incursions by the unknown at a tender age, I accepted the explanations given by the adults in my life, and still find myself slipping back into that terminology even now.

At some point, the idea of a veil began to make less sense to me. The experiences I was having simply didn't fit the model I'd grown up with. Moreover, outside of those experiences, I realized that "the veil" as a concept could not explain the fact that not all cultures consider the same times of year to be liminal.

When discussing liminal times of the year, we often use phrases like "the veil is thin" to describe the increased liminality of the period. The underlying implication is that the liminality is a feature of the time period itself. But if there truly is some kind of barrier that separates the world of the living from the dead and numinous that differs in thickness due to the time of the day/month/year, then surely that liminality would then be experienced at roughly the same time in all places, right? When we approach the problem from even a limited cross-cultural perspective, we find that this is very much not the case. Take Yule, for example. Yule was the time of year when the dead traditionally returned to haunt the living in Germanic cultures, yet relatively few people in North America associate the twelve nights of Yule with any sense of liminality. Instead, the howling horrors of the Wild Hunt have been replaced in the popular imagination by a jolly old man in a red and white suit. Halloween is the time of year most North Americans now would associate with the dead.

So what could account for this lack of cross-cultural concordance? Are there several veils of varying thicknesses? Or is it simply the case that some parts of the veil become thin depending on the cultural consensus of the area?

As with so many areas of life, I believe the answer lies within us, the humans, and the way in which we perceive our worlds.

The human brain is an incredible machine. We take in something like eleven million bits of information through our five natural senses per second, and somehow the brain condenses it down to around fifty bits of information for storage. In order to do this, the brain must edit, distort, and delete the vast majority of what it receives in terms of input. Moreover, the parts that are retained are mostly the parts that accord with your current view of the world, the experiences that have molded you, and the societal consensus within which you live.

In other words, if your society holds that ghosts can be seen at Halloween, then you are theoretically more likely to see ghosts at Halloween because your societal consensus has effectively told you that you can and your brain allows you to see it. For all you know, you're seeing ghosts and other "impossible" beings all the time, but because your brain stores information in accordance with existing consensus, you would never know it because the entire editing process takes less than a second.[242; 243]

Because of this editing process, I believe that most kinds of liminality are *formed* by our collective consensus in a way. Consensus delineates the limits of what is possible with regards to the kinds of experiences that can be had, and level of magic that can be performed. So if we are to work with the liminal and find our pathways between, we need to first tear down the veil and wrestle with our relationships to the consensus instead.

Trance

Out of the various methods for challenging the grip of consensus reality in our perceptions, trance journeying is one of the safest. This is all relative of course, because any practice that enables a person to step away from normative ideas of reality is inherently dangerous. Practices that take a slower, more graduated approach will always be safer than ones that figuratively quickly crack the head open.

---

242. George Markowsky, "Information Theory, Physiology," *Encyclopædia Britannica*, Encyclopædia Britannica, June 16, 2017, accessed November 13, 2019. https://www.britannica.com/science/information-theory/Physiology.

243. Timothy Brady and Adena Schachner, "Blurring the Boundary Between Perception and Memory," *Scientific American*, December 16, 2008, accessed November 13, 2019. https://www.scientificamerican.com/article/perception-and-memory/.

Although a popular practice among modern Heathen seið-workers, there is no historical evidence that the elder Heathen ever went on trance journeys. That's not to say that it cannot be an effective practice, just that it doesn't seem to have ever been done in the past. As we saw in chapter 5, we have evidence of *hamfarir* and mentions of something called *hugspæi*, or "mind-spæi/seeing" (whatever that was).[244] We do not have evidence, however, of trance journeying to other worlds.[245]

Despite the lack of historical evidence, trance journeying can be an effective practice if approached correctly. Like all forms of trance work, it begins with the use of breath, sound, and/or dance to enter an altered state of consciousness. But whereas other types of trance may be receptive in nature, the kind of trance we enter for journeying is more active and resembles a controlled dream.

Nowadays it's popular to say that there are no right or wrong ways of doing things. But when it comes to trance, I think there *are* right and wrong ways of working with trance journeys.

The "Where" of Trance

One of the biggest issues I see with trance journey is that there seems to be some confusion among practitioners about whether the journeys they take are inner, outer, or somewhere in between. Knowing your destination is important, because it allows you to frame your expectations and behavior accordingly. Moreover, there's also an element of risk here that needs to be addressed. Trance can be, and is often used as, a method for encountering a wide range of beings. Practitioners regularly report interactions with everything from gods, to the dead and elves. If you are unclear on the "meta-destination" of your journeys, you run the risk of not recognizing who or what you're actually encountering. And there's a big difference between encountering Óðinn the god as opposed to a part of your psyche masquerading as him. This issue is further exacerbated by the belief that trance journey (at least within a Heathen context) always takes place within the cosmology as described in the Eddas. There is nothing inherently wrong with this, but it leaves little room for a more *liminal* view of trance. Because when we approach religious cosmology within a magical setting, for some reason, we only ever seem to think

---

244. See chapter 5 for more information about hamfarir and hugspæi.

245. Clive Tolley, *Shamanism in Norse Myth and Magic* (Helsinki: Academia Scientiarum Fennica, 2009), 139.

in terms of "inner journeys vs. outer journeys that take a part of the person outside of the body." This, in my opinion, is an unhelpful dichotomy.

Earlier in this section, I described trance journeying as being like a controlled dream, which is where I think we need to focus our attention when considering what actually happens in trance journeys. Like trance, dreams can be a place in which you can encounter a wide range of beings. Sometimes, dreams may bring you into what I can only describe as the otherworld for these interactions, or you may even find yourself encountering these beings during spontaneous hamfarir while sleeping. For the most part, our encounters in dream seem to take place in a kind of in-between place that is neither the Other nor wholly our minds, and it's this kind of common ground that I aim to journey to when engaging in trance journey.

Trance, Liminality, and the "User Interface"

As we will see later in this chapter, the use of what might be termed *intermediary technologies* makes up an important component of interacting with the dead and Hiddenfolk. These intermediary spaces are inherently liminal and constitute what might be thought of as "common ground" between ourselves and those with whom we would interact. Within this wider cultural context, journeying with the intention of going to this kind of common ground or user interface makes a lot of sense.

How your user interface looks in practice can be highly individual. There's nothing wrong with rooting your user interface in personal cosmology, but it's important to remember that the map is not the territory, nor should the two be equated. Things can and will look different, and unless you are constantly thinking about what "should" be there based on half-remembered myths, you will come across some things that simply don't fit. As with all magical work involving cosmologies, it's best to have a flexible approach and keep only what is helpful.

Alternatively, you may wish to create your own user interface, and there are a number of ways to do so. The easiest way, by far, is to adapt an already-existing trance induction.

Generally speaking, all trance inductions follow a similar series of stages. First comes the relaxation stage, and then once relaxed, the inductee is verbally guided to some kind of threshold. This threshold can be everything from a doorway, to a curtain that is pulled back, or even a thick mist that slowly clears after depositing the inductee in the desired world, so to speak. From there, the inductee is then guided into the desired user interface. For example, if the user interface is Norse-themed, the guide may supply the appropriate descriptive details for the inductee's mind to fill in the world tree Yggdrasil.

To adapt a trance induction to find your own user interface, simply remove the theme details from the rest of the trance induction script or recording. If I were adapting the Norse-themed trance induction in this way, I would remove all the descriptive details that came after passing through the threshold point of the induction and instead allow my mind to spontaneously fill in the details as I explore. Once the designated time for exploration is ended, then I would return to the trance induction and allow it to guide me back.

Finally, because of how pervasive consensus reality is, it can be helpful to incorporate tools from self-hypnosis into any trance induction process that you create or use. Simple additions—like elements that progressively relax the body or counting down to symbolize a deepening of trance—can be incredibly helpful when you're struggling. The sample trance induction at the end of this section incorporates some of these hypnotic techniques so you can see for yourself if they are useful to you.

⭤ Experiential: Trance Induction ⭤

The aim of this induction is to help you get into a trance state and to enter into the space that might become your user interface. The trance induction given below will take you only as far as to the bottom of a set of steps, and from there it's for you to figure out how that user interface is going to look for you.

You may decide that you find a path at the bottom of the steps and that it takes you to Yggdrasill, or you may find that you encounter a different landscape. Whatever you find, you're effectively mapping this space, so write down everything you encounter in your explorations.

The induction given here incorporates self-hypnosis techniques that may be adapted as you practice. In order to do this exercise, you will need a working name, and a glass of water and journal for when you return. When working in liminal space, it's advisable to never tell anyone or any being your true name, as the knowing or having of someone's name can often imply control. Instead, decide on a pseudonym or working name for this purpose. Along similar lines, never let anyone have your name either as many otherworldly beings (should you encounter them) can be quite literal in their interpretation of anything you say. Answering "Can I have your name?" with "You can call me _____" is perfectly acceptable.

Many people (myself included), find that journey is often easier when the head and eyes are covered, and that one can become quite cold when in deep trance. You may want to find something breathable to cover your head with and a blanket to keep warm.

For best results, either have someone else read this to you out loud or make a recording. Pauses in the script are denoted by "…"

You will need

A recording of the script or a friend to read for you

A working name or alias that you can go by while journeying

A glass of water

Journal

Pen

Veil (optional)

Script

Begin with your breath. This is the engine of your vision. This is the steed upon which you will ride … Make it the center of your focus … feel the air as it moves in and out … the sensation of its movement in your airways … the cyclical filling and emptying of your lungs …

Allow this movement of breath to relax you … Feel your body slowing down as you breathe … With every breath you take, you feel more relaxed and at peace … Your body continues to slow down, but your mind becomes as clear as a pool …

As your mind clears, you draw three, deep, slow breaths … and focus your attention on the darkness behind your eyes … Feel it surround you as it does before you fall into dream …

Continue to breathe … and as you breathe, feel your body become lighter with each breath … With each in-breath, feel yourself as you lift up from your body … Allow the breath to fill your intangible self like a balloon, and feel yourself begin to float through the darkness … Feeling calm and at peace, you float in what seems like an endless night, but this night is not so endless, and you become aware of a light in the distance... You begin to move toward it, and it becomes larger as you draw closer...

This is your guiding star. This is the light which guides you to the portal through which you will pass...

You draw closer still, and as you do, you see a doorway. It looks ancient, and at each doorpost stands a man...

As you draw closer, the men become clearer and you see that they have similar facial features and that each man carries two spears...

Below you forms a path leading up to the doorway, and you feel your feet making contact with the ground below you as you continue to move closer... When you come to stand before the two spear carriers, greet them and introduce yourself by your working name... Explain your reason for needing to pass through the gate, and ask them if they will allow you to pass...

If they say no then simply remain where you are until you hear the instructions for returning from the gate. Perhaps you can ask them why you have been barred from passage while you wait? But if they say yes, then thank them and go through the gate...

When you have passed through the gate, take a few moments to allow the world to become clear around you. Try not to stare too intently at anything—at least not at first — but simply accept that the details will become clearer the more you journey...

Return your attention to the path beneath your feet and notice how it leads downward—you're in a high place... How does this path look for you? How does the landscape look?

When you have oriented yourself somewhat, begin to make your way downward along the path... With every step you take, you feel your trance deepening and the world becoming clearer... What do you see as you walk? What is on your left?... Now what about your right?...

You continue to follow the path down, taking yourself yet deeper into trance with every step... Your mind remains alert...

After a while, you see that the path leads to a small staircase carved in stone. You notice that there are five steps, and know that each one represents another level of deepening your trance. Beyond the staircase, you see a path and little else. This is the beginning of the liminal space between. It is only for you that it will begin to take shape...

Do you see anything yet? Do not worry if you cannot yet, it will become clearer the closer you get...

Feeling confident and safe, you count your steps down with me as you go.

Five... You feel yourself descending effortlessly as you move toward the path.

Four... The world around you becomes clearer still as you move deeper into trance.

Three... Sounds and smells come into focus.

Two... The path before you is clear now, and you notice the world around it beginning to take shape.

One... You are now deeply in trance and prepared to proceed. Whatever you experience you will remember with ease. Your between space awaits...

From the bottom of the steps, begin to move along the path... What do you see? Do you encounter anything or anyone interesting? Take several minutes to explore this space...(10-minute pause).

With your exploration for today complete, you make your way back..coming the same way you came...(2-minute pause)... Coming back now to the bottom of the steps, you find them awaiting you...

This time when you ascend the steps, know that each step is a step back to your regular state of consciousness; count the steps with me as you ascend.

One... You are preparing to return to the gate. Whatever you experienced, you will remember with perfect clarity.

Two... Looking back, you see your between space losing a little of its clarity, but know that it will always be here for you when you return.

Three... You notice once more the sounds and smells of this world you're in, but this time, once you have acknowledged them, they slip away.

Four... The world around you becomes a little softer in focus as you move toward the path and the gate.

Five... You are now ready to continue your ascent up to the gate.

Move along the path as it leads up and up... notice that around you, the world is becoming increasingly softer in focus... Every step you take is a step back to you, and to consensus reality...

Up and up you go... the world around you becoming increasingly misty as you ascend the path to the gate... When you reach the gate, pass through...

The spear men meet you on the other side. Take a moment to thank them for their guardianship and for allowing you passage... See if they have any words to share with you before proceeding...

When you feel it is time and that the conversation with the Twins is at an end, continue to follow the path back into the darkness of the eternal night... Moving away from the guiding star and doorway... allowing them to fade in the distance as you follow your instinct back to yourself... And when the path falls away, you find yourself floating once more as you return... Don't worry about being unable to find your way back. Know that the part of you which goes is always connected to the part of you which stays. You cannot get lost here. Continue to follow your instinct until you find yourself... See yourself in body surrounded by the darkness of that eternal night... Pay attention to how you are seated, and move yourself to seat yourself once more in your body...

Return your attention to your breath and feel yourself getting heavier as you settle back into yourself... Notice the sensation of air moving in and out of your lungs... Feel the weight of your limbs... Allow the eternal night to become dark behind your eyes as you return fully to consensus reality... And when you are ready, open your eyes, drink some water, and write down everything you can remember about your journey.

If you find that you are still not completely back, take a few moments to ground and center yourself. If you still don't feel one hundred percent back after that, try eating a small amount of salt.

With this kind of trance journey, the possibilities for exploration are endless. But you will probably find yourself coming across the same set of places the more you practice this skill—this is the user interface becoming more reified as a place between in which you can not only meet with the numinous Other, but also practice various magical skills before having to do them in the real world. If you come to work with a staff elf, it will be here where you will have some of your most meaningful interactions. But none of that is possible without regular practice, so do be sure to put the work in.

Going Under the Cloak

From the liminality of user interfaces in trance, to a different kind of liminality now: the art of being everywhere at the same time. We first encountered the practice of going under the cloak and its pivotal role in Icelandic history in chapter 1. But although this practice is well (and famously) attested, the practice of going under the cloak remains mysterious, and we still do not know exactly what this entailed beyond the obvious act of lying under one's cloak for a prolonged period of time. There is, however, evidence to suggest that it was probably a method of seeking out mantic knowledge, and it was this suggestion that initially interested me in the practice of going under the cloak.

As I've said a number of times throughout this book, my process for uncovering the kind of magic I practice is a combination of historical reconstruction, experimentation, evaluation (making changes where appropriate), and a whole lot of experiences and unverified personal gnosis (UPG). This is difficult enough even when you have lots of evidence for a practice, but it is far harder when the evidence is sparse.

In the following section, I will show you how the magical reconstruction process can look when you don't have a lot of historical information, in addition to how you can still create a workable magical practice in an authentic way despite having very little information to go on.

Step One: Research

Over the years, I've nursed the suspicion that the process of going under the cloak was a way of seeing and interacting with the spirits of the land. In the book *Under the Cloak*, Icelandic scholar Jón Hnefill Aðalsteinsson links the practice with folkloric accounts of necromancy as well as the inspiration-seeking practices of the Old Irish poets. While I agree with the theory that the practice was mantic in nature, I disagree with his ideas on the mechanics of the practice.

There's a common problem here. When non-spinners attempt to formulate theories about the mechanics of spun seiðr, they miss what is immediately obvious to the spinner. And when non-magic workers write about the mechanics of magic, they omit what they cannot imagine. It's an issue with modern culture in general. We often use the word "magic" as a placeholder word for "I don't know how this works." Yet as we have seen, there is an underlying logic to the different forms of Heathen magic. It couldn't have been as simple as "person + cloak = mantic knowledge," or "Irish poet + dark cave + getting out after a while = inspiration." Magic works and is worked on both outer and inner levels, but yet again we are missing the inner and so it is to the world of theory and experimentation that we must go. Like Aðalsteinnson, I looked to the Irish sources. I wanted to understand the kind of inspiration they sought in the practices described by Aðalsteinsson and how that inspiration may have looked in the people said to possess it.

The breakthrough came when I encountered the poem from the *Book of Invasions* referred to as the *Song of Amergin*. Amergin was a poet and druid, or in other words, a person for whom inspiration was important to his practice. In the *Song of Amergin,* Amergin addresses the "spirit of Ireland" in order to part a magically created storm that was preventing his ship from making shore. It's impossible to know the magical processes by which he parted the storm, but the words he speaks as he sets foot on shore may provide an important clue.

The effects of this magic are similar to the effects of the magic performed by a man named Loðmundr the Old in the Landnámabók. In this section of the Landnámabók, Loðmundr and his family are leaving to move elsewhere. But instead of just leaving as soon as all the belongings and people are packed on the ship, we are told that Loðmundr lay down and told people not to speak his name under any circumstances. There is no explicit mention of a cloak in this account, but shortly after he lay down there was a loud noise from the land and people saw a landslide fall on the farm where they had previously lived. The implication here is clear: the landslide was caused by whatever Loðmundr did when he lay down.

Like Amergin, Loðmundr was known for his skill in magic, and also like Amergin, the effects of his magic seemed to be carried out in partnership with the land and/or her unseen inhabitants. But where we are told nothing of Loðmundr's magic beyond a basic description of "he laid down and things happened," the description of Amergin's activities in the Irish sources are more explicit.

Step Two: Cross-Cultural Comparison

As previously mentioned, there is no information in the Icelandic corpus to indicate what a practitioner thought when doing magic. There does seem to be a common strand of inspiration emerging when we look to the Irish sources that seem to describe similar practices or magical effects to the Icelandic accounts of going under the cloak. Amergin was both a poet and druid. He was a man for whom inspiration (as insufficient as that word is here) was important. His words to the spirit of Ireland are reminiscent of the kind of prophecy that is made real through speech. But his words as he sets foot on land may provide an important clue as to his state of being as he parted the storm:

> I am a wind on the sea,
> I am a wave of the ocean,
> I am the roar of the sea,
> I am a powerful ox,
> I am a hawk on a cliff,
> I am a dewdrop in the sunshine,
> I am a boar for valor,
> I am a salmon in pools,
> I am a lake in a plain,
> I am the strength of art,
> I am a spear with spoils that wages battle,
> I am a man that shapes fire for a head.[246]

In these opening lines of the *Song of Amergin*, we possibly see Amergin expressing a sense of "pervasive oneness" with everything. He is both himself and all other things at the same time, and by being so, potentially inhabits a different kind of liminal space.

Interestingly, we find this same sense of pervasive oneness mirrored in the words of the great poet Taliesin from Welsh tradition. In the following quote taken from the poem *Cad Goddeu*, or *The Battle of Trees*, Taliesin expresses the sentiment of having previously inhabited a variety of forms:

> I have been in a multitude of shapes, before I assumed
> a consistent form. I have been a sword, narrow, variegated,
> I will believe when it is apparent. I have been a tear
> in the air, I have been the dullest of stars. I have been
> a word among letters, I have been a book in the origin.

We also see this claim of having previously inhabited a multitude of forms repeated in the following excerpt from *The First Address of Taliesin*:

---

246. Mary Jones, "Awen," *Jones' Celtic Encyclopedia*, 2004, accessed November 13, 2019. www
.maryjones.us/jce/awen.html.

> I have been with skilful men, with Matheu and Govannon,
> with Eunydd and Elestron, in company with Achwyson,
> for a year in Caer Gofannon. I am old. I am young. I am
> Gwion, I am universal, I am possessed of penetrating wit.[247]

Again, the pervasive sense of oneness is expressed in these poems, but in the Taliesin poems is a oneness that transcends the limits of a single human life and form. In doing so, the oneness is again situated in liminal space.

Experimentation, Evaluation, and UPG

There is no way of knowing if people like Loðmundr and Þorgeir had the ability to enter this kind of liminal space (if indeed it was a space rather than a way of being). However, the experiments I conducted with this kind of magic that were based on this idea of pervasive oneness (which I take to mean "dissolving the barriers between myself and the rest of the world around me") yielded the best results. In each attempt to work in this way, I found myself coming into contact with and able to communicate with the álfar and other kinds of Hiddenfolk resident in the land. Moreover, these results were replicated in a group setting with two of us describing encounters with the same beings. This, I believe, was the ultimate purpose of going under the cloak: it was a way to communicate with the unseen beings of your land.

From the perspective of reconstruction, we cannot say that the method of going under the cloak that I have been working with is the same as that depicted in the Icelandic accounts. However, from a practical standpoint, I seem to have found a way of going under the cloak that yields results.

In terms of insights gained, this practice feels very much connected to the elves, and not just because they may be encountered during this work. There's something very *moundlike* about lying on the ground as though asleep or dead and covering yourself with a cloak. That is, after all, the meaning of the word *Hel*. On one level, Hel is the goddess of the dead, but her name is thought to derive from the Proto-Indo-European word *kolyo*, meaning "the coverer."[248]

---

247. Ibid.

248. Bruce Lincoln, *Death, War, and Sacrifice: Studies in Ideology and Practice* (Chicago: University of Chicago Press, 1991), 78.

In a sense, the burial mound (that archetypal realm of elves) *is* Hel; it is that which covers the dead. By covering myself with the cloak, I symbolically enter the mound in order to go into the world around me in much the same way as the dead themselves eventually do.

⇥ Experiential: Going Under the Cloak ⇤

In the following exercise, you will have the opportunity to practice my method of going under the cloak as a way of encountering and communicating with the Hiddenfolk and álfar in the land where you live.

The ability to not only meet but interact with the Hiddenfolk is an important part of my practice. Not only does it allow me to understand what is going where I live and the various unseen beings who live there, it also gives me the opportunity to interact with them in a relatively safe way should any issues come up.

However, there are a few practical considerations you will need to take into account before attempting this practice, and the first is the choice of place. Ideally, you want to do this in a place that feels friendly to you and where you will not be interrupted. You can do this pretty much anywhere, but my personal preference is outside. If you do not feel safe going alone, ask a friend to accompany you. Just be sure to make it clear to them that they absolutely should not say your name while under the cloak. This is a detail that is mentioned over and over again in the sources.

The second consideration is the cloak. Comparatively few people nowadays own cloaks, let alone go off on magical adventures in them. All you really need in my experience is a blanket that is breathable, yet big enough and dark enough to prevent light from getting in and distracting you. The cloaks that Icelanders would have used for going under the cloak were woolen, but yours can be made out of whichever material you find most comfortable in terms of warmth and breathability. Depending on the weather and time of year, you may wish to vary the size and thickness of the "cloak" you use. When working in winter, I layer up and then sit under one of my knitted woolen shawls; in summer, my preference is linen.

Speaking of the weather, are you warm enough? In cold temperatures, exposure is a real risk when engaging in trance-based activities outside for prolonged periods of time. Be sure to take into account the temperature and weather conditions before practicing, and don't forget to bring water!

The following script is quite long and takes roughly twenty minutes to complete. Until you become accustomed to the process, I recommend making a recording that can be played back while under the cloak.

You will need

Cloak or large blanket made out of a breathable material

A bottle of water

Your journal

A recording of the script (optional)

A friend (optional)

Script (Learn or make recording before attempting this practice)

Take a little time to get comfortable in your chosen spot. Make sure you're warm enough, that you are not out of breath, and that you have your water ready for when you get back.

(Pause a few moments before continuing.)

Begin with your breath. This is the engine of your vision. This is the steed upon which you will ride... Make it the center of your focus... Feel the air as it moves in and out... the sensation of its movement in your airways... the cyclical filling and emptying of your lungs...

Allow this movement of breath to relax you... Feel your body slowing down as you breathe... With every breath you take, you feel more relaxed and at peace... Your body continues to slow down, but your mind becomes as clear as a pool...

Now turn your attention to the world around you... Concentrate on the sounds you hear... the smells you pick up... the feel of the ground beneath you...

Think about the parts of your body that make contact with the ground... your clothes... and the covering on your head... Allow that sense of otherness to fill you for a moment... Allow yourself to be filled with the awareness of what is of you and what is not of you... Then simply let it fall away until all of those things feel a part of you.

Realize that there is no difference between you and the world around you... that there is no difference between you and the earth, or you and the air, or you and every other person here... You are all part of the self-same tapestry... each person an intersection point of the whole... Without you, there couldn't be anything else... Without everything else, there could be no you...

Take a few moments to rest in this state before proceeding...

Now, in a state of equipoise, expand your awareness outward... Remember, there is no difference between you and the world around you. This is merely checking in with more parts of yourself than you are used to...

What do you notice? Does anything grab your attention?

Take some time to explore...(Allow at least 10 minutes here.)

The time has come to return to our usual sense of self... Thank any numina that you worked with and take your leave of them as politely as you may... Now slowly, begin the process of contracting your awareness... You are still part of all of this, but you have only one body to move... So return... Re-seat yourself within your usual boundaries, and when you feel you have done so, take some time to move your fingers, wriggle your toes, and get reacquainted with the old meat sack. Laugh too. It's good for you!

Now go make those offerings of thanks, drink some water, and write everything down so you don't forget it.

Like any other practice in which you meet with and potentially form relationships with other sentient beings, this method of going under the cloak is best practiced regularly. It's not just about honing your skills, but creating and keeping good relationships with your unseen neighbors, and that takes work.

Calling the Dead through Intermediary Spaces

So far, we've concentrated on the kinds of liminal practices that enable us to go to those with whom we wish to communicate, in a sense. In this section, we're going to take a look at ways in which we can create liminal, intermediary spaces in this world through which the nonhuman (in this case the dead) can come to us.

As a general rule, it's not good for the living to get too close to the dead, and it is my sincere belief that those who do so anyway pay in terms of luck and health. Not all places are for us, and outside of spontaneous encounters in trance, dream, or while under the cloak initiated by the dead, we must bring the dead to us if we wish to communicate with them.

Ancestor veneration and necromancy can be somewhat controversial topics among modern Heathens. As a group of religions that practice varying degrees of reconstructionism, our beliefs and practices are often shaped to some extent by the available evidence. Until relatively recently, that evidence was primarily derived from the textual sources, which is where the controversy begins.

Outside of more mythological ideas about the afterlife such as traveling to Hel or going to Valhalla, the evidence presented by the textual evidence suggests a very *physical* conception of the dead. There is no mention of the disembodied dead in the earlier sources, which has led some to suggest that the arrival of ghosts represented Christian influence in the later sources. Instead, the textual sources present a world in which the dead inhabited their mounds in much the same way as they did their homes in life, receiving offerings from the living at the grave site, and when encountered outside their graves, taking the form of a revenant (*draugr*). Historically, this has presented quite a unique quandary for modern Heathens, and especially for those of us who are magically inclined.

However, more recent work by archaeologists has highlighted a group of structures, grave features, and funerary practices that might best be referred to as "intermediary technologies." The function of these features, structures, and practices seems to have been necromantic in nature—in other words, they seem to have been created with the intention of calling up the dead.[249; 250]

Despite the focus on physical remains and revenants in the textual sources, these heavily necromantic intermediary structures do not just exist where physical remains are present. A significant number of these structures are associated with cremation burials and in some cases even where *no remains* are present, suggesting that the necromancy practiced in these places concerned the disembodied dead rather than physical remains.[251]

But this practice was not just necromancy—there are indications that these necromantic practices were combined with acts of veneration as well. For example, there is evidence of ritual feasting and food offerings at some of these sites, including at sites where no physical remains were found.

---

249. Marianne H. Eriksen, "Doors to the Dead: The Power of Doorways and Thresholds in Viking Age Scandinavia," *Archaeological Dialogues* 20, no. 2 (2013): 187–214.

250. Neil Price, "Nine Paces from Hel: Time and Motion in Old Norse Ritual Performance," *World Archaeology* 46, no. 2 (2014): 178–191.

251. Neil Price, "Dying and the Dead: Viking Age Mortuary Behavior," in *The Viking World*, ed. Stefan Brink (New York: Routledge, 2011), 261.

The evidence of these sites has profound implications for anyone who would do the work of the helrune. Not only is it possible to conceive of Heathen-period ancestor cultus that did not exclude the disembodied dead, but we also have examples of the necromantic technologies through which the dead were interacted with.

Doorways

The first and most obviously necromantic of these technologies is the doorway.

Doorways are symbolically potent places, existing between spaces yet able to be closed off. To stand inside a doorway is to be neither here nor there; it's a liminal space through which liminal things may be glimpsed or pass.[252]

Where doorways appear in Old Norse texts, they're often necromantic in context. In an account from 922 CE written by the Arab writer Ibn Fadhlan, a slave girl is lifted three times over a door-like structure prior to being sacrificed, and with each ascent, she claims to see her ancestors calling her to join them.[253]

When Óðinn rides to Hel in the Eddaic poem *Baldrs Draumar*, he goes to consult the völva buried "east of the door," and in the poem *Svipdagsmál*, Svipdag raises his mother with a formula that references the "doors of the dead."[254]

Doors were also used judicially for dealing with the disruptive dead. The dead would be summoned to a "door court" or *duradómr* and were then judged in accordance with the law before being expelled.[255] Finally, in the Laxdaela saga, a dying man was buried in a doorway only to return after death to terrorize the living, seemingly able to do so by virtue of having been buried in that liminal space in the first place.[256]

The archaeological record is equally productive. In southwest Norway are several examples of people being buried in doorways.[257] And in Sweden, there are roughly eighty burial mounds that are largely empty of remains but that originally had doorposts set before them.[258]

---

252. Marianne H. Eriksen, "Doors to the Dead," 189.

253. Ibid.,191.

254. Ibid.,192.

255. Ibid.,194.

256. Ibid., 196.

257. Ibid., 197.

258. Ibid., 200-201.

Ships

The second intermediary technology is the stone ship setting. These graves contained by boat shapes outlined in stones date back to the Bronze Age and are the oldest form of intermediary technology.[259] Ships, like doors, are symbolically potent and have carried a number of meanings throughout the years. In Scandinavia, their very earliest associations were with the dead.[260]

The vast majority of stone ship settings contain cremation burials. However, as with the previously mentioned doorway sites, there are some that are completely empty of remains. Despite the lack of remains, these empty ship settings show evidence of fires and meals within, suggesting feasting and food offerings.[261] Although I have only discussed two of these intermediary technologies, there are at least two more. However, as I have not had the chance to work with them, I did not think it right to include them.

In my experience, these intermediary technologies are powerful tools, and ones that I've progressively experimented with over the past couple of years. I initially began entering trance states while standing in doorways before moving onto constructing temporary doorways for ritual use when engaging in psychopomp work on old Civil War battlefields. These doorways are used in conjunction with a song that helps to guide the dead as well as speak their fate. As always, magic works on multiple layers all at once.

⟶⟶ Experiential: Calling Up the Dead ⟵⟵

The following ritual is intended for both ancestor veneration practices and more clearly necromantic operations in which you call up disembodied dead that you do not know in order to gain knowledge. I'm not going to lie: necromancy is never safe, but it can be somewhat safer when dealing with dead you know and who hopefully have a positive view of you. For the first few times you perform this ritual, I recommend performing it as an ancestor offering ritual until you are more

---

259. Peter Skoglund, "Stone Ships: Continuity and Change in Scandinavian Prehistory," *World Archaeology* 40, no. 3 (2008), 392.

260. Chris Ballard, Richard Bradley, Lise N. Myhre, and Meredith Wilson, "The Ship as Symbol in the Prehistory of Scandinavia and Southeast Asia," *World Archaeology* 35, no. 3 (2004): 389.

261. Neil Price, "Dying and the Dead," 261.

accustomed to this kind of work. If you do not have a good relationship with your ancestors or family in general, you can perform this ritual as an offering ritual to any dead you have reason to believe would be well-inclined toward you instead.

The ritual requires that you create a doorway effigy. This does not have to be a complicated affair. You can easily make a doorway effigy by binding two longer sticks of equal length to a third stick. This third stick will be shorter than the other two, and serve the crossbeam to the longer doorpost sticks. Then, depending on if you are working indoors or out, you can either stand the bottom of each doorpost in a pot of dirt, or (if working outside) drive the ends into the ground.

Aside from the doorway, you will also need to learn a song (or at least the tune). The song I use for this ritual is an adaptation of the old dirge "A Lyke Wake." In its original form, "A Lyke Wake" was designed to be sung over the corpse of the recently deceased and guides the dead through the various obstacles between this world and the afterlife. The version used here is a Heathenized version of the same. It's a haunting song that lends itself to a wailing, keening kind of singing. There is an abundance of music videos on YouTube where you can learn this tune for yourself.

When people begin to work with the dead in this way, one of the first questions is "How do I know that it worked?" As with all things of a magical nature, there are no hard and fast signs (except in very rare instances), but you may feel a cool breeze or coolness in the room after you sing the song. Alternatively, you may find that it's significantly colder around the doorway than the rest of the ritual space. In my experience, that cool breeze or coldness is usually one of the baseline signs that the dead are present.

From there, any number of different things may happen with communication. It's not easy for the dead to come to the world of the living or even to a liminal space set aside within the world, and the capacity for communication can vary from dead person to dead person. Some dead may be able to give you disembodied voices, but you may need to use your divinatory tools as a method of communication with others. How much you perceive will also depend on your capacity, and this is something that will develop over time if you continue to do this work. Whatever you do, never assume that you are alone. Always act as though spirits are present and work the ritual accordingly.

It doesn't matter if no one is really there; you have still opened a way between and created liminal space in the world. All of it will need to be put back.

You will also notice that this ritual instructs you to circumambulate counterclockwise as opposed to clockwise. This is because we are intending to go against the natural order of things by calling up the dead from their usual abode. You may also see counterclockwise circumambulation in baneful workings or when creating space for ritual with the Hiddenfolk. We use it here to help create a liminal ritual space for the dead to temporarily inhabit.

One of the major differences between working in the kind of sacred space that allows us to enter the time beyond time, and the kind of space through which we can access the dead, is that there is no inherent protection in the latter. This is not a situation where you can rely on your circle to protect you. It is, at best, containment. I therefore recommend wearing some kind of iron or steel pendant as an amulet for this rite, and keeping apotropaic substances such as salt, mugwort, and iron/a blade close by. Afterward, be sure to purify physically and energetically.[262]

You will need

Knife

Censer

Charcoal disc/s

Lighter or matches

Apotropaic substances (at the very least mugwort and salt; see chapter 11 for more suggestions)

An iron/steel amulet

Two cups of red wine as offerings for Hel (some people also like to give her dark chocolate as an offering)

Offering for the dead/ancestors you call (this can be a cup of beer, tea or coffee, and/or a portion of food without salt)

Bowl of water

Offering bowl

Preferred form of divination

---

262. Please find further information about staying safe and troubleshooting issues in chapter 11.

Red yarn (enough to mark out your circle)

A doorpost effigy

Ritual Procedure

1. Make sure that you have all your supplies to hand and that you're wearing your amulet. If there are any deities you feel closest to at this point, make offerings and ask for protection. Soak yarn in water and set up the doorway so that it is in a north/northeast direction and place the offering bowl before it.

2. Take the red yarn from the bowl of water and wring out a little so it's easier to handle. Then walk in a counterclockwise circle around your ritual space, laying the yarn as you go and saying:

> With wool and water I walk this round
> And make a path against the sun
> The waters bless
> The yarn ensnares
> Hallowed ground within
> Profane without
> I found my space between the worlds.

3. Set aside the yarn and water. Ready Hel's offering (one of the cups of wine), and go to kneel before the doorposts facing north. Knock on the ground before them three times before speaking the following prayer:

> I pray to mighty Hel,
> To the coverer whose realm lies down the sloping path
> Whose walls are high and gates impenetrable
> Who wields in the Hel-ropes the mightiest of magics
> Lady Below, hear me! I stand at the doors of the Dead
> And beseech thee to allow (Name of person/people you wish to summon)
> To gain temporary passage to the Around World of man
> So that I may gain their counsel!

You may need to say this more than once; if that is the case, do so. Sometimes the dead can take a little while to respond. When you sense that you have gotten Hel's attention and things are beginning to feel different in the room, make the offering to Hel and thank her.

4. Now it is time to sing the song. For added efficacy, sing while in a light trance and visualize the dead encountering and overcoming the various obstacles as you sing them.

"A Lyke Wake" (Summoning Version):
This one night, this one night
Every night and all
Fire and sleet and candlelight
Dead, I call you forth

From Hel's halls thou comst to us
Every night and all
Through Hel's great gates you shall pass
Dead, I call you forth

From Hel's great gates when thou may pass
Every night and all
To Brig o' Dread thou comst at last
Dead, I call you forth

From Brig o' Dread when thou may pass
Every night and all
To thorny woods thou comst at last
Dead, I call you forth

When through thorny woods thou pass
Every night and all
To our fires/this ring/our place here thou comst at last
Dead, I call you forth

This one night, this one night
Every night and all
Fire and sleet and candlelight
Welcome Mighty Ones!

5. Welcome the dead you have summoned and make an offering of whichever substance you brought for them. If this is an ancestor offering, then feel free to take the time to chat and/or pray.

6. At this point, you may wish to ask them for a message or omen. Depending on the strength of the spirit you are dealing with, you may get disembodied voices or receive psychic communication if you have that capacity. If nothing is forthcoming, try performing divination. This is also a good time to invite them to enter your dreams and communicate with you there.

7. When you are finished, thank the dead for coming and then sing the psychopomp version of the adapted version of "A Lyke Wake" (even if nothing happened in the rite). Again, try to do this in a light trance state so you can guide them through and ensure that everyone who is supposed to be in Hel, ends up there again.

"A Lyke Wake" (Psychopomp Version):
This one night, this one night
Every night and all
Fire and sleet and candlelight
Dead, I guide you home

From our fires/place/ring here you shall pass
Every night and all
To thorny woods thou comst at last
Dead, I guide you home

Through thorny woods when thou may pass
Every night and all
To Brig o' Dread thou comst at last
Dead, I guide you home

From Brig o' Dread when thou may pass
Every night and all
To Hel's great gates thou comst at last
Dead, I guide you home

From Hel's great gates when thou may pass
Every night and all
To Hel's halls thou comst at last
Dead, I guide you home

This one night, this one night
Every night and all
Fire and sleet and candlelight
Rest, for you are home!

8. If you feel as though you have some hangers-on, try singing the song once more, each time *politely asking them* to disperse. When you have sung the song three times and asked them each time to go, then it is time to knock on the ground before the doorway again and tell Hel that some of her people do not wish to return and ask her to pull them back down.

   By now, you should be alone again (you will likely feel a temperature difference). Thank Hel and pour her her second cup of wine. Take down the doorway and fumigate the space with mugwort rēcels (see chapter ten for information on how to make rēcels).

9. When you are sure that you have returned the space to how it was before, then begin the process of taking up your circle. This time, walk clockwise, taking up the yarn as you go and saying:

I walk this round with the sun
And declare what was made now undone
I return this space to the world.

Finish by tidying up. Bathe or shower with salt and perform the purification exercise from chapter eleven.

One thing I've found to be true about working with the dead over the years is that necromantic rituals of this sort often beget spontaneous visitations in dreams. When it comes to working with family dead, this ritual and the ensuing visitations can even form the basis for ancestor cultus in your home. You may find your dead asking you to set up a shrine and make offerings.

This shrine doesn't have to be a complex or grandiose affair. It can be as simple as a side table with photographs of your dead, a couple of candles, and offering bowls. You may even encounter ancestors who were themselves involved in magic. I have one such ancestor whom I deal with quite regularly and who is progressively teaching me different ways of working with the dead.

But if you find the work of the helrune attractive, you probably don't want to just stick to ancestor veneration. If you are anything like me, you are probably drawn to the places where the dead still linger and have a drive to not only interact with them, but help them on to whichever afterlife they will go to. But that kind of practice is something you will need to work up to. The ritual provided here is a good set of magical training wheels.

Nine
FIBER MAGIC

In our society, fiber arts have a benign appearance, conjuring up imagery of cardigan-wearing people knitting or crocheting placidly. There's something *homey* about the sight of someone knitting or working with fiber in some way, something about it just seems to inspire feelings of nostalgia and safety.

Like seiðr in general, the fiber arts are a gendered set of activities, with traditional associations placing them firmly in the female purview despite the fact that both men and women have historically engaged in fiber arts. This was especially the case in the Viking Age, and remnants of this association still persist today. For example, one way of referring to the female side of a family is the "distaff side" (as opposed to the "spear side," which denotes the male). Due to these long-held associations, female-presenting people are still far more likely to be in fiber arts than male-presenting people due to social stigma against male participation in what was seen as being a feminine art.[263]

As seen in chapter 5, women have always been associated with fiber arts such as spinning, weaving, and embroidery. Where men have historically spoken their shaping words in the halls of power, women have woven and embroidered theirs. Men kept land, and women stitched portable heirlooms to pass down to their daughters so that they might always carry a piece of

---

263. Thankfully this is changing now; more people of all gender identities are becoming involved in fiber arts.

home with them wherever they went. Knowledge of the fiber arts and items crafted with love are the traditional inheritance of women.

Though still popular, fiber arts are no longer commonly taught in the home. Instead, they are typically acquired through other avenues. The perception of fiber arts as being womanly, uninteresting, and something that only older people do also does not help. Despite this homey image, there's also something about the fiber arts that lends itself to magic—and not just any kind, either. Where fiber magic appears in Norse sources, it is usually a life-or-death matter. The comforting, loving, and homey becomes transgressive and dangerous.

So far, this book has predominantly focused on spinning and weaving (as well as embroidery to some degree). However, these are not the only forms of fiber art that can be used magically (nor do you need fiber to spin magic, but more on that later). Pretty much any type of fiber art can be used to effect magical change or create items for use in magic.

In this chapter, we're going to take a look at the various kinds of fiber magic that may be practiced within a Heathen magical context. We'll begin by taking a look at the properties of fiber and why it's so useful in magic, as well as some of the mechanics of spun magic. Then we'll move on to the use of different washes and water in fiber magic. Finally, we'll take a deep dive into the art of crafting with intention, and examine the ways in which you can create charms that can be sung over your work.

The Magical Characteristics of Fiber

One of the most common responses I get whenever I talk about my love for fiber magic is confusion. Fiber magic seems to be one of those areas that we *know* existed but is hard to conceptualize nowadays, as comparatively few people spin. This is an important distinction to make because the way in which spinners experience fiber is far different from how knitters, crocheters, or even weavers experience it. There's a big difference between working with the raw product as opposed to the end product, and it's only through exposure to the raw product that the why of fiber magic becomes obvious. For the purpose of this discussion, I'm going to separate the different kinds of fibers I work with and limit myself to discussing wool and flax (and, to a lesser extent, nettle): the type of fiber magic I practice is rooted in Northern Europe practices, and these were the most common fibers available to the Heathen-period Northern European person.

Wool

Wool has several qualities which would have made it an obvious choice for magical use to the Heathen-period spinner. One of the first things you learn about sheep's wool is that it is naturally sticky. There is of course lanolin in the wool, which makes it physically sticky to the touch. But when viewed under a microscope, each individual wool fiber also has hooks on it that, when combined with the twist from spinning and the tension provided by the weight of the whorl, lock together. You don't even need to spin the fiber to see this effect in action, either—anyone who has taken two tufts of wool and brushed them together in opposite directions can see it quite clearly. Even without the benefit of a microscope, many people would come to the conclusion that there's something about the woolen fibers themselves that hook onto each other. In other words, woolen fibers naturally ensnare, trap, and bind on their own. And these fibers don't just stick to each other—it's not uncommon to find small pieces of leaves and grass in wool even after processing. At times it can feel as though the wool even attracts these particles, and unless you're very careful, it can be difficult to keep your wool clear of everything from pet hairs to crumbs and vegetable matter (VM). Yet again, wool appears to have the intrinsic qualities of ensnaring, trapping, binding, and also attracting things to it.

Fiber magic is inherently sympathetic, functioning by mimicking the desired magical effect in both choice of material and type of fiber art being practiced. For seiðr, a magic particularly associated with ensnaring, attraction, trapping, and binding, wool is the perfect choice of materia magica.

Flax

But wool is not the only kind of fiber that holds magical associations. Flax is also significant for its associations with deities such as Freyja (who was also called Hörn, a word believed to derive from the word for "flax") and Frau Holle.

Wool and flax are very different fibers, however; as a spinner, I tend to divide the different varieties of fiber into animal fibers and plant fibers, as both sets of fibers behave and must be worked with quite differently. As a general rule in fiber magic, you can apply this dichotomy to other types of fiber: all animal fibers may be considered magically similar to wool, and all plant fibers to flax.

Unlike wool, plant fibers such as flax are far smoother and lack the kind of hooks or jaggedness on the surface that wool and other animal fibers have. This means that when you work with plant fibers, you have to not only work with them differently, but they also lend themselves to quite different kinds of magic.

The process of spinning flax is simple. You have to ensure that your fibers are straight, then spin them as you would ordinarily spin wool. But when you spin flax, you're essentially spinning long lengths of plant fiber that must be wetted to join them together. Many flax spinners simply lay the new lengths of fiber on top of the lengths currently being spun, then use their spittle to create the join.

Because of this key difference, plant-based fibers such as flax do not lend themselves to any of the same magical applications as wool. There is a sense of compliance and order here—of consent, even—that is absent from wool-based magic. The flax fibers are not hooked together while trying to pull away but must instead be intentionally placed together and then joined with water or spittle. Because of this, flax lends itself to workings for community or for any other occasion in which you need to bring different elements together to create a greater whole.

Ready-Spun Threads and Knots

One final characteristic of fiber that must be covered before moving on to a deeper examination of the mechanics of spun seiðr concerns fibers that have already been spun. Regardless of the type of fiber used, yarn, thread, and string all have the same propensity to spontaneously become knotted. The phenomenon of spontaneous knot formation is something that has fascinated physicists for quite a while now, and these scientists have carried out experiments testing the precise conditions under which thread spontaneously knots itself. Seemingly all that is required for a piece of spun fiber to form a knot is enough string and some kind of random motion. Once again, we follow the natural inclinations of the fiber when we work magically with knots.

The most obvious use for a knot is to bind something together or prevent it from pulling away. In this, knot magic shares similar magical characteristics as woolen fibers. But where woolen fibers can only ensnare, trap, and bind in an enclosed fashion, the energy and intent stored in magical knots can continue to affect those who come into contact with them for as long as the knots are present.

Out of the various forms of fiber magic you will find among modern magic workers, knot magic is the most common. This can be as simple as a braided and knotted thread created with magical intent, or as complex as a knitted or crocheted blanket or garment. We'll get into some of the ways in which you can knit, crochet, and knot magically toward the end of this chapter, but for now we're going to return to the less common practice of spun magic and take a look at how it may have worked.

The Mechanics of Spun Magic

As previously covered, one of the ways in which seiðr was practiced in the historical sources was as a form of spun magic. This kind of seiðr is, at least in my opinion, the oldest and deepest form of the practice. But very few modern magic workers think of spun magic when they think of seiðr, and even fewer can imagine it, let alone think about how it may have worked.

Theories and Method

Ever since scholars first began to discuss the possibility of seiðr as a spun form of magic, a number of theories surrounding its mechanics have been proposed by practitioners and scholars alike. Typically, these theories involve shamanistic elements, such as sending out spirit emissaries (that travel out from the whorl as a wind), or using the movement of the whorl to enter trance.[264] However, many of these theories unfortunately make little sense on magical or practical levels.

We once again arrive at the same issue of observer perspective versus practitioner perspective covered in chapter 1. Most scholars do not spin or perform magic, and in my experience, most magical practitioners do not spin or engage in scholarship, which leads to a shortfall of relevant experience across the board. Theories often work within the context of the available evidence but fall down both magically and practically. More commonly, a theory may work in terms of the available evidence and hold a grain of something that can work magically but fail on a practical level.

---

264. Eldar Heide, "Spinning Seiðr," 164.

We can never truly know how seiðr was spun in the Viking Age. The sources we currently have simply don't have enough information on how this art was historically practiced for that to ever be the case. However, we can, I think, get somewhat close and at least build a workable modern practice that is clearly rooted in those older practices.

Practical Concerns

One of the biggest hindrances to anyone who tries to put forth a workable theory on seiðr is the inability to spin. People who observe spinning tend to be drawn in by the spinning motion of the whorl and assume that the spinner is also similarly affected.

However, no spinner focuses on the whorl in the same way that a non-spinner observer does. The focus of the spinner is always on the area referred to as the drafting zone, the area in which the spinner pulls out and separates the fibers (i.e., drafts them) so that they're not only straight but will create the right thickness of yarn once spun together. This is where the fibers (along with anything else that might be stuck in them) are ensnared, trapped, and bound in place by the twist created by the spinning motion of the whorl below. What the spinner sees during this process is not just the organization and setting "flat" of fibers but also the incredible trapping ability of the twist to ensnare, trap, and bind. This is something obvious to spinners and would have been obvious from the first time a person picked up a stick and used it to add twist to fibers.[265]

It's entirely possible that people in the Viking Age spun differently to how we spin today. The style that most spinners use nowadays is actually based on Andean styles of spinning, quite different from traditional European styles that are still in use in more remote areas of Eastern Europe. In these more traditional European styles, the spinner does not allow the spindle to drop, but instead manually twists the spindle in order to add the correct amount of twist to the yarn. Theories that focus on the idea of the spinning whorl and spirit emissaries that travel like winds may be appropriate for Andean styles of spinning, but they certainly fall down when the spindle is not allowed to drop (if that is indeed how they spun).

---

265. "Stick spinning" is believed to be the oldest form of spinning and is still practiced by some spinners to this day.

Magical Concerns

Scholars such as Eldar Heide have pointed out an association between seiðr and a type of spirit referred to as a *gandr* (plural *gandir*), characterized as a kind of spirit emissary that was sent out to do the work of the seiðrworker. For Heide, the gandr was connected to spinning through its derivative *göndull*, a word that generally referred to coarse yarn and other twisted items. This association led Heide to conclude that the gandr is a mind emissary that is spun and cites folkloric accounts of sightings of gandir that describe them as resembling a rope or a thread that comes in a whirlwind.[266] Other scholars classify gandir as actual spirits that must be summoned with the use of certain tools.[267]

However, this theory is incredibly problematic from a magical perspective. Is the gandr a mind emissary or a spirit that must be summoned? Because those are two very different things and imply two very different ways of working. If the *gandr* is a "mind emissary," then how is it different from the wandering "free soul" or hugr/hyge covered in chapter 5? Moreover, why would one need to spin in order to send it forth? From my perspective as a magical practitioner, the gandr as spirit is the most logical possibility here.

But if the gandr is a spirit, it must come from somewhere. Even more curiously, the fact that it has its own distinct nomenclature suggests that a gandr was a particular type of spirit.

Given the connections between völur and álfar explored in chapter 3, as well as the possible associations between elves and the often distaff-shaped völva staff discussed in chapter 7, I believe it likely that elves and gandir are one and the same. This interpretation would also potentially align with the tales described by Heide in which the gandr seems to travel in a whirlwind. Whirlwinds feature as a form of fairy transportation in a number of tales from Ireland, and as with their counterpart stories from Scandinavia, throwing an iron knife into the whirlwind was believed to stop it.[268; 269]

---

266. Eldar Heide, "Spinning Seiðr," 164.

267. Neil Price, *The Viking Way 2nd Ed.*, 134.

268. Joshua Cutchin, *Thieves in the Night: A Brief History of Supernatural Child Abductions* (San Antonio: Anomalist Books, 2018), 34, 88.

269. See chapter 3 for a brief comparison of the Irish *aes sidhe* fairies and elves.

From Theory to Method

As mentioned numerous times, my approach to Heathen magic involves both research and experimentation, or in other words, taking information from both primary sources and more recent scholarship and testing the theories out for myself to see how they work. This was a major factor in my learning how to spin. I *wanted* to test out these theories to see what actually worked and what didn't.

In my experience, theories centered around practitioners being lulled into trance by the motion of the whorl do not work because of the simple fact that spinners don't focus on the whorl while working. Moreover, it would be impossible to successfully spin in this way for a long enough period of time to enter trance while focusing on the whorl without the spindle dropping. In my experience, the idea of spinning magic being worked in concert with *gandir/*staff-elves works both practically and magically, especially when emulating older European forms of spinning mentioned above. I've found this method of spinning the most effective when working magic.

I have worked spinning magic both with and without the help of a staff elf, and the processes I have found to work are different for each, as one might expect. When working without a staff elf, I've found it best to focus on the thing that I want in a very general way as I spin and "pull" it to me. The kind of pulling I'm referring to here is the kind that involves your will—in other words, you have to really want it to come to you. A good comparison for the kind of sensation you should be looking for when pulling in this way is if you have ever been in a moving vehicle going in a direction you don't want it to. Depending on what is happening, you may have noticed that your entire torso feels like it's trying to pull the car in a different direction. Your gut lurches and tries to exert something akin to a will—this is what you need to work with.

When spinning in the European way, the motion of twisting the spindle can feel almost like you are landing a fish. Only instead of winding the reel and fighting the fish to shore, you are chanting while twisting the spindle to pull the thing toward you to potentially trap and bind in the drafting zone. This works, but you have to really focus on what you want and want it with your whole being. That sensation of wanting something and pulling it with everything you have is key to the success of this method.

However, when working with a staff elf, you tend to focus more on what your magical partner is doing. This is more like fishing with a self-guiding fishing hook. The gandr helps with targeting, so to speak. You still need to pull, chant, and twist, but it's not all on you.

For pulling luck and other positive things to me, I turn my spindle in a clockwise direction, but for more baneful purposes, I turn the spindle counterclockwise. When I have ensnared something (with or without the help of my staff spirit), I have noticed that it becomes much harder to spin and pull it back. Spinning in the style that I do makes it easier, but there is still a discernible change in how the spinning goes once you have ensnared something. This is what I believe happened to our bond spinner in the story at the beginning of this section. For me, this is hardtwisted sorcery because it feels as though I must fight and force whatever I have ensnared to come to me so that I can trap it in my yarn, and if I'm successful there's a sensation of release, an inexplicable slub appears in my yarn, and I can spin normally again.[270]

→))o Fundamentals: Spinning Magic (Visualization) o((←

When I first began to learn from Óðinn, one of the first things he taught me in dreams was how to "pull" spirits. This was many years before I came across the concept of seiðr as a spun form of magic. But in hindsight, by teaching me how to pull in this way, he was teaching me one of the fundamental skills of one of the forms of seiðr that I would come to practice.

In the following exercise, you will have the opportunity to practice not only the art of pulling, but visualizing your targets too. This will teach you the inner processes of spun magic without a staff elf as I perform it. You will notice that I have included a spindle as an optional tool for this rite, but you do not need to be able to spin to do this exercise. The physical spindle here is a physical support for the inner work for those who would like to use it.

As with other forms of magic, it's very important to have a clear idea of what you are working for when spinning seiðr, especially if what you are working for is something specific like "I want _____ to come home now." Like all magic, spun seiðr accomplishes your goals in the most direct way possible. Moreover, because you are actively pulling your desired outcomes or items to

---

270. A slub is a lump that forms in the yarn, usually as a result of clumped-up fibers that weren't combed or drafted out.

you, the effects can be a lot more spectacular (for the good and the bad of that). For example, if you work to bring someone home, they may come home because of an accident (usually to those around them). Often it's best to just spin for luck in a very broad sense without any specifics, and visualize the luck as golden light. If you are not sure what you would like to spin for while performing this exercise, my recommendation is luck.

You will need

A comfortable place where you can sit upright

10 to 15 minutes of undisturbed time

A spindle (optional)

Journal

Pen

Practice

1. Begin by seating yourself comfortably in an upright position and take a few minutes to meditate before beginning.

2. When you feel relaxed, imagine yourself sitting as a spinner would. Imagine the spindle in your dominant hand, and distaff and roving in your non-dominant hand. Build this picture as clearly as you can before proceeding onto the next step.

3. Now, without letting the visualization of yourself as a spinner drop, allow yourself to think about the thing you wish to pull to yourself. Visualize it in as much detail as you can, and allow your desire to have it grow. Let it fill your body as completely as you can, but especially your torso and pelvis.

4. When you have this item clearly in mind, visualize it caught in a noose surrounded by a whirlwind that connects back to your distaff and the wool upon it.

5. When you have this item clearly in mind and feel as though you could not want it any more, then begin to visualize yourself pulling it to the wool upon your distaff via the noose and whirlwind with each visualized twist of the spindle. If you are working with a spindle as physical support for this activity, this is where you would begin to twist it.

Regardless of whether or not you have a physical spindle, try to feel the sensation of pulling in your torso and pelvis as strongly as you can as you pull.

6. In your visualization, you may "see" your item or an abstract representation of it drawing closer to you with each visualized twist of the spindle. This is a good thing. Depending on what you are pulling to yourself, you may wish to allow it to settle around you, or to continue to pull it into the wool to be spun into the yarn. If you want to stop the pulling, simply allow the sensations and desire to dissipate and stop turning the spindle.

7. If you intend to pull your desired item/thing into the yarn, continue working as you are until the desired item enters into the wool and then is spun into the yarn. You may feel the wool become almost electrified as your target enters it, then feel that electric sensation move down into the yarn as it's spun in. The spinning may also become more difficult at this point, but keep at it until you feel as though you have captured it all!

8. Regardless of whether you trap your target or not, when you are satisfied with your work, speak the following charm:

> Well I worked and well I spun
> Well I pulled and brought to me
> What I have gained I hold until I say
> I put up my work now for the day

Now allow your visualization to fade, but know that what you pulled will remain with you. When ready, open your eyes and note any impressions and changes in your journal.

Once you have become proficient in this method of spun seiðr, you will probably find it quite easy to incorporate the physical act of spinning into this work. The method presented here is designed to be used with or without a spindle; even if you never learn how to spin, this method can still be used to work a spindle-less variant of seiðr with practice. However, I would encourage you to learn how to spin all the same, as this method is far more effective when you do.

⇥ Experiential: Twelve-Day Spinning Rite ⇤

In the following ritual, those of you who spin will have the opportunity to practice the method described in the fundamentals exercise. The series of rituals presented here was originally designed to be done over the twelve nights of Yule but can be done as needed at any time of year. Aside from your spindle, you will need three half-ounce lots of roving: one natural/white, one red, and one black. Before beginning the ritual, it's best to divide each half-ounce lot into four portions of wool (one for each night), so that you have an equal amount to spin each night. My preferred time to begin this ritual is at nine o'clock on a Friday, then continue the theme of nine in the evening on each of the subsequent nights.

When I designed this ritual, I did so because my family had endured a bad year and it felt like we had a lot of ill luck hanging around our house and lives in general. But a more immediate concern was that my husband's work situation was fast becoming untenable. Within a month of doing this, our lives had drastically improved and my husband started a new and better job.

This ritual takes place in three stages over twelve nights, with each stage of the ritual lasting four nights. During the first four nights, you spin black wool to pull the negative energy and ill luck from your family and home. During the second set of four nights you spin the red wool to pull in luck, and the final four nights are prayer and devotion spun into an offering of white wool.

At the end of each night, simply put your spindle somewhere safe until it is time to take it out again for the next night's work. After each set of four nights, clear your spindle and wind the yarn into a ball. After the twelfth night of spinning, I burn the black yarn to destroy the ill luck, bury the white yarn as an offering to the Spinning Goddess, and keep the red yarn for use in future magical workings.

You do not need to set up for ritual space while working this series of rituals. Working within a space that is ritually separated from the rest of the world is not conducive to a rite focused on pulling different energies from the world around you. That said, I do begin by reciting a short prayer to the Spinning Goddess because in doing this work, I am swimming in her waters (so to speak) and it's good to acknowledge that.

You will need

Your spindle

½ ounce of roving each in white, red, and black

Ritual Procedure

1. At the beginning of each night, take your spindle and wool in hand and begin by spending a few moments meditating as you did in *Fundamentals: Spinning Magic (Visualization)*. When you feel ready, speak the following prayer to the Spinning Goddess:

> As I take your tools into my hands
> I ask that you empower my work
> Goddess of witches and wives
> Goddess of distaff and flax
> May the work of my spindle be blessed.

2. Now begin to visualize yourself in your home with spindle and wool in hand. Once you have this image clearly in your mind, start spinning as you visualize and, as you spin, "see" a snare come from the roving yet to be spun, moving out in a cone of wind that turns as you spin. This is how you should begin every night.

3. For the first four nights, you'll spin the black and practice and seek out the negative energy and ill luck with your snare. Focus on that ill luck as a concept and how it may be manifesting in your home and life as you visualize your snare; allow your snare to search for it as it moves through your home. At some point, what you see may take on a life of its own—that's when you generally find what you're looking for. When you get the feeling that you have found something, begin to pull as you spin.

4. After each spinning session, put your spindle and wool somewhere safe. On the fourth night, clear your spindle and wind the black yarn into a ball.

5. On the second four nights, you spin with the red. This time your goal is to seek out and ensnare luck that you can then pull to yourself and use. When I envision luck in the world, I see it as a beautiful, golden thing—this is the visual I begin these second four nights with. Once again, put

your spinning somewhere safe between sessions. Clear your spindle on the fourth night. Be extra careful when winding your ball from these four nights as a badly wound ball of yarn can become difficult to use later on.

6. The final four nights are spun with the white/natural wool. Unlike the other eight nights, there is no pulling or ensnarement required. These final four nights are about spinning as an offering to the Spinning Goddess, so try to spin with a mindset of devotion and gratitude. Again, keep your spinning safe between sessions and clear the spindle on the final night.

7. At the end of the twelve nights, you will need to burn the black yarn to destroy the negativity and bury the white wool as an offering to the Spinning Goddess. The red wool is for you to keep for future magical workings.

As previously mentioned, there is no way to know if this method is the same one practiced by the spinning witches in the Norse sources. However, it is a *workable* method that can be used for a wide range of purposes. To date, I have used it for everything from clearing out ill luck and trapping spirits, to pulling apart magic worked by others, and, yes, bringing my husband home.

Washes

Water features heavily in Old Norse and Germanic ideas of fate and the goddesses who are most associated with it. The Norns presumably put the slips of wood they write on into the waters of *Urðrbrunnr* ("Urðr's spring"). Frigga (a goddess who is believed to know the future and is therefore tied with fate) dwells in *Fensalir* ("marsh halls"), and one of Freyja's names, *Mardöll*, is believed to relate to the sea.[271] On the continent, the Germanic figure Frau Holle is associated with watery places such as the Hollenteich (a body of water on top of the Hoher Meißner mountain), and she's associated with herons and geese, which are both aquatic birds.

Throughout my years of magical fiber practice, I have found that water also has a role to play in fiber magic. In my experience, there are four main ways in which water may be used in fiber magic: washes, as a blessing water, and in the production of flax.

---

271. Rudolf Simek, *Dictionary of Northern Mythology*, 81, 202.

Using Washes

One of the first things that a fiber artist does after finishing a project is to gently soak the project in a mixture of soap and water. This not only helps to ensure that the item that has been handled over a prolonged period of time is clean, but it also helps to open up and make any patterns worked into it more obvious. If you have ever knitted lace, for example, you know how magical it can be to see the pattern finally revealed in its full glory as you pull it from the water.

Note that while all kinds of fiber can be soaked in this way, you have to be gentle. The soap used cannot be harsh, the water cannot be hot, and the piece must be treated in such a way that it is not scrubbed or otherwise agitated. The following recommended washes are for a second soaking. The first wash will be with soap—ideally one created for the purpose (you can buy specialized soap formulations for this purpose from online vendors like Knitpicks). The second wash can be where you use more specialized ingredients, depending on your purpose. This final wash can be an opportunity to reinforce and further imbue your creation with your intent.

⇥○ Recipe: Protective and Blessing Washes ○⇤

The most common category of wash that I make is a protective and blessing wash. I especially like to do this with any baby blankets that I make. Young children have a lot of fears, and to make matters worse, they also tend to attract attention from various kinds of spirits far more easily than adults do. So when I make a baby blanket, I make it with the intent that it becomes a protective and comforting item for the child. This is something I believe children can sense in the blankets I make as well, and baby blankets that are made in this way seem to become firm favorites with the children I gift them to. The following recipe is the recipe I use when finishing the things I make that are intended to bless and protect.

You will need

3 t of rosemary

3 t of vervain

3 t of mugwort

1 T salt

9 juniper berries

1 pint jug

1 soup spoon

1 tea "egg" (for drinking loose leaf tea)

A water boiler/kettle/pan for boiling water

A basin

Procedure

1. Using whatever utensils or appliances you have to boil water, put some water on to boil. It should be enough to fill a pint jug three-quarters of the way.

2. While you are waiting for the water to boil, add 1 tablespoon of salt to the bottom of the jug, speaking the following charm and making sure your breath goes wholly in as you do so:

> A foundation of earth for the brew I make
> Of holy salt, a burden to the wicked
> What you touch you cleanse
> You drive evil out
> Leaving space only for the sacred.

3. Now add 3 teaspoons of mugwort, vervain, and rosemary to the tea egg as well as the nine juniper berries. Close your egg and place it in the jug.

4. When the water boils, add ¾ pint of water to the jug. Then, leaning over the jug so that your breath goes in, recite the following charm over the mixture three times, stirring clockwise as you do so. As you chant, visualize your words exiting your mouth as golden light that fills the water, enlivening the herbs and causing them to infuse the water with their powers:

> Over waters clean, wise words I speak
> With loving heart I breathe my charm
> Address myself to salt and herb
> To juniper and vervain
> Mugwort and rosemary

To the bane of evil and herb of witches
To the the first herb and dew of the sea
You mighty herbs, strong in power
Hear me now as I chant
Protect and bless the work you touch
Fix your power to always remain
Apply yourself to my purpose now
Blessings to _____, keep them safe!

5. Leave the mixture to stand for five minutes before repeating the chant. Now fill whichever basin you typically use for washing your magical fiber until it is full enough that it will not overflow when you add your fiber and the ¾ pint of herbal mixture. Speak the following charm over the water in the basin:

Over good water a galdor I speak
With wise words I will it
and my breath goes wholly in
Making clean waters holy
Fast flee the evil from it!
Fast flee evil magic from it!

6. Remove the tea egg of herbs and pour the mixture into your basin of hallowed water. Stir clockwise three times, then add your fiber work to the waters and leave for an hour. Pull your work from the water and lay it out to dry (you may wish to retain the water for further work). If possible, dry your work in the sun to imbue it with further blessings.

Depending on what you are making and the intent you are making it with, there are many different potential combinations of herbs that you can use depending on your needs. You can also customize the herbs you use to reflect any deities you call upon while creating your magic. For example, as I associate roses and elderflower with the Spinning Goddess, I might add roses and/or elderflower to washes where her specific blessings are desired.

Although I have only given the procedure for creating a wash for blessing and protection, you can adapt this procedure according to your needs. One of the ways in which you can do this is to look up which herbs align most closely with your magical purpose in either the magico-medical manuscripts or magical correspondence tables, incorporating them into your wash, and adapting the incantation accordingly. If you choose to do this, check that the herbs you use are not skin irritants, toxic or corrosive, especially if you intend them to be worn against the skin.

Blessing Water

When working with magical washes, you may also want to retain the waters after you have soaked your fiber work. These washes often make quite good additions to other spell work, especially if you have used them for soaking spun skeins of wool.

To provide a quick explanation for non-spinners, skeins of newly spun yarn must be soaked so that the twist is set. The process of spinning adds a lot of energy to the yarn in the form of twist, but unless there is too much twist, a soak in water followed by hanging to dry with weights attached is all that is required to settle that energy. When yarn has too much energy, it curls and loops back on itself. This is usually not by design; most people want balanced yarn to work with. However, some people work with this "energized" yarn by preference... and the use of the term "energized" here is curious, seemingly one of those instinctively-given terms that touch on something deeper, often without the labeling parties even realizing it.

To soak a skein after spinning is to leech off the excess energy contained within the yarn. Most people simply allow the water to drain away once the yarn has been soaked. However, several years ago I noticed that the water had a curious *magically* energetic quality too. There was a feeling of stored potential springing outward, so I began to retain this water—often full of apotropaic herbs from the wash—and use it in my clearing practices. While using water in this manner is ideal for environments where smoke cannot be used, this mixture cannot be kept for long (no more than a day or so), and must be kept in the fridge or you may as well be flinging bacteria around your home.

Flax Water

Another way in which we can use infused waters is during the spinning of flax. As mentioned in the section on flax at the beginning of this chapter, you need to wet the flax in order to make joins in the different lengths of flax fibers. Many flax spinners use their own spittle, but my preference (especially if it's for others), is to use a bowl of water. Hard experience has taught me that it's rarely a good idea to give something as personal as spittle away to other practitioners. Moreover, a lot of people find the idea disgusting.

Once again, where there is water, there is an opportunity to add layers of magic to whatever you are making. When spinning a three-ply flax for delineating ritual space, for example, I will brew my waters in such a way that they're not just apotropaic but also reflect each of the three deities I associate with Heathen magic.[272] One length I spin as a prayer to the Spinning Goddess, and the water I use while spinning contains roses and elderflower. The second length I spin in honor of the Spear God, and the water is made with mugwort and salt. The final length I spin for the Mound God, and I brew some barley for this water. Through the act of prayer while spinning and the use of apotropaics such as salt and mugwort, the vé bonds I spin for delineating my sacred space are both apotropaic in nature as well as a spun form of prayer.[273] You can use the same procedures when creating these different waters as given above for creating washes.

Crafting with Intention: Knot Magic

In this chapter, we've predominantly focused on the inherent qualities of fiber and spun magic. However, as I said at the beginning, you do not have to spin in order to practice fiber magic. In fact, as you will see, a lot of people (witches and non-witches alike) do it without even realizing it.

Without a doubt, the most accessible form of fiber magic is knot magic. Almost everyone has the ability to tie a knot, and unless you make a point of learning the different kinds of knots, you do not need any special knowledge or ability beyond the magical mainstays of visualization and will or intent.

Knots have long been used by witches for a wide variety of magical purposes—everything from binding spirits and other magical practitioners to the creation of healing talismans and love spells. The topic of knot magic is broad

---

272. "Three-ply flax" is composed of three separate lengths of spun flax that are spun together (in the opposite direction from how they were originally spun) in order to ply them.

273. See pages 294–296 for more information on vé bonds and how to make them.

enough to fill entire books, so I will be brief here (look at the Recommended Reading section if you are interested in exploring the topic further).

Knot magic can be as simple or as complex as you want or need it to be, and you can work it with any old piece of string you happen to have to hand, or use it to create something that resembles a piece of knotted art.

The simplest form of knot magic involves the tying of nine knots. These are worked with intent while visualizing what you wish to happen and reciting a certain charm as you do so. The charm in question is something of a mainstay in modern witchcraft practice, and there are a number of variations that can be found online. However, I personally do not use it; instead I speak my will as I work each knot using words that come to me as I work. I've found my approach to be more effective over the years, and fate is a thing that must be spoken and named in Heathen magic—especially when performing an otherwise silent magical act like making knots. As you will see if you take the time to look up the charm in question, the common knot magic spell does not do that.

Beyond this more simple practice, knot magic can become quite complex, and involve everything from color and number correspondences, in addition to different types of knots and other materia magica such as dried berries, feathers, or beads. You don't have to adhere to these correspondences—after all, knot magic only ever requires you, a piece of string, and some knots to work.

Knitting, Crochet, Macramé as Long Forms of Knot Magic

Not all knot magic even looks like magic. Many fiber arts such as knitting, crochet, and macramé require the craftsperson to make a series of knots in order to create fabric. When worked as magic, these crafts can be a sustained, long form of knot magic. The average sweater, for example, has tens of thousands of stitches! This complexity presents a problem for anyone who wishes to craft with intention. It's easy to maintain one's focus when there are only nine knots to be made, or the work can be finished within a couple of hours, depending on what you're doing. But what about the tens of thousands of knots representing countless hours of work?

The fact of the matter is that it would be impossible to maintain the same level of focus in these larger projects as you would during shorter forms of knot magic. Even if you were the most disciplined person on the planet, without any other distractions in life, it would still be impossible! But there is one way in which you can maintain a thread of focus throughout your work regardless of what distractions may come.

Adding Words to Your Work

Most people who try to work magic into larger knotting projects such as sweaters or shawls work solely with intent. They think about the person they are crafting for and the love they have for them as they work—a completely valid way to work. Mothers and grandmothers have done this while making clothes for their family members probably since the first person figured out how to create fabric from making groups of knots. Recall from chapter 5 that spoken words were a key part of setting ørlög or speaking the kind of prophecies that come true. It's one thing to work with silent intent, but it's far better to speak the words into being.

Before deciding on which words to speak, you first need to be clear about your purpose. For example, I recently began work on a shawl for use in trance work. That right there is my purpose, but there are many different ways in which an item can be used in trance work, and so more specifics were needed.

When planning those specifics, I find it helpful to sit down with a pen and paper, and simply brainstorm ideas around that core purpose. Don't hesitate to add any planned physical characteristics as well as the specifics of how it will function in your practice. If I were to create one for my shawl, my brainstorming might look something like this:

Shawl for Trance
Shawl for Trance → Green → Must have wing-like
characteristics → veil → for wandering → aids flight → protection

From this point, I like to sit down and compose a spoken charm for use while working. My favorite way of doing that is by using one of the old poetic meters known as *galdralag* or "spell meter." Galdralag can be a little confusing to learn because there seem to be a number of different interpretations among scholars of how to form galdralag. The method taught here is simply how *I* do it; it may not be galdralag proper.

The easiest way to teach a poetic form is to give an example, so here is the charm I created for use while knitting my shawl:

With stitches *green*
I *grow* my wings
To *wander* *wide* among the *worlds*
A *veil* of prayers
Victory's cloak
Well I fly upon these *wings*
Well I fly throughout the *worlds*
Well I fly then safe return

Old Norse poetry is alliterative, which means that it doesn't have to rhyme. Instead, the focus is placed on the letter sounds of the *stressed* syllables in each line. One easy way to figure out where the stressed syllables are in a sentence is to speak it in time while tapping out a beat on a desk or drum. The stressed syllables are the ones that you speak on the beat.

In the example I give above, the stressed syllables I have chosen to alliterate are written in bold type. In this form of poetic meter, lines 1+2 and 4+5 are paired. In these lines, the rule is that you need one word in each line that alliterates. In lines 1+2, this is the letter g, and in lines 4+5, the letter v. When we get to line three at least two words must alliterate with each other on the same line. So we have "*To wander wide among the worlds.*"

Lines six and seven is where the magical transformation takes place. Line six is a mirror of line three and also requires that two words alliterate within the same line. But then line seven (and eight, if you have that many) comes along and it takes line six and *transforms* it. Galdralag is about transformation. It's about taking an expected end and changing it in an unexpected way, and in doing so, bringing about transformation with that speech.

The final test of any galdralag charm is through recitation, in my opinion. It's no coincidence that a lot of rap is alliterative—alliterative poetry is best when spoken in time with a beat, and it either works or it doesn't. You can test your poetry by tapping out a steady beat on a desk or with a drum and chanting your galdralag along with it. If it works, you will find that the words flow well with the beat.

Sometimes you can come up with the most technically perfect poem but it's missing something. Or your poem looks good on paper but doesn't sound so good to the ear. Alternatively, you may find that you make mistakes but the version with the mistakes actually works better than a corrected version. In my experience, it's always best to go with what sounds good, because that's usually what turns out to work the best.

Unfortunately, not everyone likes or is particularly gifted at writing. If this is true for you, come up with a simple statement for what you want to happen. It does not have to be fancy, especially if you're going to follow the advice of the next section and hide it in a song. Above all, what you write should be clear and concise. If I were writing a statement for my shawl, for example, something like this would suffice: "Make my shawl wooly wings that help me to fly around the worlds in journey, protect me, and help me get back safely again."

Hiding Words in Song

It's not always feasible to chant a galdor or an intentional statement again and again while you work. Fiber arts (and, by extension, fiber magic) is magic that is worked on the fly and over a long period of time. We deal with distractions and often find ourselves crafting in a wide range of places. This is magic that can be done in full view of the world. And due to the portability and range of settings, it can be all too easy to forget to chant or remember the purpose of your work.

The easiest way to maintain a thread of focus—even if only on a subconscious level—is through song. There was a point in time when work songs were traditional; people had songs for everything from washing clothes to ploughing fields. I like to imagine that the weavers in the dyngja (or half-sunken weaving rooms) had their songs too.

It can be hard to turn a galdor or statement into a song, and especially a song you make up yourself! It's easier if you begin with the rhythm and build the tune from there, but don't worry if you are having absolutely no luck coming up with a song of your own. Some charms lend themselves to music better than others. In these cases, you can try to filch an existing song (any that work will do) or, failing that, you can distill your poem or statement down into a rhythmic drone.

Regardless of what you come up with, it will probably sound strange at first—forced, even. But stick with it, because every time you sing it to yourself, you're teaching your brain to associate the song with the galdor or statement, and with enough repetition, it won't matter if you do little more than hum when you work. Your subconscious will fill in the rest for you.

Story in Fiber

The final element of fiber magic to be covered in this chapter is embroidery and weaving, or the depiction of stories in fiber. As we saw in chapter 5, woven tapestries and embroideries could each be considered a form of silent storytelling—a woman's corpus of literature, if you will. There's something powerful in setting pictures or words into cloth, especially when chanted over and done with intent. The Nornir may speak fate and write on slips of wood, but I chant galdor and write with needle and thread.

Unfortunately, I've never had the chance to take up weaving, but I know embroidery well. I began embroidering as a tween after finding my grandmother's embroidery basket under some very mysterious circumstances. I knew what to do almost instantly, and within the week I was churning out (and selling) stitched pictures to the amazement of my parents.

Over the years, I've embroidered gifts, fold-away shrine pieces, and worked magic with my needle and thread. I've used it for offerings, to record family events, and to completely change my life.

The advantages of arts such as embroidery and weaving is that the use of pictures makes it much easier to remember the purpose of what you're creating and why. When you're embroidering a charm, it's hard to forget it or zone out because otherwise you'll make a mistake. You always have a point of focus when you work with pictures.

But as with every other form of fiber magic, the silent has to be spoken into the world. It's not enough to simply embroider with intent; you also need to speak of what you're embroidering and why. If you're embroidering a charm, you need to repeat it intermittently as you work. When stitching bind runes or sigils, you may want to focus intently on the forms and lines of what you're working on, and if you know the meaning, to remind yourself of it as you work.

Songs have their place here too, and can present a way of hiding your incantations from untrained ears. This is especially important if the pictures you are creating with your needle are what most people would consider strange.

When you are done, don't forget to soak the finished piece in water. If your finished cloth is your slip of wood, it should find its way into the waters of Urðr's spring so that it might eventually become real.[274]

---

274. See chapter 13 for full ritual instructions.

Ten

SPOKEN MAGIC AND HERBAL CHARMS

For the elder Heathen, speech could be a magical thing. In the mouth of a völva, it could reify a "fate" and make it real, and in the mouth of a Norn, it could set down the ørlög of a child. In each case, there's the implication that both völva and Norn have some agency in this process, and that it is one fate out of a number of *potential* fates that are chosen.[275]

The magician who wields speech is different; in an active-versus-passive dichotomy, galdor and spoken fate sit at opposite ends of the same spectrum of magical speech. When the völva wields magical speech, it seems to be an act of choosing and can be flexible depending on the desires of her audience.[276] But when a magician wields magical speech, it is because the magician has already decided upon a desired outcome—perhaps independently of any existing choices—and is now actively working to bring it to pass.

Galdr/galdor ("charms") is Óðinn's magic, and although his galdr is reputedly able to raise the dead and turn back curses, it is his connection with magical galdor within the context of healing that we are going to focus on in this chapter.[277]

---

275. Karen Bek-Pedersen, "Nornir in Old Norse Mythology," 67.

276. Ibid., 201–202.

277. *Galdr* and *Galdor* are Old Norse and Old English variants of the same word.

The idea of the Spear God as a healer is not particularly common among modern Heathens. Yet he is depicted as a god of healing in every culture in which he is found. In the Norse poem *Hávamál*, "Sayings of the High One," he tells us that he knows a spell "which the sons of men need, those who want to live as physicians".[278] Among the early English, we find him in the Old English magico-medical text *Lacnunga* under the name Woden, where he is depicted as engaging in healing magic; in the Old High German Second Merseburg Charm, he heals a horse with spoken charms. These sources are admittedly sparse yet present a picture that is consistent across three different but related cultures. Moreover, in two out of the three attestations, not only is he connected with healing; he uses galdr to enact that healing as well.

One of the problems facing the modern Heathen attempting to work with galdr in a historically authentic way is the precious little information about how to actually create and perform this art from the Old Norse sources. As with all forms of historical Heathen magic, here again we face the issue of sources written from the observer perspective rather than that of a practitioner. But what if there *were* sources on galdr written from the practitioner perspective? As unlikely as it may sound, there may very well be.

Introducing the Old English Magico-Medical Manuscripts

Like many of the Old Norse sources, the Old English magico-medical manuscripts are the product of post-conversion authors. They are somewhat older than the Old Norse sources, dating back for the most part to the tenth and eleventh centuries.[279] But due to the earlier conversion of England to Christianity, in addition to the Christian veneer of many of the remedies, they are often overlooked by modern Heathens as a magical resource. To further complicate matters, there is also a clear thread of classical influence that runs through these texts as well.[280] Texts such as Pliny's *Natural History* as well as Old English versions of the *Herbarium Apulei* and *Medicina de Quadrupedi-*

---

278. Carolyne Larrington, *Poetic Edda*, 35.

279. Pollington, *Leechcraft*, 69–72.

280. Although given the early influence of the classical world on Germanic cultures, the usefulness of this is questionable.

bus were known to Old English healers.[281] Despite these foreign influences, I believe it is still possible to discern the threads of what might be considered traditional Germanic healing practices.

To understand why these healing texts are valuable sources for galdr/galdor, we must first understand the role that galdor played within the Old English healing tradition and how sickness itself was perceived.

Old English Approaches to Sickness and Healing

A lot can be learned from the way in which a culture approaches healing and perceives the causes of illness. For example, to most modern humans living in the industrialized world, the cause of sickness is purely physical, and our ideas of healing reflect that view.

We can infer a number of different ideas surrounding sickness and healing from the Old English sources and, as you will see, use these ideas as a kind of filter to (hopefully) tease out Christian and classical influences from the Germanic. Although this process requires some degree of knowledge about early Germanic Christianity and classical healing modalities, it is much easier than one might think. For example, we know from Old English sources that for the devout early English Christian, suffering was sent by God to test mankind, and prayer was the only acceptable form of healing.[282] Sickness was something that had to be endured and was considered entirely in God's hands. Even the use of healing herbs seems to have represented a potential spiritual risk to the devout; where used, great care had to be taken that only God's blessings were spoken over them before ingestion.[283] So when we find the use of spoken magical charms (galdor) coupled with ritual actions and herbs, even when the charms appear to be Christian, we can be quite confident that the underlying magical methodology was not.

We can apply a similar process of elimination to classical influence as well, and use it to tease out the lapidaries, non-native plants, and any remnants of the Hippocratic theory of the Four Humors from the texts.[284]

---

281. Pollington, *Leechcraft*, 28.

282. Ibid., 32.

283. Ibid., 32–33.

284. Ibid., 28–29.

Once Christian and classical influences are removed, what remains is a vibrant and deeply animistic healing tradition in which disease seems to have not only been perceived as an invading force, but one that was alive and had agency to boot. It's not always certain whether these invading forces were considered to be "natural" or "supernatural" to the early English healers, but it's entirely possible that the early English did not distinguish between the two concepts in the first place. The most useful thing we can say about how they saw these invading beings is that they seem to have been external and were possibly considered able to either deplete from the *hælu* of a person or introduce a source of unhælu to the body.[285; 286]

As beings possessed of agency, the sickness-causing entities addressed in the verbal formulas were rarely considered to be faceless and instead were often personified in charms, even when the identity of those beings was unclear. Moreover, certain groupings of symptoms seem to have been clearly associated with specific types of being. For example, there were some types of digestive issues as well as illnesses involving impaired perception that were considered to be related to either witchcraft or elves.[287]

The underlying rationale of any treatment was simple: remove the depleting or unhæl force from the patient by either driving it out with purifying salves or smoke, or cursing the invading force in order to eventually banish it. Far from the white-coated materialism of modern medicine, this was a form of healing that was more at home with the witch and exorcist than anyone we would recognize as a doctor today. It was a magician's art, of chanted spells that addressed herbal allies and invading enemies alike, cursing and banishing as necessary. In short, it was precisely the kind of magic we are searching for when we set out on our modern quests for *galdr*.

'Magico-Medical'

Before digging deeper into the galdor of those texts, we must first cover what is meant by the term "magico-medical" within the context of these remedies. As one might expect, the magico-medical manuscripts are both magical and

---

285. Ibid., 453–468.

286. See chapter 5 for further discussion of hælu.

287. Alaric Hall, *Elves in Anglo-Saxon England*, 96–119.

medical in nature, which means that they combine elements of both the medical and the magical in order to effect cures for suffering patients to varying degrees. You will find remedies that are purely herbal, remedies that combine herbal cures with magical acts, remedies that combine spoken charms with magical acts, and remedies that combine herbal cures with both magical acts and verbal formulas.[288] It is in the categories of remedy, those containing verbal charms or *galdor*, where I believe we find not only the most potential remnants of Heathen magic but also our best source of practitioner perspective information on the art of galdor.

Introducing Galdor

The word *galdr* (or *galdor/gealdor* in Old English) relates to the verb *galen*, or "sing, twitter."[289] This is the art of crafting or reciting intentionally magical speech or, in other words, charms.

There are three different types of galdor I have found in the primary sources. The first is the magical formula that was passed down through oral tradition before finally being recorded at a later date.[290] (You will have the opportunity to use the most famous of these old magical formulae in the procedure for making depossession oil at the end of this chapter.)

The second type of charm is already familiar from chapter 9; it is galdralag, or "spell meter," the art of magical poetry. Finally is the narrative charm, the charm that affects magical change through the telling of story.

Narrative Charms

Narrative charms are found in Old English, Old High German, and Scandinavian sources, with a greater proliferation in the former than the latter two. As the label suggests, these are charms that in some way *narrate* the circumstances of illness and then the cure in order to effect the desired change.

The chosen narratives of these charms are often mythological in nature, calling to mind the successful resolution of similar problems by the Holy Powers in sacred (or mythic) time, and drawing power from those myths to

---

288. Ibid., 470.

289. Simek, *Dictionary of Northern Mythology*, 98.

290. Ibid.

work a cure. The art of storytelling is central to this art, both in terms of the knowledge of stories that may be told, and also the ability to create charms based upon those stories. Sometimes the mythological stories and references used in these charms are quite clear and easy to track down. But other times, they are not so clear, and the mythological "origins story" of the cure is lost to the ages.

An excellent example of this kind of confusing reference can be found in *Lacnunga* charm No. 162:

> Nine are the sisters of noðþ, then the nine became eight,
>   and the eight to seven, and the seven to six, and the
>   six to five, and the five to four, and the four to three,
>   and the three to two, and the two to one, and the one to none.[291]

This charm (which purports to be for a swelling, "worm," or "every evil") is a banishing charm that progressively diminishes the invading force through the act of counting down. This is a technique we can use today in our modern rites, and I will show you a way to combine this method with propitiatory offerings at the end of this chapter.

Returning to the content, the question of who *noðþ* and her sisters are is something of a mystery. Some scholars have suggested that noðþ is linked to the word "node" and tie it to "ganglion," which suggests that noðþ was possibly a personified cyst or something similar. But it has also been suggested that the use of noðþ here parallels the use of the word *nouþær*, or "needs," found carved in runes on a staff that was found at Ribe, Denmark.[292]

Regardless of whether or not noðþ can be taken to refer to "needs," the use of "nine needs" is significant and merits further exploration because the use of "nine needs" is a theme that crops up again and again as a form of curse. In the following charm, which was found inscribed on an eleventh-century amulet from Sigtuna, we see the use of "nine needs" and "three pangs" to curse a "wound-fever":

---

291. Stephen Pollington, *Leechcraft*, 235.

292. Ibid.

> Ogre of wound-fever, lord of the ogres! Flee now! You are found.
> Have for yourself three pangs, wolf!
> Have for yourself nine needs, wolf!
> ice [runes]. These ice [runes] may grant that you are satisfied, wolf.
> Make good use of the healing charm.[293]

Once again, we see the personification of illness (this time "wound-fever"). Here it is labeled as both "ogre" (þurs) and "wolf," beings considered to ravage a man as a fever would. At the beginning of the charm, the wound-fever is an ogre, a great supernatural beast considered uncontrollable and ravenous. But by the time it is cursed to three pangs and nine needs, it is addressed as a wolf, something far more controllable. Then finally this far more manageable and less deadly wolf is given ice runes to alleviate the effects of the curse in exchange for leaving. This use of cursing to compel a non-human person to a course of action is a method we can still use today, and we'll be discussing it in greater depth as we go on.

Not all magical cures were martial in nature or required personification —some relied upon the retelling of a mythological healing instead. You will likely already recognize part of the following charm from the section on hamingja repair in chapter five. It is the Old High German Second Merseburg Charm, here quoted in full:

> Phol and Woden rode to the wood;
> Then Baldur's horse sprained its leg.
> Then Sinthgunt sang over it and Sunna her sister,
> Then Frija sang over it and Volla her sister,
> Then Woden sang over it as, he well knew how,
> Over this bone sprain, this bone sprain, this limb sprain:
> Bone to bone, blood to blood,
> Limb to limb, such as they belong together.[294]

---

293. Taken from Ben Waggoner, *Norse Magical and Herbal Healing* (Morrisville, NC: Lulu.com, 2011), xxxi.

294. Taken from Godfrid Storms, *Anglo-Saxon Magic* (Gravenhage: Martinus Nijhoff, 1948), 110.

Here we have an example of a charm that is not only founded in some mythological time but also recounts a tale of healing. One interpretation of charms such as these is that by rooting the current healing in a mythological time of gods and greater magical powers, the success experienced by the gods in those endeavors might be repeated by the healer.

Moreover, the underlying mechanic of the Second Merseburg Charm was in all likelihood quite old. Most of the charm is narrative, but within that narrative is seated a magical formula ("bone to bone, blood to blood, limb to limb, such as they belong together") that is believed to be quite ancient.

The charm itself is believed to date to the ninth or tenth centuries, but the formula appears to be much older, with close parallels to horse-healing charms in both Hittite and Vedic texts. To provide some context here, the Hittites ceased to exist as a culture by 1200 BCE.[295] It is possible that the parallels between these charms from vastly different eras and geographical locals indicate either a possible link to otherwise unknown Proto-Indo-European healing practices, or early cultural and religious transmission between Europe, Asia Minor, and India.

Animism?

Compared to the Norse, the Anglo-Saxons converted to Christianity relatively early, officially succumbing to the rood over the course of the seventh century.[296] However, official religion and folk religion are often quite different, especially when that official religion is new to a land. It's one thing to live as a member of a new religion when surrounded by fellow co-religionists. But for the everyday seventh-century English person (who presumably lived much closer to the land and saw no difference between supernatural and natural)— the concerns of the clerics would have probably seemed quite alien.

As far as we can tell, the world of the early English healer seems to have been quite animist in nature, even as far removed from Heathenism as those healers were. Homilists and law-makers writing three centuries after conversion were still railing against the worship of celestial bodies, water, wells,

---

295. J. P. Mallory, *In Search of the Indo-Europeans: Language, Archaeology and Myth* (London: Thames & Hudson, 2001), 25.

296. Gale R. Owen, *Rites and Religions of the Anglo-Saxons* (New York: Dorset Press, 1985), 148.

stones, trees, and the earth herself.[297] These are all classically animist expressions of worship, at least as viewed through the eyes of an outsider.

There are also hints of animism in the charms themselves. We have already discussed some of the more "animistic" causes of sickness in the personified illnesses and angered elves we encountered earlier in the chapter. However, in my opinion, the best evidence for animistic thought in the Old English magico-medical tradition can be found in the *Lacnunga* charm known as the Nine Herbs Charm.

From an animistic perspective, this charm is interesting on a number of levels. Like remedies and charms in which the number nine features, the *Nine Herbs Charm* purports to heal all kinds of invisible, malicious ills. The charm (which also references Woden) begins by directly addressing each of the nine herbs as though they are beings with agency, reminding them of their abilities and power. Beginning with mugwort, the healer then goes on to address plantain, cress, nettle, atterlothe (identity uncertain), chamomile, crab apple or nettles, chervil, and fennel in turn.[298]

Like a well-trained army, each of the plants addressed share the ability to stand against poison and various other foes, however, with some plants additional details are supplied. Some of these details are confusing and have been theorized to have been preserved fragments of now-lost mythological references and folklore. Mugwort, we are told, is the oldest of herbs, and as such was present at the "great proclamation," where she declared her strengths and abilities. Another such reference is *maythe*, or chamomile, the apparent victor of a now-unknown event that seems to have taken place at *Alorford*. The final herb to receive an origin story of sorts in the Nine Herbs Charm is crab apple (or nettles), who was allegedly sent by a seal over the "sea ridges" as help against poison.[299]

So far, the picture that has emerged of the magico-medical tradition and the narrative charms in general is one in which story is king. To heal or effect any change with this kind of magic, one must not only know the stories within

297. Richard North, *Heathen Gods in Old English Literature*, 205–207.

298. Storms, *Anglo-Saxon Magic*, 191.

299. Karen Louise Jolly, *Popular Religion in Late Saxon England, Elf Charms in Context* (Chapel Hill, NC: University of North Carolina Press, 1996), 127.

which cures or magical effects might be rooted, but also be able to manipulate them and their cast of characters.

Important though they may be, the storied charms are not the only useful tools in the magico-medical tradition—numbers and certain ritual actions also have their roles to play.

Other Elements of Magico-Medical Charms

As important as the spoken story is in these charms, speech is not the only way in which narrative can be created and reinforced in these charms. There is also an entire language of ritual action to take into account. The following section is a look at the most necessary elements of that language for creating your own charms.

Numbers

Whether it's in the number of times a chant is to be sung, the number of days the charm should be carried out, or even as a specific feature of a charm, numbers and repetition play a significant role in many of the old magico-medical charms.

There are a number of suggested reasons for the relative importance of numbers in these texts. Some appear to be practical in nature and, according to herbalist friends, likely served as a way to time the stages of preparation in order to achieve the desired potency. However, there are also examples of number use in the charms that seem to hint at a correlation between the desired outcome of the charm and the numerical themes present.

As one might expect, some numbers are used far more commonly than others. In the magico-medical tradition, the most commonly used numbers are three and nine. Three (as always) seems to be the magic number, with no fewer than twenty-nine of the one hundred and ninety-four charms of the *Lacnunga* containing a link to the number three. In eight of those charms, the number three appears as a way to time preparation, dosage, and even length of treatment. However, the rest seem to be more magical in intent, with recommendations that the galdor or prayers be chanted three times (or that three different prayers be chanted three times for a total of nine).

When creating my own charms, the number three is at the most basic level a way of building layers of holiness into what I make. This is important if I am creating something to drive out the unholy and ill from a person or place. But on a deeper level, in using the number three to create my charms, I connect with the creation story of the first people, and the three life-bringing gifts of breath-soul, color and warmth, and mind or inspiration that enlivened them.

The number nine occurs fifteen times in the *Lacnunga* text. In nine of those examples, it is used in conjunction with treating skin growths or inflammations, and in the remaining six, nine features as part of a blessing or purification used before drinking medicine. Finally, like the number three, nine could also refer to the length of time a treatment should be carried out.

When I incorporate the number nine in my magic, I mostly use it when creating purifying oils, or galdor to curse and banish unhale beings. However, that is not all there is to the number nine or its applications for ritual use. As the number three may be thought to relate to creation and the beginning of life, nine can be just as readily associated with the end of life. Because as the Norse sources tell us, the realm of the dead, or Hel, is nine nights'" ride from the land of the living (or only nine great paces if you are Þórr/Thor).[300]

The number nine is also strongly associated with the Spear God, Óðinn (or *Woden* in Old English). As previously discussed in chapter two, the Allfather is a complex of many faces. In the Norse sources, he hangs on the world tree Yggdrasil for nine days and nights in a quest to attain the secrets of the runes, and in the Old English magico-medical manuscripts he's the magic-wielding healer of the Nine Herbs Charm. As the god I look to the most for this kind of work, I often include the number nine in my magic as a way of better connecting the stories I build in my charms with the god of healing and magic.

Directionality, Turning, and Circumambulation

The next element of this ritual language is directionality, turning, and circumambulation. In the Old English tradition, to turn with the sun (clockwise) seems to have been a way of asking for blessings. For example, among the many instructions contained in the famous *Field Remedy Charm* (a charm used to restore land to fertility), the healer is instructed to stand facing east.

---

300. Price, "Nine Paces from Hel," 184.

Then they are to bow nine times before speaking a prayer asking for help and turning three times in a clockwise direction.[301]

This is not so different from walking the boundaries clockwise with fire in order to create hallowed space. To walk with the sun is to walk the path of cosmological order and blessings. This is something I also incorporate into the creation of hallowed waters. For example, I will stir the waters in a clockwise direction with my right hand in order to imbue those waters with further blessings.

According to the scholar Godfrid Storms, there are no mentions of walking counterclockwise in the Old English magico-medical manuscripts, but as these texts are predominantly concerned with healing and what might be thought of as the restoration of order to the body, this is not entirely surprising. In the Icelandic sources, the act of turning counterclockwise could be preparation for (often baneful) witchcraft or the giving over of one's claim to the land to the wild unseen. To walk against the course of the sun was to go counter to the ordered world of gods and man, and as we saw in chapter eight, a way of creating liminal space for calling the dead and/or interacting with the unseen Other.

There was also an additional parallel here with left and right hand use. To turn right is to go clockwise, but to go left is counterclockwise. Over the years, the left side has gained a reputation for being *sinister* (a word which means "left" in Latin), and is often taken to signify a reversal of all that is good, right, and holy. However, left is not always bad in the early English sources. There is still a sense of reversal, but not all reversal is bad, and there are examples of the left side being used to reverse or turn back illnesses or recover stolen goods in these texts.[302; 303]

Spitting

Although considered unhygienic by modern standards, there are no fewer than five remedies in the *Lacnunga* in which the healer or patient is instructed

---

301. See chapter 13 for my adaptation.

302. Storms, *Anglo-Saxon Magic*, 183–184.

303. Ibid., 90–92.

to either spit or use spittle as a tool.[304] This could and has been the topic of entire presentations in and of itself, but for the purposes of this chapter, it's enough to say that spitting can be a powerful barrier between yourself and something you wish to make separate from you.[305] One way in which I use spitting is when disposing of something nasty that I've caught in my home or just something with bad vibes. I will dispose of it (preferably on the other side of running water if it's that bad), and then spit three times before leaving.

Breath

The final ritual action is breath, or rather the use of breath in the creation of remedies. We have already encountered the use of breath in breathing charms "wholly into" whatever it is you are chanting over. However, breath is used in some other useful (though not unrelated) ways too.

The breath of the magician is like the horse ridden by either the charm or the cure to its final destination. For example, when singing over a drink, the final destination is the drink. Similarly, the examples of singing charms into the mouth and ears of a patient might be thought of carrying those charms to their final destinations within the patient's body. However, breath didn't just serve as a horse for charms. Liquid cures could also be administered in this way through a straw with the cure itself being blown at the patient.[306]

The elements of ritual language presented in this section are far from exhaustive. What follows is more of a rough guide to some of the parts I consider essential to the creation and working of Heathen magic. In the next section, we're going to take a look at one of the most important tools in my magical arsenal: smoke fumigation or rēcels. Then, I'll cover the most essential herbs in your magical herb collection before providing some recipes you can try out for yourself.

How to Work with Charms: A Basic Framework

So far in this chapter, I've discussed the historical background of the magico-medical charms and demonstrated how we can tease out the potential Heathen

---

304. Ibid., 61–62.

305. Ibid., 165–166.

306. Ibid., 62–63.

magical survivals through a process of elimination. I also gave an overview of the different kinds of narrative charms, and explained some of the most common and useful elements of ritual language found in the charms. In this section, I'm going to tie it all together and present ways in which you can adapt existing historical charms for your modern rites.

Getting Started

The first stage when creating or adapting existing charms is always contemplation. This is where you think about why you need to create a charm. For most people, that "why" is something simple like "purify my home." But because we are dealing with a kind of magic that's arguably animistic, and in which personalization also plays a role, we need to reframe that purpose into a *metaplot*.

If there's one thing I've found about Heathen magic over the years (or indeed any form of animistic magic), it's that story is important. So you not only need to be clear on the purpose of the charm, but you also need to reframe it as a metaplot. Put another way, you *storify* the purpose of your charm. When reframed in this way, "purify my home" can easily adopt any one of the following metaplots:

+ Holy substance causes unhæl beings to flee.
+ Magic worker curses invading forces in order to force them to leave.
+ Magic worker emulates the mythological actions of Holy Powers and emerges victorious against a foe.

You may have noticed that these metaplots read like news headlines, but this is precisely what you want; complexity isn't needed at this stage. This is just to help you find existing charms with similar metaplots. Find recommendations for books containing translations of magico-medical charms in the Recommended Reading section.

Using/Adapting Existing Charms

For the most part, you will probably find that the older charms require varying degrees of adaptation. It's a rare charm that you can use within a Heathen context directly out of the book and without adaptation. If you believe you have found such a charm, please make sure that you take the time to look into the toxicity of any associated herbs before use. Not all of the recommended herbs of the tenth-century herbalist would be recommended by a herbalist today. For more magical preparations in which the herbs clearly serve a magical purpose rather than medical (e.g., in the charms concerned with elves), the toxic herbs can easily be substituted for less toxic herbs with similar magical associations.

There are roughly three stages to adapting existing charms: deconstruction, research, and replacement.

Deconstruction

The first step of adapting charms is deconstruction. This is the process of teasing out and identifying the various contributing cultural elements in each charm so that you can see what needs to be replaced.

When I deconstruct a charm, I begin by reading the charm through, then drawing up a table with four columns. In the first column, I break the instructions/ritual actions down into a numbered list. For example:

1. Take equal parts of herbs and tie in cloth.

2. Dip in holy water three times.

As you can see, these are really barebones descriptions of ritual actions. You don't need to be super detailed in this column. In the second column is where you're going to write any herbs used, and what you believe their intended purposes to have been. Try to keep your numbering system consistent, or things can get confusing. For example, the numbers you assign to the herbs in column two should be the same as those assigned to the ritual actions in which the herbs feature.

The third column is where you write any accompanying incantations or prayers. Again, it's a good idea to make sure you assign the correct corresponding numbers to the items in this column as you do the other three.

Finally, we have the fourth column, which is for any items or tools that are made or used when working the magic or as a product of that magic.

Research

The second stage of adapting charms is research. Here you're looking at each of the ritual actions, the herbs used, any incantations spoken, and any tools or items produced either as a byproduct or result of working the magic.

At this stage, you're trying to figure out two main things: the purpose and meaning of each element with regards to the larger metaplot of the charm, and which (if any) cross-cultural elements are present. I have already provided some brief guidelines for the process of teaching out these cross-cultural elements toward the beginning of this chapter. But if you intend to work regularly with these charms, it's a good idea to read widely about early Germanic Christianity, classical ideas on healing, medicinal herbs, and later runic amulet finds. The more background knowledge you have, the easier this background knowledge will be.

The research done at this stage needs to reflect both the magical and medical concerns of the magico-medical nature of the texts themselves. For example, you need to research the practical and/or medical elements of ritual actions and herbs as well as the magical. Some of the most common and important ritual actions found in the manuscripts have already been covered; here is where that knowledge can be applied.

When researching any herbs used, you will generally find that some tend to be used in the same kinds of charms. This is important to note because the contexts in which you find herbs can often give you important clues about their purpose, magical and medical. Other herbs you may find correspond well with classical ideas of healing, or even more modern magical correspondences.

The greatest amount of metaplot exposition will be found in the spoken incantations. You will thus need to research the incantations and prayers you find as well as the stories they tell. Even the most overtly Christian charms contain discernible threads of connection to the charm's metaplot or purpose.

Finally, you will need to try and understand the purposes of each of the tools used or created as a result or product of the working. Some of the tools you will find are strictly practical in use, while others clearly have a more magical purpose and so must be understood within the wider context of the metaplot.

Replacement

The final stage of the adaptation process is replacement. This is simply when you take a look at the results the research stage has yielded and decide what needs to be replaced and how. Typically, you're looking to replace the Christian (and, if you choose, classical) elements with things rooted in Heathen belief but which convey the same metaplot elements as whatever you're replacing. So, instead of washing herbs with holy water (as in the example given in the subsection on deconstruction), you're hallowing water in whichever way you see fit and washing the herbs in it. Or if you have prayers depicting the beating back of demons by angels, you'll want to create a narrative charm depicting the beating back of baneful giants by Thor (for example). As long as your replacements largely mirror the elements you are replacing in terms of their function within the wider metaplot of the charm, they should work.

Once you have completed these three stages, I recommend taking the time to write out your new charm neatly and read it through. For one thing, you'll be able to spot any mistakes or missed details—after all, it's better to spot them at this stage than in the middle of a working—it's also just good to have a nice copy already written out and ready for use. Most importantly, writing and reading your charm lets you get a feel for how it flows—and not just the flow of your physical actions; try to visualize the energetic flow as well. When I read workings that have good energetic flow, the part of me that responds to magic in other people seems to awaken and enter a state of excitement and readiness. This is generally a good sign that what you've created is going to work.

Taking Things Further

Once you have become more familiar with the magico-medical charms and their magic, you may decide that you want to try your hand at creating your own charms. As exciting as this may sound, this is not something I recommend for beginners. Most beginners just don't have the depth of knowledge or experience with the material to teach this skill effectively. There's also a lot to be said for having a feel or instinct for the material; in your early days of creating new charms, you will likely find it is this instinct which guides you far more than any systematized process.

Once you are more experienced with the charms and have developed that instinct for them, there is absolutely nothing to stop you from creating your own. Because if we are to move our magic from recreation to living tradition, it's important that we also create.

Rēcels and Fumigation

The topic of holy smoke and smoke fumigation can be quite controversial in modern Pagan and Heathen communities. Most within those communities are aware of smudging and the various issues of cultural appropriation surrounding the use of smudge. Relatively few (even those within modern Heathenism) are aware of the use of smoke fumigation or *rēcels* in the Old English magico-medical texts.

For the early English healer, the use of rēcels was medicinal, belonging to the banishing branch of the tradition, and was recommended for the treatment of "elf-disease." Different charms involving rēcels recommend different herbs. However, not all that are recommended are considered safe to burn nowadays and so the herbs themselves should be considered open to substitution. Whichever herbs you opt for, preparation seems to have been an important step.

To summarize the preparations given in folio 123v of *Bald's Leechbook III*: First the healer is told to take a handful of each of the plants and bind them in a cloth. After this, the bundle of plants are dipped into a fountain of holy water three times, then taken to have three masses sung over them. Once those steps are complete, then the healer is instructed to put hot coals in a chafing dish and lay the plants in it so that they may fumigate the person with the plants both before 9 a.m. and at night.[307]

From these instructions, it's easy to see how the layers of holiness are built into the rēcels. These layers are key to how rēcels work. To clear a person with rēcels is to introduce something so holy to that person that the unholy flees. Once again we see the number nine used here, as we might expect within the context of banishing or exorcism. Unfortunately for us, it's not exactly clear

---

307. Brooke Bullock, "Leechbook III: 123v," *Leechbook III, A New Digital Edition*, accessed November 11, 2019. https://leechbookiii.github.io/123v.html.

as to whether the patient is to be fumigated before 9 p.m. too, or if only the morning time is significant.

As we have seen throughout the course of this chapter, the healing magic of the Old English magico-medical tradition (and potentially Norse tradition too) is not so much healing as we would think about it nowadays. Rather than the usual placid images of modern spiritual healers, the early English healer that worked with these more animistic forms of cures was something akin to a battle mage, banishing, cursing, and binding where necessary. This is a magic of both silent and vocalized story, starring a whole cast of agency-filled characters. These charms were never meant to be dead words on a page, but living magic. The only question that faces us now is how to bring it back to life.

Preparing Rēcels

I try to cleave to the instructions given in *Bald's Leechbook III* as closely as is reasonable when making rēcels. The process outlined in that book is complicated and made up of several stages that begin with the foraging of the herb and end with the burning.

Despite the recommendations in the *Leechbook*, my herb of preference for rēcels is, and always will be, mugwort, followed closely by a mixture of rosemary, vervain, and juniper. Over the years, I've found these herbs to be incredibly effective and—most importantly—relatively safe for use.

When foraging or buying my herbs for rēcels, I try to do so on a Friday, due to the mythological and/or folkloric connections between mugwort and Diana (who was also equated with Freya), so it seems appropriate to obtain them on a day associated with her. There is mention of ritually "killing" some plants before harvesting in the primary sources, but I do not believe this to be appropriate with mugwort.

Once obtained, I dip the herbs three times in water I have hallowed using the following charm:

> Over water and salt,
> A galdor I speak
> With wise words I will it
> And my breath goes wholly in
> Making clean waters holy

Fast flee the evil from it!
Fast flee evil magic from it!

Although the *Leechbook* gives the instruction to wrap these herbs in cloth first, I do not generally do this unless dealing with loose herbs bought from the store. Freshly foraged herbs are far more likely to hold up to being dipped without breaking off and getting lost in the water. As the emphasis is on purification and building a general theme of purification in these rēcels, I try to use spring water for this (collected from a known source if possible). Once the herbs have been dipped, I dry them before placing them on my altar.

In the next stage of the process as outlined by Bald, the herbs are to have three masses sung over them. However, as I am a Heathen, I substitute this with a nine-day cycle of offering rituals to Wōden as healer.[308] One additional recommendation I would make at this stage is to take the time to chant the mugwort verse from the Nine Herbs Charm during these rites, allowing of course, your breath to go wholly in as you do so:

Remember, Mugwort, what you revealed
What you set out in mighty revelation.
"Una" you are called, oldest of plants
You have might against three and against thirty.
You have might against poison and infection
You have might against the evil that travels around the land.[309]

By the end of your nine-day cycle of rituals, the herb should be completely dried and ready for storing. For portability and ease of use, I tend to bind the herbs into a stick when using whole foraged herbs, not unlike a Native American smudge stick. I do a lot of my work on the fly and setting up a censer is often not practical.

When I work to fumigate a person, thing, or place, I chant the mugwort verse again as I do so, doing so in multiples of nine. As mentioned in the sub-

---

308. You can use the ritual format given at the end of chapter 2 for this, inviting only Wōden if you wish.

309. Taken from the Nine Herbs Charm in Pollington, *Leechcraft*, 215.

section on numbers, nine is the number for purification and banishment and so I try to include it as often as I can in work of this kind.

To give a quick summary of the process:

1. If using mugwort, collect or buy your herbs on a Friday (Wednesday or Thursday would be my choices for other herbs).[310]

2. Depending on whether you have the whole herb or a bag of herb pieces from your local occult store, wash/dip your herbs in spring water and then spread out on a towel to dry.

3. Once dry, hold offering rituals to Wōden for nine nights in a row. If using mugwort, include the mugwort verse from the Nine Herbs Charm, and make sure you chant so that your breath goes on the herbs.[311]

4. At the end of the nine-day cycle of rituals, either store in a dry container like a mason jar or bind into a stick for future use. Chant the mugwort verse when you use it. Try to keep things in multiples of nine.

Smokeless Alternative

Smoke fumigation is not suitable for everyone. A patient or occupant of a space may have lung or allergy issues that may preclude them from using smoke in this way. If you are unable to use smoke fumigation, then my suggestion is to add an additional step between steps two and three, and make your herbs into a tincture before proceeding with the nine-day cycle of rituals. You can make a tincture by filling a mason jar half to three-quarters full of dried herb, then filling to the top with 80- to 90-percent proof vodka and seal. When using fresh herbs, fill two-thirds to three-quarters of the jar then fill to the top with 80- to 90-percent proof vodka and seal. Shake regularly. It should be ready in around 6 to 8 weeks. Top up alcohol amounts as needed. Herbs *must* remain covered. When ready, strain, rebottle, and store in a dark place.

---

310. Wednesday is associated with Wōden and Thursday is associated with Þūnor/Þórr, the defender of mankind.

311. If you use other herbs, try creating your own galdr to be spoken over each herb using the instructions in chapter 9.

Once the tincture is ready in roughly six weeks, you can add some to a spray bottle of water to create a cleansing spray. This cleansing spray should be used immediately but may be kept in the fridge for up to a week.

Recipes

In the following section are some of my most commonly used recipes, as well as the processes used when creating them. Due to toxicity issues with some items, substitutions are common. Moreover, like the Icelanders who adapted the Old English remedies for their own use, I am also not the kind of person to worry about finding every single ingredient, largely because I don't have the time, space, or resources to obtain and maintain such a wide collection of herbs as was seemingly available to the early English leech. Instead of the recommended fifty-seven herbs, my version of the holy salve, for example, has nine.

The Basic Herb Chest

In contrast to what appears above, there are some herbs that I recommend keeping at all times. Not all of the herbs recommended here are used as I use them in the Old English magico-medical sources, but I include them because of their proven usefulness in my practice. The herbs listed here are intended to be used in fresh or dried form (as opposed to essential oils). I also recommend that you always keep an extra bottle of olive oil to hand, and that you acquire a small Crock-Pot for making magical oils, as it really does make the process much easier.

Broom (Cytisus scoparius)

Uses: Depossession

Parts Used: Flowers

Safety Concerns: Do not ingest; fatal if eaten. Does not produce contact dermatitis so use in very limited quantities in oils.[312]

---

312. "Cytisus Scoparius," North Carolina Extension Gardener Toolbox, North Carolina State Cooperative Extension, accessed March 10, 2020. https://plants.ces.ncsu.edu/plants/cytisus -scoparius/.

Hyssop (Hyssopus officinalis)
Uses: Protection, purification

Parts Used: Leaves

Safety Concerns: Essential oil should be avoided by epileptics and pregnant people.

Juniper (Juniperus communis)
Uses: Driving back or repelling evil spirits, purification

Parts Used: Branches, berries

Safety Concerns: Do not ingest berries if pregnant or suffering from kidney disease.[313]

Mugwort (Artemisia vulgaris)
Uses: Purification, protection, driving out evil, blessing, consecration, and for increased psychic awareness. A very holy plant!

Parts Used: Leaves, stems

Safety Concerns: Mugwort is considered by some to be an abortifacient; avoid ingestion while pregnant.

Rosemary (Rosmarinus officinalis)
Uses: Blessing, purification, protection, curse-breaking

Parts Used: Leaves and stems

Safety Concerns: Poisonous if ingested in large doses.[314]

Salt
Uses: Blessings, banishing, purification, protective magic

Safety Concerns: Safe unless ingested in extreme amounts.

St. John's Wort (Hypericum perforatum)
Uses: Depossession, protection from fairies and hostile magic

Parts Used: Flowers

---

313. John Michael Greer, *Encyclopedia of Natural Magic*, 136.

314. Ibid., 180.

Safety Concerns: Skin irritant, especially when skin is exposed to the sun after application.[315]

Vervain (Verbena officinalis)
Uses: Purification; driving back or repelling evil spirits
Parts Used: Whole plant
Safety Concerns: None.

Additional Items
Olive oil (base for making magical oils)

Recipe Notes
The following recipes are either adaptations of charms and procedures pulled from the magico-medical manuscripts, or created as needed using magical techniques pulled from the early charms. Where possible, I have included what I see as the necessary layers of story (either through speech or ritual action). In cases when reconstructing charms in which the original story is Christian, I have deconstructed the various components of the story and sought out a more Heathen story that has many if not all of the same components, then adapted my ritual actions accordingly.

As you will probably notice, the majority of these recipes are for items of a banishing or protective nature. This is because the majority of the work I am called to do involves either stepping in when things get bad, advising people on what to do when things get bad, or working with the dead and unseen. But even if your life is much calmer than mine, these are generally good recipes to have to hand.

⟶ Recipe: Depossession Oil ⟵

I created this oil after receiving a dream in which many people were becoming possessed or having to deal with spiritual attachments of some kind. Since its creation, I have used it successfully many times and a roll-on bottle of this oil has become a permanent part of my magical go-bag.

---

315. John Michael Greer, *Encyclopedia*, 186–187.

The procedure for making this oil includes the use of the *acre arcre arnem nona ærnem beoðor ærnem nidren arcum cunað ele harassan fidine* formulae, perhaps the most well-known of all the magical formulae found in the Old English magico-medical corpus.[316] These formulae have already been covered to some degree in the section on narrative charms. They seem to originally derive from oral tradition, and their meanings have largely been lost. To make matters even more confusing, there is a wide variety of spellings for formulae such as the *acre arcre* given in this charm, which means that not only is it impossible to translate, but there is no way to give an accurate pronunciation, either. What we can say, however, is that this formula appears in multiple depossession charms, and early English healers themselves probably didn't know the original form of the formula. Don't worry too much about the pronunciation; you can use the pronunciation guide at the back of this book to help you with pronouncing the letters *æ* and *ð*.

To use, apply the oil sparingly to the skin of the patient. When using on other people, you will need to have a conversation with them about it first. Do not proceed if you do not have consent, and be sure to let them know that the oil contains St. John's Wort and that some people experience skin sensitivities with this herb.

Often, this oil will remove or drive away whatever attachment or being is exerting influence on a person almost instantaneously. But when the attachment is more established, or the possessing being more powerful, its action is more of a loosening effect that allows for easier removal by other means.

You will need

Mugwort

Broom

St. John's Wort[317]

Birch

Salt

---

316. Stephen Pollington, *Leechcraft*, 203.

317. Please be aware that some people experience skin sensitivity issues with St. John's Wort. Amounts have been kept low in this recipe for this purpose but some people may still have a reaction. Be sure to inform any potential users of this risk.

Oil

A Crock-Pot

Procedure

1. As I see this oil as a tool of war, my preference is to make it on a Tuesday, but Wednesday would also be appropriate.[318] If you are dealing with an acute situation, you can make this oil as needed. Magical timing of this kind is largely optional in Heathen magic.

2. Begin by cleaning down your work area. Plug in your Crock-Pot and set it on "low." This does not need to be a dedicated Crock-Pot; many of the old magical tools were things that were used for everyday activities as well as for magic.

3. Spend a few moments in meditation. It's also a good idea to ground and center at this stage. You do not need to create sacred space when making this oil, but you should at least begin work in a ritual headspace and with all your faculties pulled to the same place and intent. At this point, I also pray to Woden as the healing god to guide my hands as I work and empower me in my act of creation.

4. Now, add the oil to the Crock-Pot. (I tend to use between sixteen and twenty ounces of oil per batch.)

5. Then, add five tablespoons of mugwort while chanting the mugwort verse. As always, lean over the mixture so that your breath goes in. Be sure to visualize your breath enlivening and calling the herb to action as you chant.

> Remember, Mugwort, what you revealed
> what you set out in mighty revelation.
> "Una" you are called, oldest of plants
> You have might against three and against thirty.
> You have might against poison and infection
> You have might against the evil that travels around the land.[319]

---

318. Tuesday is associated with Tiw, the god of war.

319. Taken from the Nine Herbs Charm in Pollington, *Leechcraft*, 215.

6. Next, add nine birch leaves while chanting the following:

> And you, birch, remember who you are.
> Your purifying and cleansing actions
> Are well-known among the children of men.
> You who cleanse sickness, you who strike
> From the body the causes of ill.
> You who make clean and new,
> Stand with me now!

7. Now add nine (small) pinches of broom:

> And you, broom of the bright yellow blooms
> You upon whom no parasites or invading forces may live
> Remember your powers and bring them to bear in this oil!

8. Another nine pinches of St. John's Wort:

> And you, St. John's Wort, you who stand at your height
> Beneath the carefree joy of the midsummer sun
> You who have the power to free from melancholy and delusion
> You who have the power to free from the pain of bone-ache
> Bring your powers to bear in this oil!

9. Then nine pinches of salt:

> And you, salt, you who are born of this very earth
> You make heavy that which was light
> Pulling to ground and binding to dirt
> You who have the power to destroy glamours
> You who have the power to restore the mind
> You are loathed by all that is hateful.
> Cause the loathsome ones to flee your touch!

10. Finally, chant the following formula over the mixture three times:

acre arcre arnem nona ærnem beoðor ærnem
nidren arcum cunað ele harassan fidine.

11. Stir clockwise with your right hand, then leave to infuse on "low" for nine hours. Return every three hours to chant the same incantations over the oil. At the end of the nine hours, chant the final round of incantations and then strain. Discard leftover herbs outside on the land. Store in dark glass jars and refrigerate. Siphon off small amounts at a time for casual use but store the bulk of it in the refrigerator. Keep for no more than six months. Apply sparingly (and with consent) to the skin of your patient to use.

—»o Recipe: Black Salt o«—

Although not a part of Heathen magic, I believe that black salt with its mixture of salt, iron, and ashes would have been easily recognizable as an apotropaic to the elder Heathen.

Black salt is a wonderfully grounding and protective tool in my go-bag arsenal; over the years, I've used it for everything from driving out unwanted spirits from my daughter's bedroom in the middle of the night, to shutting down a portal.

The ashes used in this salt may be taken from a hearth or a ritual fire. Alternatively, if you do not have access to either of those sources, you can create your own ashes by burning blessings and prayers written on paper along with protective herbs such as mugwort, juniper, rosemary, and vervain. This is best done outside and in some kind of fireproof container.

As I use a cast-iron Dutch oven for my cauldron, I also take the opportunity to collect some iron scrapings from my cauldron when cleaning it out after creating the ashes. However, this only ever renders a relatively small amount and so it's good to also obtain some iron filings even if you have iron cookware you can scrape from.

The recipe I include here is of my own creation and was created with the same underlying worldview that I learned from the magico-medical tradition.

You will need
Iron filings
Salt

Ashes

A small bowl (a cereal bowl will do)

Let's Create!

1. First, collect or create your ashes.

2. Now, take a bowl, mix your ashes with equal amounts of iron shavings/ filings and salt. Then, chant the following charm as you mix, allowing your breath to go in:

> Black salt, black salt, the ally in my pocket
> With sacred ash were you made, and the ill-wights scream
> With iron you were strengthened, and the ill-wights flee
> And with salt you were grounded, and delusion falls away.

Chant the charm three times, each time changing the effect of each ingredient. So for example, instead of "*With sacred ash you were made, and the ill-wights scream,*" say, "*With sacred ash you were made, and the ill-wights flee.*" Do this for each repetition, ensuring that each ingredient ends up associated with each effect.

3. Store in an airtight container and stash somewhere where it will be of most use. Use as needed. This salt can be cast at unwanted entities, scattered over portals, or even used to delineate boundaries when working in more hostile places.

⊸⟩○ Experiential: Propitiation and Banishing Rite ○⟨⊷

The following charm was designed for those times when you either need to work magic in a place that is less than ideal or you find yourself dealing with troublesome beings on your own land. However, this charm is not designed to be a blanket remedy for all kinds of beings you may find yourself interacting with; it is only focused on some of the most destructive beings you may encounter. For the others who do not fit the given description, I recommend trying to make respectful propitiatory offerings first before escalating to something like this.

In this charm, we make use of the methodology from both the Sigtuna amulet charm and the counting charm from the *Lacnunga* as discussed in the Narrative Charms section. We begin by naming the troubles and cursing them to nine needs and three pangs. Then, with a mug of ale which serves as both propitiatory offering and the "ice" to sate those needs, we diminish their presence by counting down.

You will need

A mug of ale

Procedure

1. Taking your mug of ale, go to either the boundary of your intended workspace, or the boundary of your land.

2. Take three deep breaths, and allow your senses to expand, allowing yourself to momentarily become one with the world around you. Pay attention to what you see, hear, sense, and feel while you are in this state, but do not allow it to scare you.

3. When you feel you have a good sense of awareness of the world around you, then speak the following charm. As you do so, try to "see" your words become real as they enter the world, affecting any beings who fit the description given in the charm:

> Ogres, Etins, unæl wanderers!
> You who corrupt and disrupt
> You ravenous ones
> Bone-breakers and gnawers of flesh
> Strength-stealers and enemies of mind
> Hear me!
> Have for yourselves nine needs, wolves.
> Nine needs and three pangs, wolves.

4. Now, draw an "ice" rune nine times over your mug of ale (the "ice" rune, *isa*, simply looks like a vertical line). As you do so, visualize the ale becoming satiating and pacifying.

5. Then, continue with the following. Where you are instructed to pour, pour out a small amount of the ale/ice runes for the consumption of the beings gathered.

Nine needs I gave, wolves
Healing ice I bring, wolves
Take the healing ale and be satisfied!
Then the nine became eight (pour)
The eight, seven (pour)
The seven, six (pour)
The six, five (pour)
The five, four (pour)
The four, three (pour)
The three, two (pour)
The two, one (pour)
The one need is now none (pour)
Now be gone from this place and be satisfied!

6. Pour out any remaining ale onto the ground and take a few moments to sense if the more destructive powers you addressed in the charm are gone. If not, you may wish to reconsider continuing with any ritual you have planned or follow up with making boundary stakes if it is your land that you are trying to remedy.

─)o Remedy: Boundary Stakes o(─

Often, resolving problems with one's land can be as simple as making offerings or using a banishing charm such as the one given previously. However, there comes a time when that isn't enough and when you may wish to consider some kind of permanent boundary.

You already know one of the simplest ways to create this kind of a boundary around your property, and if you have been working on the activities in this book, you have already done it multiple times when creating sacred space. Carrying fire around the boundaries while chanting a charm is incredibly powerful but far more effective when combined with iron or steel stakes or pins at each corner of your land.

My preferred objects to use for pinning boundaries are railroad stakes. This is because they're big enough for carving or writing charms. You can often find them littering the ground along old railroad tracks. If you don't live near old tracks, you can use iron or steel nails instead. The only difference is that you won't be able to carve or write your charm on the nails because there won't be enough room, but don't worry—you can still imbue the stakes with your intent, and they will still work.

You will need
5 old railroad spikes or 5 large iron or steel nails

A candle (a tealight will do)

A lighter or match

A small bowl of hallowed water (see Preparing Rēcels for the water-hallowing charm)

Dremel or Sharpies for writing your charm (optional)

A few paper towels

A copy of the galdor

Procedure
1. Begin by cleaning down your work area and gathering the stakes/nails and carving/writing tools (if needed). Hallow your water using the charm from the Preparing Rēcels section.

2. Spend a few moments in meditation. It's also a good idea to ground and center at this stage. You do not need to create sacred space when making these stakes/nails, but you should at least begin work in a ritual headspace and with all your faculties pulled to the same place and intent. At this point, I also pray to Woden to empower my hands in this act of creation.

3. Now, take the stakes or nails and breathe into them three times while reciting the following words:

> Önd I give you, Óðinn's gift
> That you might breathe and know life.

At this point you may feel the energy begin to awaken within the stakes/nails with each breath. To me, this feels like a crackling heat that works its way from my mouth and through the material of the tool.

4. Now, bring the stakes/nails close to your mouth and say:

> Óðr I give you, the gift of Hœnir.
> Hear my words and be shaped by them!
> Boundary markers
> Made of iron/steel
> Repulse and repel evil from your bounds
> Burn the baneful
> Hurt the harmful
> May the walls you pin stand strong
> May the walls you pin stand long.

Repeat the charm as many times as you feel is necessary. As a rule, I repeat three times as a reflection of the three life-giving gifts of Óðinn, Hœnir, and Loðurr.

Then, dip the stakes/nails in the water, dry with the paper towels, and pass the stakes/nails over the candle, saying:

> Lá and Litr I give you, the gift of Lóðurr
> That you might gain color and warmth.

If you are using stakes, you may wish to also mark the sides of each stake with the following charm at this point. You can either carve it with a dremel or write with a permanent marker. If you know how to write in runes, you can also write/carve this in runes:

> Boundary markers
> Made of iron/steel
> Repulse and repel evil from your bounds
> Burn the baneful
> Hurt the harmful
> May the walls you pin stand strong
> May the walls you pin stand long.

5. Once your spikes or nails are ready, go to your front door and stand facing outward. You need to begin at the left corner of your property as you see it when looking out from your front door. If you live in a row house, simply place the spike or nail along the left boundary line. This is where your first spike/nail will go.

Place your first spike/nail and drive it into the ground as well as you can. Begin the following chant as you work:

> With spikes of iron
> I spear the ground
> And bury my boundary deep
> Impassible to evil
> Woe and ill-wights
> Þūnor watch over my home
> Þūnor protect my home.

6. Continue this chant as you walk the boundaries of your land, stopping at each corner to drive a stake/nail into the ground. You will need to go in a clockwise direction. Do not worry if you are in a row house; simply walk around the whole block and pin the corners of your property line on each side.

7. Drive the fifth and final spike/nail so that it overlaps with the first in the corner where you began your walk. This symbolically and magically closes the boundary for you.

Once placed, these boundary stakes are one of the easiest and most effective methods of warding your property. Moreover, they are the ultimate in "set it and leave it" magical technology. This makes them ideal for setting up on the property of friends and loved ones who do not practice magic themselves, but who have been experiencing strange and possibly scary goings-on.

⟶⟫∘ Experiential: Wayfarer Charm ∘⟪⟵

The following charm is an adaptation of the *Old English Journey Charm*. As its title suggests, this galdor was created as a protection for travelers. In the charm, the traveler casts a portable circle around themselves, holding their walking staff out and turning once in order to delineate the space around them.

This is one of the most useful older charms in my experience; I use it before entering wild spaces, before trance journey, and cast it regularly on the family car. If you are hiking with a staff or walking stick, you can use that to cast this charm. But this also works if you hold your finger out so that your arm is fully extended and use that as your "wand" or "staff."

When speaking the first line of the charm, turn 360 degrees in a clockwise direction while holding out your staff, wand, or finger, and visualize the boundary shimmering to life around you as you do so. The Old English Journey Charm enumerates different possible hazards that may be encountered on the roads, and this is where I have made the majority of my adaptations, adding potential dangers such as "fae-trickery" and "harm from ill-wights" (spirits), and removing others. The enumeration of potential dangers is an important element of charms such as this, and I encourage you to alter this section to reflect what you might face as needed.

You will need
A staff/wand/your finger

The Charm
I encircle myself with this rod/my finger
And entrust myself to the protection of Þunor,
Against the sore stitch, against the sore bite,
Against fae-trickery and harm from ill-wights,
Against the grim dread, against the great fear,
And against all evil that enters the land.
A victory charm I sing, a victory rod I bear,
Word-victory, work-victory.
May they avail me.

⟶⟩o Recipe: Juniper Door Oil and Charm o⟨⟵

The final charm in this chapter takes its inspiration from an Icelandic door charm for keeping out evil spirits.[320] In the original spell, the person wishing to use it is instructed to draw the accompanying sigil above the house door with a juniper awl.

As this is not particularly practical for many people (including myself), I adapted the spell by creating a juniper oil that can then be used to paint the sigil above the door. This can either be painted and repainted as necessary, or retained and used on an "as-needed" basis.

Unfortunately, I can't make any promises that this oil will not damage the surfaces upon which it is painted. But if that is a concern for you (or if you simply prefer a physical sigil in general anyway), I recommend that you purchase a blank wooden plaque from a craft store and paint or burn the sigil upon it. Once you have done this, you can then paint over the sigil with juniper oil and hang the plaque above your door.

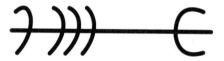

Image 2: Juniper Sigil

You will need

9 juniper berries

Pestle and mortar

Measuring jug

9 oz. of olive oil

A Crock-Pot

A dark glass bottle or jar to store the oil

Funnel (for decanting)

320. Magnús Rafnsson and Museum of Icelandic Sorcery & Witchcraft, *Tvær galdraskræður: Lbs 2413 8vo: Leyniletursskræðan Lbs 764 8vo* (Hólmavík: Strandagaldur, 2008), 116.

Procedure

1. Begin by cleaning down your work area. Plug in your Crock-Pot and set it on low.

2. Spend a few moments in meditation. It's also a good idea to ground and center at this stage. Once again, you do not need to create sacred space when making this oil, but you should at least begin work in a ritual headspace and with all your faculties pulled to the same place and intent. At this point, it is also my habit to pray to Woden as the god of healing and magic to guide and empower me in my work.

3. Now, add the oil to the Crock-Pot. For this particular infused oil, I use 9 ounces of olive oil for 9 juniper berries. As mentioned previously in the Numbers section of this chapter, the number nine is associated with purification and driving out evil, which makes it the perfect choice for an oil of this type.

4. Taking your pestle and mortar, crush your juniper berries. They do not have to be obliterated; you only need to crush them enough to release their oils. Chant the following once as you work:

> Remember, Juniper,
> What you are known for, the skills you possess
> Mightly cleanser, hated by evil, you who cause ill spirits to flee
> Bane of the baneful, protector of homes
> Awaken now, and marshal your powers
> Where you exist, may evil flee!

5. When the berries are crushed to your satisfaction, bring the pestle to your mouth so that your breath may go wholly in and chant the charm once again before scraping the berries into the Crock-Pot with the oil and stirring three times clockwise to combine.

6. Then, lean over the Crock-Pot, and chant the charm a further seven times. Imagine your words leaving your mouth as gold that imbues the oil, awaking the juniper, and filling it with your magic.

7. Replace lid and leave for nine hours on the low setting. Return every three hours to chant the juniper charm over the oil. At the end of the

nine hours, chant the juniper charm nine times more and then turn off the slow cooker. Pick out the juniper berries and discard outside on the land.

8. Allow to cool before pouring into a dark glass bottle or jar and refrigerate. Siphon off small amounts at a time for casual use, but store the bulk of it in the refrigerator. Keep for no more than six months.

9. To use, simply use a paintbrush to paint the sigil above the front door of your home.

We've covered a lot of ground over the course of this chapter, wandering through a storied realm of magical battles with unseen beings and digging deeper into more of the mechanics of this kind of Heathen magic. We've introduced yet another type of spoken magic, one that works with story to effect change rather than ensnaring change through the application of poetic meter. Both forms of spoken magic are effective, and as you get a feel for them, you'll develop preferences depending on the kind of work you're doing. But in the meantime, please don't be afraid to try things out. Begin by looking at mythological and folklore stories, and think about how they could be used in different magical applications. For example, the binding of Loki would make an excellent foundation for a galdr to bind an enemy. Moreover, the rock and binding is easily represented in ritual action too. See how easily this can come together? All it takes is practice.

Eleven
SAFETY AND TROUBLESHOOTING

For all of its wonder, magic can be dangerous, and Heathen magic is no exception. Sometimes these dangers are physical—not all sites where you might want to work are safely or legally accessible at night and there is always potential danger from other humans (especially in the wild and secluded places). At other times, these dangers are otherworldly and magical in nature but are just as able to cause harm.

The world of a Heathen magic worker is an inspirited and interconnected one. It's a world of both seen and unseen powers, and webs of reciprocal relationships that stretch between both. For a Heathen, nothing done is without effect; deeds come from deeds and in turn create more opportunities (or necessity) for action. What we do to others can almost always be done to us in return, and this is not just true of the human world, but of the otherworld too.

As has hopefully been made clear, much of Heathen magic concerns interacting with and creating relationships with numinous powers. The world we inhabit is rapidly changing too. I believe that the Hiddenfolk are increasingly becoming more active and the limits of what is possible with magic are expanding as a result. I am not alone in this belief either—many bloggers and authors have also observed that the otherworld seems to be "bleeding through." As a form of magic that involves otherworldly beings in all their glorious agency, Heathen magic has always been high-stakes magic. But in our current age, I believe those stakes are rising and the need to do what we can to keep ourselves and our loved ones safe is growing with them.

When angered or insulted, both the otherworldly and the dead are capable of cursing us to sickness, bad luck, and infertility of people and land. Both are able to take us from this world, and both are able to make us insane. Danger is unavoidable in this kind of work, but thankfully much can be mitigated with proper planning. In my experience, there are three keys to remaining safe as a practitioner of Heathen magic: preparedness, relationships, and purification practices.

Magical Preparedness

The bulk of the work of staying safe in magic (or at least as safe as you can be) begins long before you initiate a ritual. It's preparedness; a continuous process of learning, honing, and making; and it's something you never stop working on.

There's a strange dichotomy between study and practice in modern Heathen communities, but in my experience, both have their place in the practice of Heathen magic. Much of the magic I experiment with and then eventually come to practice is taken from accounts of historical practice and trying to figure them out on a practical level. However, this is not the only way in which study plays a role in Heathen magic.

There's an oft-quoted adage, "knowledge is power," that can also refer to a form of preparedness. For example, when you're working outside, simple things like knowing the lore of the place, the kind of beings you might encounter, and any etiquette or offering preferences they're known to have, can go a long way toward keeping you safe. You may also visit the site several times to get a feel for a place before going there to work magically. Often you can turn up some helpful information, and a bit of reconnaissance during the day can give you a good idea of what you might encounter after the sun goes down.

But this kind of preparedness isn't foolproof. For example, despite the research I did on a mound I once worked in, there was nothing about the massacre that archaeologists would later discover because it simply hadn't been discovered yet. (Guess which spirits I encountered while sitting out?) Moreover, a place can be vastly different depending on time of day and time of year. You can literally encounter entirely different groups of beings!

Where there is little to no information about a place and/or its inhabitants, it's generally a good idea to follow what might be called "fairy-tale rules" while there. Boiled down, these usually amount to remaining polite and respectful, making propitiatory offerings as a first response if things begin to go wrong, not telling lies, and never agreeing to what you are not prepared to keep or fulfill. There are many more of these "fairy-tale rules," as well as multiple facets of the same rules, so I would encourage you to read widely on the subject of fairies and fairy tales. There are a lot more clues there for surviving these encounters than most people realize.

The second kind of preparedness is keeping your magical skills sharp. If you don't practice regularly, your skills can become weak, just like any other muscle. While the weakness isn't as noticeable in day-to-day magic, you will most definitely notice the difference in more dangerous situations. Neglecting what should be your baseline practices of meditation, visualization, energy manipulation, and the main derivations of these skills (shielding, grounding, and centering) makes you slower and less focused. It also becomes harder to shuck off worries and fears and get into the right head space to work when out of the habit.

One of my teachers has a saying—"It's called 'practice' because you're practicing for when things get real"—which is one of the truest things I have ever been taught throughout my decades of practice. Your grounding, centering, and shielding need to be as automatic as you can make them because if you enter into wild witchy situations without the ability to do these things, then you're not only a danger to yourself when alone, but a liability to others when working in groups. So, learn to walk before you can run and keep practicing that walking; there will be times when you'll be glad you did.

The third category of magical preparedness is basically your "bag of tricks" (or magical go-bag) for when things look like they're going wrong. For some people, this is a dedicated bag that can be easily grabbed on the way out of the house. But for others, it's a pocket in whichever bag you use the most on a daily basis. I have a tendency to encounter odd things even when going about my mundane life; it's not uncommon for me to be called upon for help when something strange or otherworldly happens. For this reason, I have a dedicated bag as well as a selection of core supplies in my other most commonly used bags.

I keep a range of protective or apotropaic items and substances in my bag(s), but what you carry will probably vary depending on how you work, what's available to you at the time, and where you live. For example, in all of my bags, I carry traditional apotropaic items like black salt, holey stones, red handspun thread, and a small bag of something to offer. But in my main bag, I carry all of the above as well as iron, mugwort, fibers for spinning, a collapsible spindle, bells, and oils for depossession and purification. Again, your bag's contents will vary. As a general rule, it's good to think of your main bag as being your "working" bag and your other stashes as emergency supplies for when the unexpected crops up. At the bare minimum, I would say that you should always have some kind of salt, iron in some form, and an easily portable offering item such as a small tin of tobacco or a couple of shelf-stable creamer pots with you. Be sure to stock accordingly and keep track of your supplies.

Relationships

In addition to the preparation of studying, stocking, and honing your skills, you should also adopt a regular routine of making offerings to the gods, ancestors, and any other beings you work with. As previously mentioned, this is a form of magic that hinges on relationships. Relationships are important to the average Heathen and critical for the magic practitioner, who must carefully nurture the reciprocal relationships with allies and the Holy Powers.

Your offerings depend on to whom they are being offered, and you can often discover the traditional offerings with a little bit of research. It is also a good idea to talk to modern adherents to find out what they have found to be good offerings for the numinous powers they worship and/or work with. I have included suggestions for the deities and beings discussed in this book in the relevant chapters. But those are not the only offerings you can make to Freyja, Óðinn, Freyr, and the álfar. Over the years, I've found the Heathen Holy Powers to enjoy a wide range of offerings. For example, as well as bread men and spun offerings, I've found Freyja to like flowers, strawberries, and drinks made of elderberry or elderflower. And while Óðinn may only be reputed to consume wine, he's long accepted poetry and (good-quality) incense offerings from me. For Freyr, I make and burn ships, horses, and boars made out of bread, and the álfar seem to enjoy boiled eggs and coins as well as shots of liquor.

Over time, you may find that the beings to whom you make offerings subtly clue you in on their preferences. Some offering substances turn moldy on the shrine of one deity but remain unchanged on the shrine of another deity, even if that second shrine is in the same part of the house. This kind of observation is a good indication of a deity or spirit's feelings about a particular offering. Alternatively, you may also receive requests in dreams. For example, my mother's side of the family sends me dreams asking for tobacco on a semi-regular basis. Finally, don't be afraid to just *ask* them how they liked your gifts via divination. A simple, "Did you like my gifts?" using runes or tarot cards for yes/no answers (with upright as "yes" and reversed as "no") can go a long way.

How regularly you make your offerings will also depend on your relationship with the beings in question. For example, my dead are fine with me offering weekly (and any time I bake a new loaf of bread); the other spirits that live in our house always get the first of the new milk and the first pancake of a batch, but a certain reputedly one-eyed god is a fan of daily offerings (even if it's just a quick prayer with some incense). If you are new to Heathen magic, I recommend that you begin with weekly offerings and go from there. However, because this is about relationships, be prepared to adapt as you get to know the beings to whom you are offering. That line of communication between humans and Holy Powers *does* go both ways.

A lot of non-magic-working Heathens tend to shy away from this kind of regular gifting relationship. But if you are involved in magical practice, it's not just desirable—it's *necessary*. The relationships you have and maintain can not only give you leverage and protection but magical authority as well. As we saw in chapter 7, it's no coincidence that the staffs of old—symbols of authority— resembled the magical tools of two of the main deities of Heathen magic and usually originated in some way with the dead or other. To wield their tools is to root yourself in their practices and essentially embody them in this world, and you can't really do that unless you take care to build those relationships with them. To quote the Anglo-Saxon rune poem for Tiw, you need to "keep good faith with the nobles."

Purification

The third and final consideration for magical preparedness recommended for practitioners is purification. In my opinion, this should be done on a regular basis and form a part of one's baseline practices.

Why Purify?

There are a couple of different reasons why I make this recommendation. The first is that as a practitioner or various forms of Heathen magic, I believe that we encounter things in our day-to-day lives that detract from our *hælu*, or "health," "wholeness," "luck."

Sometimes these things may seem insignificant, like an argument with someone or simply being ill-wished. But there are more serious examples: for example, you can inadvertently anger wihta while just going about your daily life without even really knowing it. A regular purification practice is therefore just a good idea. The most important reason I make this recommendation is that the magic itself can also be a danger, a topic not really discussed much in modern traditions. Magic and the energy involved affect the practitioner's body and mind. The otherworldly and dead bring a lot of it (I believe we get a lot of our propensity for magic from them), but there's also the energy intrinsic to your body. Over the years, I've found that not everyone is "wired" for magic and what is a perfectly comfortable level of magic/energy for one person can be uncomfortable for others.

Signs You Need to Purify

This kind of magical/energetic overload comes with some very physical symptoms. For example, you may find yourself feeling more anxious and restless for no discernible reason. There may be times when you find your heart racing, and you may be unable to sleep. Once, I even had one of my eyes stop seeing! Moreover, you may find that there are times when (depending on what you're doing and who you're working with) your digestive system feels off.

The only way to really counteract these effects is through purification practices. Proximity to the dead and otherworldly, as well as carrying a lot of energy in the body can be unhealthy over the long term. Not all of the numinous beings you work with nor energy you carry will be of a particularly healthy or "positive" kind, so you need a way to slough off the negative. This observation isn't attested in Heathen sources but is included here because it is something that I've found to be true on a practical level.

As with all magic, purification has to involve both outer and inner work. The thing about energy is that it doesn't just stay on your outer skin—it goes inside you and runs through all the places where your energy flows (however you imagine that subtle body to look). Purification is therefore best practiced on both the outer and inner levels.

Outer Purification of Body

The most common forms of outer purifications involve water with salt, blessings, or herbs (or all three). To pull from what you've already read in this book, either the salt water or herbal infusion used when sanctifying the cauldron will serve. It can be in the form of a spiritual bath, but I've personally found it very effective to make a bundle of birch and use it to gently beat my skin with rainwater that has been prayed over.

Items and substances that are used for outer purification should in some way reflect an idea of purity. For example, in using rainwater for purifications, I am using water that has not been touched by human or animal. Until it falls into my receptacle, it can be considered "pure" in a sense. This sense is further reflected in the choice of birch for the bundle, as birch has long been associated with purity and cleansing. Similarly, salt may be considered to be both purifying and grounding.

Inner Purification of Body

One form of purification that may be considered both outer and inner is rēcels, or smoke fumigation. Purification by smoke is not only experienced upon the skin but also through inhalation, which allows the purifying substances to be taken within and work internally as well as externally. You can find instructions on how to prepare and use rēcels in chapter 10.

The beauty about working with herbs for purification in this way is that they will work regardless of what you do on the inner level. They are, after all, beings in their own right and by partnering with them in your work, you are asking them to bring their competencies to the table in order to help you. However, when it comes to inner purification, what you do on the inner level is everything.

Here is one of those areas in which the ability to visualize becomes key. Your average visualized purification is roughly one-part cosmology and one-part grounding and centering, with purification a thread that runs through all of the above. There are many different visualizations for purification, but the one given here is inspired by Heathen cosmology. Like all purifications of this type, efficacy increases with use; the more you do it, the more "real" it will become to you.

→)⊷ Fundamentals: Sunna's Light ⊷(← Purification Visualization

For the peoples of northwestern Europe, the sun has always been a blessing. She is both the welcome light at the end of the cold, dark winter, and the chaser-away of unhæl beings when she rises from the horizon at dawn. To move with the sun in the Old English magico-medical tradition was to align yourself with holiness and the sacred order set into motion by the Holy Powers in order to effect a healing.

In the Germanic world, the sun deity is always feminine, a goddess by the name of Sunna (ON)/Sunne (OE). In the following inner purification exercise, we're going to ground ourselves in the earth, then reach up to the heavens to bring down Sunna's purifying light into ourselves in order to not only realign ourselves with all that is holy and hæl in the cosmos, but also cause any ill energies or beings to flee.

You will need

Somewhere where you can sit comfortably

10 to 15 minutes of undisturbed time

Practice

1. Seat yourself comfortably in an upright position. As with meditation, you should ideally be in a position in which your back is straight. This visualization can be practiced standing as well, but until you get the hang of it, I recommend that you begin this exercise seated.

2. Once you have arranged yourself comfortably, take nine deep breaths, breathing in through your nose and out through your mouth. Remember, nine is the number of purification and banishing in the Old English

magico-medical manuscripts! It's a good idea to include the number nine in your purifications as much as possible.

3. Now, become aware of your feet on the ground; feel them become roots that dig down deep into the rich, loamy soil of the earth. This isn't hard for you. In a sense, you are born of trees, so lean into that connection. Feel your roots become more wooden and tree-like as they root down, digging deeper as you work. When you feel that you have gone as deeply as you need to, take a moment to release any spare energy you are carrying into the earth where it may be grounded out. Then, turn your attention skyward to Sunna's light.

4. After rooting as deeply as you can, become aware of Sunna. See her in the sky as both a fiery star and a goddess. Concentrate on her until she is as clear as you can make her, then when she is clear, visualize a single ray of light coming from her down to the top of your head. Know that everything she touches that is impure will either be chased out by her touch, or become a lighter energy. Try to feel the movement of energy as tangibly as you can, first as Sunna's warm light upon the crown of your head, and then as it moves down through the center of your body, chasing out dross and purifying as it goes. Although this is the sun's light and she may cause you to feel warm when doing this exercise, hold onto the concept that she is not so strong that she will hurt you.

5. Visualize the accumulated dross falling from you as a kind of oiliness that oozes from your skin and slides down until it reaches the earth where it's absorbed. Continue the visualization until the warmth reaches the ends of your roots and then rest in the visualization for as long as you wish. Allow the warm light of Sunna to move wherever it needs to in your body and, if you wish, intone runes like *sowilo*, *kenaz*, and *berkano* as you work. The addition of chanting can be incredibly powerful when used in conjunction with this kind of purification.

6. When you feel it is time to finish, simply thank Sunna and allow her light to retreat back to the skies. Then turn your attention to your "roots" and visualize them receding and returning to you where they become feet again. Once you have returned to your original state, spend a few moments in meditation in order to allow yourself to settle.

If done regularly, this exercise will not only purify you, but it will also enable you to remain grounded and centered and keep an even keel … all necessary things for the practitioner of magic when it comes to staying as safe and well as possible.

Purification and the Home

One area where you should establish a regular purification routine is in the home. In much the same way that we take on energy from the numinous, we also give off energy to the people around us. Depending on their "wiring," it can make for uncomfortable living. A home filled with ungrounded and possibly negative energy can attract all kinds of problems. At best, family members feel restless and on edge. You may find that you're having more arguments with each other. And at worst, it's possible to attract some really nasty beings that can bring their own (far worse) problems.

There's a saying that cleanliness is next to godliness, which is a good rule to keep in mind when it comes to keeping your home comfortable for everyone. The very act of cleaning itself is purifying, and there are a range of products on the market nowadays in the "Natural Cleaning" sections of supermarkets that contain herbs and oils that are associated with purification. There are also a number of floor washes available from various hoodoo retailers online that work well.

As with your body, it's best to purify from the top down. Homes differ in design, but ideally you want to start from the top and end up by your back door in order to let out any bad energy that you've managed to sweep up and move through the house. After physically cleaning my home, I then follow up with smoke purification, or recels.

The herbs that I use for this purpose differ, but as a general rule mugwort is my go-to. Some people have issues with mugwort and find it hard on the lungs. Because of this I try to mugwort my house when I'm home alone so that my family doesn't have to breathe it in. An alternative to smoke here is making an infusion of mugwort and then putting it in a spray bottle to spray the home. Just be careful of any electrical devices or outlets if you do this.

Troubleshooting

No matter how careful you are in your practices and work, there will always be things that go wrong and need troubleshooting. In my opinion, this is just the nature of the beast when it comes to this kind of magic. And it doesn't matter how "good" we think we are at what we do, there is *always* something we get wrong, or some being out there who is more powerful and more capable of doing harm to us than we to them.

However, not all forms of magic and venues of working come with the same inherent risks. For example, people who work indoors out of either choice or necessity face very different potential issues than someone who is out in the woods or on top of a burial mound. Generally speaking, there are two main hazards to this kind of work: infestation of your home, and personal attachments that range from obsession by spirits to full possessions. While I have dealt with many home infestations and some attachments, I have thankfully only ever dealt with one actual possession case.

Dealing with a "Null" Reaction

Sometimes the problem is that we can make all the preparations and practice skills religiously but when it comes down to it, what we're trying to do just doesn't work out. We feel nothing, we see nothing, and nothing is working. It can be embarrassing and disheartening. Even worse, it can chip away at our faith in ourselves that we *can* move away from our consensus reality, experience something "other," and practice magic. If left unchecked (even if you've had previous experiences and successes), disbelief can set in and a vicious cycle begin.

Null reactions can occur for a variety of reasons: sometimes it's an issue with the ritual technology we're using, or we need to reassess our magical goals and what we think we know of a situation. It's also entirely possible to get a big fat "no" from the spirits you're working with. Other times, it's because we need to further develop our faculties of perception, or the ones we do have are blocked in some way.

Self-doubt can play a huge part here too and can cripple a practitioner. So much of what we do relies on our ability to maintain our break from consensus reality, and our successes and experiences help to reinforce that. Without those successes and experiences, it's easy for the weight of consensus reality to push in and reframe our perceptions and ability to perceive so that we effectively lose the ability to see. In these cases, I recommend a return to working on basic skills, especially meditation. Meditation forms the basis for so much of our practice and wellness in this work. It's also a good way to see what comes up, if there *are* any blockages there, and eventually receive the inspiration to clear them.

Baseline Measures

For those who have no difficulties in obtaining a reaction, one of the first things I encourage practitioners to do is to set aside one room in the home and make that a kind of safe room. It does not need to be a special temple room but simply a single room designated as being the safe room. Make this space the most warded room of the house with the intention that if anything goes wrong and you're faced with terrifying circumstances in the middle of the night, you at least have somewhere to go in your own home where your family can sleep with some degree of safety. I also advise keeping a bag of salt handy for when things go bump in the night and you're not with it enough to properly deal with whatever it is.

There is a lot to be said for choosing your battles, and it's often far better to fight in daylight when fully awake than half-asleep at 3 a.m. It's important to know your limits, and it's wise to plan for the times when you really can't or shouldn't fight. The salt is helpful for pushing back against whatever is there so that you get your loved ones out and into the safe room. In my experience, this is especially important if you have children and more so if those children are showing signs of magical and/or psychic ability.

Signs You May Have a Problem

As with many things in magic, prevention is always far better than cure, and many would-be infestations can be headed off by sharing your home with helpful animistic powers. If you are Heathen, these will most likely be your ancestors and house spirits as well as any allies. When things don't quite feel right in your home or when your dreams begin to feel like attacks (particularly around the fifteenth lunar day), your first port of call is your allies. In my experience, the fifteenth lunar day is the most common day for dreams that indicate psychic or magical attack. These dreams usually involve (but are not limited to) themes of being shot by arrows, stabbed, or bitten by snakes. When I have these dreams and sensations, I set up a ritual to make offerings to my allies and then enter trance in order to speak with them. It can be really useful to see what your non-human housemates have noticed.

If your home is becoming infested, you may notice a sensation that you're being watched even when you're not and that things start to go missing. You may find that your relationships with loved ones are becoming more combative and that everything just *feels* unsettled. You may even start to experience the "psychic bell" (a ringing sound or series of knocks with no discernible cause that often signals something otherworldly seeking an invitation in). The psychic bell can also be an indicator of magical or psychic attack. The last time I experienced this, I heard knocking noises whenever I tried to go into trance or work ritual. They only stopped after I followed the advice of a spirit I work with to perform protection magic focused on magical defense. You may also see darting figures in your peripheral vision.

Diagnosis and Discernment

Your first task when you notice these signs is to figure out who is causing these effects and whether you can propitiate them so that they leave you in peace. Oftentimes, this is all you need to do, and sometimes some of these beings may even become a regular among your household crowd (as long as they agree to abide by the rules of residency, of course!). Although many people tend to think in terms of ghosts and demons when it comes to household infestations, there is a wide range of beings that might decide to try to take up residence in your house. For example, some of the worst cases of infestation have been fairy-related.

As always, discernment is key, and there are a few key signs that what you're dealing with is a fairy as opposed to a member of the human dead. Fairies (a term I use here to refer to the various kinds of otherworldly beings), for example, tend to be associated with things going missing, strange dreams, fairy rings appearing in the garden, and tangling people's hair while asleep (a phenomenon referred to as "elf locks"). Tangled hair may not sound like much of a sign; most people's hair gets tangled to some degree when they sleep at night. However, when a fairy or fairies are involved the degree of hair tangling is much more pronounced than usual. It usually manifests in a way that is abnormal for the person who is experiencing the issue.

Dealing with Fairies

If you find that it is a fairy at the root of everything, then your first action is to attempt to bribe them. Always remain polite, and remember that any attempts to boss them around will be the equivalent of pouring gasoline onto a fire. The traditional "fairy repellents" of iron, salt, St. John's wort, mugwort, and rowan are your friends here, so make sure to ward as many areas as you can, and especially the rooms of any children present. You really don't want an angry fairy getting access to children. I would also advise that you use a combination of these "repellents" too, because different types of fairy are affected by some apotropaic substances but not others. For example, most types of fairy flee exposed iron, but some fairy beings, like redcaps, are completely unaffected and have even been depicted as wearing and carrying iron! So do not just rely on one apotropaic substance. Try to mix it up.

Lastly, if you have to try and get rid of them, then you need to make sure you go all in. There can be no half measures here, because things will likely get even worse if you underestimate the problem and fail. In more traditional communities in Ireland, people used to go to a kind of specialist called a Fairy Doctor when faced with this kind of problem. If you ever find yourself facing this issue and have the option, it's a really good idea to get a similar expert in to help you. Failing that, if you work with or know of a group, don't be afraid to call for backup. I've seen incredibly experienced practitioners having to move house to get away from fairy infestation.

Dealing with the Dead

If you find that you are dealing with a member of the dead who has stuck around after one of your necromantic rituals, things are somewhat easier to deal with; there are various ways in which you could make them leave. The first is to try telling them to get out of your house. When you do this, you cannot be afraid. Fear has the unfortunate side effect of handing over power to whomever you are facing. If you are commanding the dead to get out of your home, you must do so with full confidence in your authority and sovereignty over your home.

If they don't leave when you ask, then it's time to take sterner measures. But here is where it can get complex, because the dead are beings of story. In a sense, we the living write stories with our actions. But the dead no longer write; they are bound by the stories they lived in life and the stories we put on them now. If you essentially "tell them the wrong" story in order to get them to leave, then they won't. A dead Jewish person is likely not going to respond to Christian prayers to Jesus any more than he or she did in life. Think about what "story" you're telling here.

One of the most common-to-humans "stories" that we tell ourselves is the law. Law as a concept is incredibly powerful and capable of not only restraining the behaviors of living people, but changing them too. When we say that something is law, there is a weightiness that is often obeyed. There's a saying that "possession is nine-tenths of the law," but few realize just how old some laws regarding property rights and ownership are; concepts of sovereignty and ownership have long formed a part of legal history. Here is where we come to a way in which law can become a useful story to tell the misbehaving dead.

One of the ways in which people in Iceland used to get rid of the troublesome dead was to summon them to a "door court," a court that was convened at the main door of the house to which the dead were summoned, judged, and then sentenced in accordance with the law. Unfortunately, this isn't nearly as effective with rental properties (unless you can convince the landlord to participate). But for people who own their own homes, holding a door court can be a useful ritual for laying the disquiet dead.

Driving Out the Disquiet Dead

Although my preference is to try to get the dead to leave on their own through making offerings (or door courts, for example), sometimes the dead person just will not go of their own volition. It's therefore a good idea to know how to drive them out forcibly if needed too.

The most basic form of exorcism is to salt and fumigate the home while calling upon the Holy Powers you worship. Again, story can play a role here too, because, for example, if your ghost was a devout Christian in life, then it can be enough to summon your own Heathen gods to scare them off. Other times, especially when working for other people, you may need to call to other gods or numinous powers in order for this to work. There are two conditions to an exorcism that need to be fulfilled in order to have a chance at success: that you yourself believe in what you are doing, and that the people who you are doing it for also believe it and have confidence in it. If you do a clearing for someone who is Catholic, for example, you need to use ritual that they understand and have faith in. Sometimes there is enough common ground here that you can come up with something that everyone can put their faith in. But if there is no common ground (such as working with Brighid/St. Brigid or other Christianized Pagan deities), it's really better to refer the client to outside help.

Assuming that both practitioner and assembled people are on board with the deities and/or spirits being called upon, if the ritual works, you will either be free of the ghost, or it will "go into the walls," something that has happened to me quite a lot over the years. I clear a spirit from a home and then it just hides in the walls and lurks there until the smoke is gone and salt water sufficiently reduced for it to reemerge and start causing trouble. If that happens, you have two options: you can either fumigate with rēcels or try trapping it.[321] The most responsible method that I use for compelling a wayward ghost to leave can be found in chapter 9. It's a form of trap and release that uses spun magic to pull and bind the spirit in the fibers. Once bound, the wool can simply be broken up into a bowl of water that has been ritually made into a passage to the underworld of the Dead, or you can take the wool to the crossroads and sing them over using the psychopomp version of the song in chapter 8.

Another way of trapping a spirit is in old shoes. Shoes have long played a part in apotropaic practices and are the most common apotropaic find in old houses in England, where they're found placed on ledges inside chimneys. Unfortunately, we don't actually know the purpose of the shoes beyond "apotropaic," but I began working with them because the most logical use for me was as a spirit trap. Over the years, they have proven to be excellent spirit traps. When I construct one of these shoe traps, I usually use both shoes in the pair and connect them with a braided string of white, red, and black, and imbue the braid with intent as I work. Finally, I leave them in the place

---

321. See chapter 10 for instructions on making rēcels.

I believe best suited for trapping what is there. If I am impatient, I also burn some mullein because it's known to attract spirits to a place.

Dealing with Deities

Generally speaking, fairies and the dead are the most common sources of home disturbance. Sometimes you may encounter beings claiming to be deities, but in my experience, deities don't tend to lurk in houses and break electrical appliances, rap on walls, and tangle hair. When a deity has a problem with a human, usually it's because the human is not doing something that the deity wishes them to do or that they themselves have sworn an oath to do. From what I've seen in these cases, this displeasure commonly manifests in a loss of luck or withdrawal of favor; from a Heathen perspective, it is incumbent on the adherent to make amends or propitiate the deity in some way (depending on what has happened). If you are not sure how to do this, seek advice from a more experienced völva.

As mentioned throughout this book, Heathenry is about relationships, and so it is from the perspective of repairing relationships that we approach this issue. There is no magic in Heathenry for binding or expelling gods.

⤜}⚬ Experiential: Holding a Door Court ⚬{⤛

You will need:

The person whose name is on the house deed

A copy of your local law codes pertaining to property ownership and squatting

Whichever items are indicated for your chosen form of necromancy (see chapter 8)

Procedure

1. Gather the residents of the home, including the legal owner, at the main door of the home, and set up any necromantic tools you may need in readiness.

2. Summon the dead using one of the rituals from chapter 8 and present your case using your copy of local law codes pertaining to property ownership and squatting. Cite your arguments as you make them in

order to root them in law. You may also wish to include a traditional "hearth ownership" argument in your case. Some of the oldest laws regarding ownership (at least in Indo-European cultures) center around the ability to maintain a hearth in the home. Although many homes no longer feature hearths in the traditional sense, this is still the best foundation for your arguments. Most of the functions of the hearth have now been taken over by electric lighting and stoves; in a sense, we still keep hearths. The dead, on the other hand, are not capable of keeping any hearths, traditional or otherwise.

3. Once you have presented the case, you need to sentence the ghost to leave the house. A lot of ghosts will go at this point. But in the cases where they do not, you need to employ much harsher measures, and this is when we get into exorcism territory. After all, through refusing to leave the home, your ghost has now made itself an outlaw.

⟶⟩○ Remedy: Creating a Shoe Trap ○⟨⟵

You will need

An old pair of shoes

9 lengths of yarn or embroidery thread (3 white, 3 red, 3 black)

Red paint and brush

A pair of scissors

Procedure

1. Take your pair of shoes and blow into each one nine times. As you do so, imagine yourself blowing out the remnants of whoever used to wear the shoes. Then fumigate them with mugwort smoke before setting them aside.

2. Take your yarn or embroidery thread and measure three lengths, the same amount in each color. You should now have three lengths of white, three of red, and three of black. A foot-long piece of each is usually enough. If you don't have a measuring tape, you can use the length from the tip of your fingers to your elbow as a rough guide.

3. Lay all the lengths of thread next to each other so they are flat, then draw the ends together on one end and pick up the bundle. You will

want to put a knot in about a couple of inches from the top to hold them all together as you braid. When you are ready to begin, divide the threads into three so that each color is grouped together. As you braid, work on the visualization that the spirit is attracted to the shoes and cannot keep away. "See" it moving closer to the shoe as you work and becoming trapped in a force that pulls it irresistibly into one of the shoes. If you wish, chant the following charm as you work:

> With every twist
> And turn of thread
> I bring and bind you to this trap
> Empty shoes
> No escape
> Without my word, no longer loose
> Without my word, never loose.

4. Braid, chant, and visualize until you have around two inches left at the bottom and put a knot into the braid to hold it.

5. Now, use the final two inches of unbraided thread at each end to connect the pair of shoes through a lace-hole on each shoe, and visualize the braid and its magic blending and merging with the shoe as you do so.

6. Once you have done this, take each shoe and breathe into it three times, chanting the following:

> I breathe into this shoe
> A life's breath for my spell.

Take some of the red paint and make a dot inside the shoe before continuing.

> Hue and heat I give that it may live
> Sense I speak
> A spoken charm
> Snare of spirits, entice my prey
> Snare of spirits, trap my prey.

7. Finally, visualize the trap ensnaring the errant spirit. Include any details you may have picked up about the spirit intuitively or during trancework so as to further "key" it to your prey. Then leave the trap where it will do the most good.

When I make spirit traps of any kind, I intentionally make them with the option of releasing whoever I have caught; the wording of the incantation reflects this. If you use this method of spirit-trapping and want to release what you have caught, then you can take it to the crossroads and sing it over to the realms of the dead using one of the adaptations of "A Lyke Wake" given in chapter 8. This trap is constructed in such a way that it is by your word only that the trapped spirit may be released.

At the end of the day, mistakes and the art of troubleshooting them are a part of magical practice. We all make mistakes and run into problems, and it can be hard when it seems like everyone else's practice is more "together" than your own. Mistakes are not necessarily a bad thing; if approached correctly, they present opportunities for learning and growth that will never be found in any book or class. Try to learn to love your mistakes, because they'll be some of the greatest teachers you ever have.

Twelve

RITES, RITUALS, AND CELEBRATIONS

M ost religions have a set of holy tides observed throughout the course of the year. While there are some differences between different sects of the same religion, holy tides generally remain the same across traditions. For example, most sects of Christianity celebrate Christmas as the anniversary of the birth of Christ, but whereas some traditions celebrate on the December 25, others celebrate on January 7. Although the date of the celebration may change, the date does not as it is tied to the central myth of the Christian religion.

There is a similar standardization of holy tides among the modern Pagan traditions that observe the Wheel of the Year. Unlike the Christian holy tides, however, these are centered around the solstices, equinoxes, and cross-quarter days. Depending on tradition, modern Pagans may also tie these holy tides to a central unifying myth.

Unlike Christians and Pagans, there is no general agreement between modern Heathens regarding the holy tides; practices vary widely. Some groups adhere strictly to the historical evidence pertaining to a specific geographical area, whereas others create an entire cycle of rituals to reflect the needs and life of the group members. Historical accounts also vary: the elder Heathen seems to have either divided the year into two or three seasons, depending on the source. For the Icelanders, the summer was divided into two seasons, summer and winter. However, the Roman historian Tacitus reports that the Germans observed three seasons: spring, summer, and winter.

The Icelandic historian Snorri Sturluson wrote of three main holy tides in pre-conversion Scandinavia. The first was observed in autumn, the second at midwinter, and the third at some point in summer. The fall festival season seems to have been particularly busy for the elder Heathen, as autumn was considered the beginning of winter in much of the Germanic world. Rituals seem to have reflected this belief accordingly. There are a number of rituals recorded in various sources as taking place within this time frame.

Although there were some areas of concordance, rituals generally varied by geography. There is also evidence of local cultic practices having their own holy tides. Among the Icelanders, the fall festival season was referred to as "Winter Nights" and generally took place in mid-October. Another fall festival that was recorded (this time among the Swedes), was Álfablót or "sacrifice to the elves."[322]

We recognize the midwinter festival as Yule, generally considered as beginning around the time of the winter solstice. This festival seems to have been a pan-Germanic feast and there are a multitude of different traditions recorded as taking place during this time period depending on geographical region. Then as now, the central theme seems to have been centered around drinking and feasting with family and friends.

Sturluson records that at some point during the summer, the elder Heathens performed sacrifices for victory. Unfortunately, we do not know exactly how the elder Heathens celebrated their holy tides, but blood sacrifice was a most likely component.[323]

Heathen holy tides have always varied by group and location. In this, we are no different from the people of the Heathen period. And despite differences, modern Heathenry is at its core a group of family- and community-based religions. We tend to cocreate the rituals with which we celebrate our holy tides and adapt our celebrations as needed. Many groups have a common ritual format that is used for all rituals (including the holy tides) and simply

---

322. Hilda R. Davidson, *Myths and Symbols in Pagan Europe: Early Scandinavian and Celtic Religions* (Syracuse: Syracuse University Press, 1988), 37–41

323. Ibid.

adapted to reflect the tide. In terms of creating your own rituals for seasonal observations, I recommend a similar approach. You have already encountered one such format in the rituals given in the first three chapters. In this chapter, you will find additional ritual formats as well as an overview of the "anatomy" of Heathen ritual as I perform it.

Because of my various cultic involvements, many of my observances are tied up in what might be considered the mysteries of a specific deity; the rituals in this chapter have been divided accordingly. You will find a number of rituals that can be used at holy tides in each of these subsections.

Anatomy of Heathen Rituals

Whether explicitly recognized or not, all groups have a format used for the rituals they observe. In Heathen religion, we often talk about these as being part of the customs of a group, but not everyone has a group or the benefit of a collective ritual format. Moreover, I believe magic workers need to be much more flexible, especially if we work with others. We need to not only be able to conduct ritual but create and adapt it too.

The model presented here is the one I use and have found to be of the most use. As you will see, I favor a modular approach to ritual design; not only is this model highly customizable to lend itself to rituals for any holy tide or purpose—it also teaches you to think about ritual in a flexible way.

Overview of a Heathen Ritual Format

Setup and Start: Participants set up the ritual space and ready any tools and offerings that may be needed. If any ritual items such as rēcels or waters need to be purified, it's a good idea to speak the charms of purification now. In some traditions, the setup is considered just as sacred as the rest of the ritual and so you may wish to give thought to how you approach this stage as well.

When setup is complete, participants get into position and ready themselves for the rite. Once all is ready, it's good to take a few moments to take a few deep breaths or intone some sounds in order to get into a ritual mindset.

1. **Opening Statement and Offering to Wīhta/Hiddenfolk:** The ritual leader makes an opening statement describing the purpose of the rite.

This can be as simple as "I have come to make offerings to _____ so that they may help me with _____."

When working outside, I also like to make a small offering to the local wihta before beginning the ritual proper. When working in the wilds, it's a good idea to remember that you are working in *their* territory and show them respect accordingly. A simple offering of cornmeal or milk and a promise to put things back as you found them can go a long way when working outdoors.

2. **Purification of Space:** Although not commonly a part of Heathen ritual, I include this stage because it's important to me to build ritual space in a hæl place—especially for magic. Like many Heathens, I do not believe that the gods are always present in either places or idols and must thus be invited in order to be present. In short, it feels more hospitable to invite the Holy Powers to a place that is ritually clean than one that is not.[324]

   NB: If working outside or with the spirits of a place, this step is unnecessary as long as you first find a hæl place to work. If you have chosen to work in an unhæl space because you wish to deal with the spirits, purification would defeat the purpose of visiting that space in the first place.

3. **Construction of Worship Space:** Here is where I ritually recreate the elements of cosmology needed for ritual. Although written as a single stage, it is made up of a number of substages. Depending on where I am situating my ritual, I may also choose to preface these substages with a small remembrance offering to Ymir.

   a. **Delineating Space:** Common methods of delineating space include (but are not limited to) erecting vé bonds, walking the boundaries with fire, and casting circles/laying compasses. As a general rule, you need to move with the course of the sun (clockwise) when creating sacred space for working with the Holy Powers. This is because when we move with the course of the sun, we align ourselves with that which is holy. Sunwise is the direction of blessings

---

324. See chapters 10 and 11 for more information on purification practices.

and holiness as well as the traditional way of delineating ordered inner space as opposed to the wild outer. However, there are some circumstances in which a counterclockwise direction is more suitable. These are usually rituals that may be thought to violate the natural order of the world in some way, or involve the otherworldly.

b. **Recreating Cosmology (optional):** Though not yet common among modern Heathen groups, scholars are finding that some Heathen ritual spaces reflected cosmology in some way. In practical terms, recreating cosmology/a section of cosmology allows you to better target your rituals and magic. However, not all rituals require this step. For example, if you are planning a ritual involving the unseen in a place, then you may want to skip this step because you're already where they are!

4. **Inviting the Holy Powers/Numinous Beings and Arrival:** As mentioned in step three, many Heathens do not believe our deities to be omnipresent, and so must be invited to a rite. The arrival of our guests may be represented in various ways, including physically carrying the idols into the sacred space and seating them at the altar. One good option for solo rituals or in situations where the idols cannot be carried is lighting a tealight before each idol to represent the deity's presence.

5. **Offering:** Hospitality was important in the Heathen period, and the primary sources are full of stories detailing the consequences of not being a good host. In one story in the *Poetic Edda*, Óðinn punishes a king for denying him hospitality and grants his kingship to the son who at least brought him water.[325] The importance of proper hospitality cannot be overstated. As our guests, the powers we invite need be treated appropriately.

Moreover, if you're inviting them to a rite, then you also probably want something from them. In *Hávamál*, we are told, "a gift for a gift." This is a wider expression of Indo-European ideas on the necessity of giving gifts in order to receive gifts in return. Offerings are the gifts we give to the gods and spirits we worship, and although different deities

---

325. Carolyne Larrington, *The Poetic Edda*, 51–60.

and types of beings often have their preferences, common offerings include alcohol, dairy products such as butter or cream, bread, and handmade items.

6. **Magical Work and/or Seasonal Observances:** Once the Holy Powers have been invited, properly welcomed, and offered to, you can begin any magical work or seasonal observances.

7. **Optional Offerings:** Depending on what you are doing in step seven, you may want to make additional offerings to the Holy Powers invited.

8. **Thanking the Guests:** Once the work of the ritual is done and any final offerings have been made, it's time to thank the guests for their attendance. Do this even if you do not sense their presence. One taboo I observe when working with any of the more otherworldly beings such as álfar or the various fairy beings I encounter is to never actually say the words "thank you." Instead, I express my gratitude with phrases like "I am grateful that you ___" or "I appreciate what you _____."

    If you marked the arrival of the deity in some way in step five, be sure to reverse whatever you did. If you lit candles, blow them out. If you carried in idols, carry them out.

9. **Deconstructing the Space:** How much you do here will depend on what you did to create space in step four, but generally a good rule is, again, reversal of whatever you did. Anything you declared to be cosmological sites must be returned to their original state in the same way.

    If you walked boundaries counterclockwise, then you must walk them clockwise again. If you erected physical vé bonds, you need to take them down in the opposite direction to how you put them up.

10. **Ending the Rite:** The rite is declared officially at an end and a final offering made to the wihta of the place if working outside. This may seem obvious, but it's good to bookend rituals in this way and make it clear when you're passing between sacred and mundane spaces. Take some time to ground at this point too. A lot of groups organize their rites so that they are followed by the feast for just this reason!

As you can see, this model provides both a sound structure for ritual and a lot of scope for individual creativity as well. In the following sections, the rituals or ritual sections are labeled with the step number to which they correspond best so that you may figure out any substitutions when creating your own.

Ways of Creating Sacred Space

In the following section are three different ways of creating sacred space for use in Heathen ritual. Each of these rites corresponds with stages 2 through 4 of the previously-presented Heathen ritual framework.

As a general rule, these rites are intended to be vehicles into that "time beyond time" where we may connect with the Holy Powers and should thus be worked in a clockwise direction. Full instructions for creating liminal space for work with the dead and otherworldly are found in chapter 8.

⇥ Carrying Fire ⇤

The method of sacred space creation presented here is the one that we were first introduced to in chapter 2. Inspired by the landtaking practices of some of the first Icelandic settlers as recounted in the *Landnámabók* (or "Book of Settlements"), this method relies on circumambulating one's intended ritual space clockwise while carrying fire. This is one of my preferred methods of delineating sacred space—especially when working in the wild outdoors, as it requires very few tools to perform. More importantly, when performed right, this method is incredibly effective.

You will need

Mugwort incense (if indoors)

Censer (if using dried herb instead of incense stick)

Charcoal disc

Lighter or matches

A handful of cornmeal/small carton of cream as offering to the wīhta/ Hiddenfolk (if working outside)

A candle/candle in a jar

Procedure

1. If you are outside, begin by making a small offering of a handful of corn-meal or half of your cream to the wīhta/Hiddenfolk. Explain in your

own words what you are doing and give them assurances that you will return the land to them when you are done. If you are inside, burn some mugwort incense and carry it around the space in a clockwise direction.

2. Take three (or nine) deep breaths, then light the candle and walk the boundaries clockwise while chanting the following hallowing charm:

Fire I bear
Bright it burns
And ask for peace from all
Fast flee the enemies
Evil be gone
Þórr make sacred this space!
Þórr keep sacred this place!

3. Proceed with the rest of your ritual.

At the End of the Rite

1. If working indoors, you do not need to do anything further. You can simply leave the space as is and tidy up the remains of your ritual. If you are outdoors, however, you will need to walk the boundaries again in a counterclockwise direction (this time without fire) in order to return the space to the land.

2. Then, make a final offering of another handful of cornmeal, or the second half of the cream as a gesture of gratitude to the Hiddenfolk before leaving. Try to leave the outdoor space as you found it (if not better).

→))o Erecting Vé Bonds o(←

In the following rite, the ritualist creates space by physically constructing a sacred enclosure by pinning out the corners with four stakes of wood (one at each corner) and running spun flax or yarn between the stakes to create a barrier. Because of the physical nature of this form of sacred space, it is perfect for public rituals or religious events where sacred space needs to be maintained for days at a time.

This form of ritual enclosure can also be used for delineating the boundaries of outdoor shrines to certain deities, and it has become increasingly common to see enclosures used in this way at larger Heathen events over the past decade or so.

You will need

Four stakes of wood

Mallet

Spun flax or yarn

A handful of cornmeal or carton of cream as offering for the wīhta

Procedure

1. As you are working outside, you will need to begin by making a small offering of a handful of cornmeal or half a carton of cream to the wīhta. Explain in your own words what you are doing and give them assurances that you will return the land to them when you are done.

2. Use a mallet to drive the stakes into the ground at each corner of your planned space. If you have appropriately placed trees, you can also use trees for this form of enclosure.

3. Take the yarn/flax you have spun/bought for the vé bonds and, beginning with the stake most closely aligned with the east, attach the end of the bond to the stake and move in a clockwise direction to each of the stakes, looping the yarn/flax around each stake as you go. Alternatively, you can use six stakes in order to create a doorway through which adherents may pass. Set up the four stakes as normal, and then add a further two stakes on the side where you wish to create a doorway. Don't forget the necromantic associations of the southwest/northeast doorway orientation (see the section on doorways in chapter 8 for a quick refresher).

4. Proceed with the rest of the ritual or leave standing for the duration of the event.

At the End of the Rite/Event

1. Deconstruct your enclosure by untying the yarn or flax from the post you finished with when creating the enclosure. Then, carefully follow

the enclosure round in a counterclockwise direction, winding the yarn into a ball as you go.

2. Beginning at the same post as you untied the yarn from, walk the enclosure counterclockwise again, this time removing the posts as you go.

3. Finally, make an offering of gratitude to the Hiddenfolk. Once again, a handful of cornmeal or half a carton of cream will suffice, but if you have kept the space for several days, you may wish to offer them more cornmeal or cream, and potentially any bread you have. If the stakes you used were wildcrafted from a forest, then return them to the same forest. Burn or bury the yarn or flax that you used for the enclosure.

→)∘ Casting a Circle ∘(←

While Heathens don't cast circles as a matter of course, I am personally a big fan of them for use in magic. There's something very instinctive about circles and the act of circumambulation. When people gather in a group, we instinctively gather in circles. Historically we have danced in circles, and some of the earliest inhabitants of Northern Europe built holy sites in circular form. Circles are a truly ancient (and customizable) magical technology.

Unlike other magic circles, the one cast here is created with the intent of enabling access to that sacred "time beyond time" inhabited by the gods. The boundaries are both delineatory as well as protective, and there is some degree of cosmos recreation to firmly root this space within that sacred mythological cosmology.

Depending on where you work this rite (i.e., indoors or out), you may wish to use wet yarn to delineate your space instead of sprinkling or pouring water. If working indoors, this will prevent your floor from becoming too wet; if used outdoors, it creates a visible boundary around your space so you do not have to guess where the limits are.

You will need

A ball of red yarn (optional)

Large water receptacle full of salt water

A handful of cornmeal or carton of cream for the wihta/Hiddenfolk (if working outside)

Mugwort incense

Censer (if using dried herb instead of incense stick)

Charcoal disc

Lighter or matches

Staff/tree/pillar

Candle

Bell

Procedure

1. If you are outside, begin by making a small offering of a handful of corn-meal or half of the carton of cream to the wihta. Explain in your own words what you are doing and give them assurances that you will return the land to them when you are done. If you are inside, then burn some mugwort incense and carry it around the space in a clockwise direction.

2. Place the large receptacle of salt water at the center of your planned space along with the rest of the ritual tools. Ring the bell 3 times to signal the beginning of the ritual.

3. Take the receptacle of salt water (or wet yarn) and pour some out to form a circle around you and your tools. If you're working indoors and/or prefer having a visual representation of the boundary line, you can also use wet yarn to mark out the boundary. To use: soak yarn in the water until wet. Remove, wring out any excess, then lay it on the ground to mark out the boundary of the circle while saying:

> With water clean
> I wind my way
> Around this sacred space
> Sained within
> Yet wild without
> Þórr make holy this place
> Þórr make safe this space.

4. Now return to the center (don't forget to bring the bowl back with you if you used it to create the boundary). If working indoors, find some

way to position the tree representation so that it remains upright. If working outdoors, drive the tree representation/stang into the earth at the center and ensure that the bowl of water is positioned at the base. These are your representations of Yggdrasill and Urðr's well. When all is secure, continue by saying:

An ash I know, | Yggdrasil its name,
With water white | is the great tree wet;
Thence come the dews | that fall in the dales,
Green by Urð's well | does it ever grow.
We stand beneath the skull of the frost-cold giant
Four are the dwarves that uphold the sky
Four are the stags that gnaw at the tree. [326]

5. Finally, circumambulate the space beginning in the east and moving in a clockwise direction while saying:

Austri, Sudri, Vestri, Nordri
I call to the Holy Powers in all directions dwelling
Come forth from your homes to this place between
Come witness and bless this rite? [327]

6. From this point, proceed with the rest of the ritual.

At the End of the Rite

1. Thank any deities you invited and declare the "well" and "tree" to be a bowl of water and stick once more.

2. Circumambulate to return the space to the land and take up any yarn you laid down when setting the space.

---

326. First half of incantation taken from the poem *Völuspá*, in Henry Adams Bellows, *The Poetic Edda: The Mythological Poems* (Mineola, NY: Dover Publications, 2004), 9.

327. See the glossary for more on *Austri, Sudri, Vestri,* and *Nordri.*

3. If working outdoors, make a final offering of gratitude to the local Hiddenfolk. Another handful of cornmeal or the second half of the cream will suffice.

Rituals to the Spinning Goddess

In this section, you will find rituals devoted to the worship and magical work of the Spinning Goddess. Although this deity is (as the epithet suggests) associated with spinning, you do not have to be able to spin to worship her. It is my sincere belief that she accepts all offerings of handmade items that were made with a heart full of devotion, and takes interest in the work of the hands in general.

Unlike the other rituals in this chapter, the rituals in this section were written with wider cultic use in mind and are taken from the liturgy of a group called the *Cult of the Spinning Goddess*.

The Cult of the Spinning Goddess was founded around Yuletide 2014 with the intent of resurrecting the cultic practices of völur that I believe once existed. Although presented as little more than wandering fortune tellers and witches, it's my intuition that völur and seiðkonur were originally the ritual specialists of cults dedicated to the deity who came to be known as Freyja in the north. The Cult of the Spinning Goddess is an attempt to recontextualize the practice of seiðr as something *holy* while rebuilding relationships with the goddess introduced in chapter 2.

Solo Rites—Taboo-Along

There are two main holy tides that are recognized by the Cult of the Spinning Goddess, Yule and Walpurgisnacht. As our goddess is predominantly associated with the Raw Nights of Yule when the Dead wander and the Hunt rides, Yule is by far the most important of the two holidays for us.[328] As such, we bookend this holy tide with both a spinning "taboo-along" before the Raw Nights of Yule settle in and a final ritual at the end of the holy tide.

The cult's tradition of taboo-alongs is a modification of the spinning taboos found in German folklore. Traditionally, the woman of the home would be forced to spin nearly constantly when not otherwise occupied with

---

328. Lotte Motz, "The Winter Goddess: Percht, Holda, and Related Figures," 152–155.

yet more work, so the taboo against spinning during the holy nights of Yule must have come as something of a relief. If nothing else, it was downtime for ladies who didn't usually get any.

The pressure to keep spinning had to have been pervasive. It can also be hard to stop doing something when you do it frequently. It's often that people feel as though they need permission to rest or believe that bad things will happen if they do. In my opinion, this is the original function of the spinning taboos: to enforce a prolonged period of rest from an ever-present chore. After all, no one wants to anger a goddess known for giving bad luck when her rules are violated or enacting violence against those who violate her rules!

The taboo-alongs in the cult are done for three main reasons: to hopefully deepen our connection with the goddess; to gain her favor so that she might bless us with luck; and as a way to remember the old taboos (albeit with a little twist).

Unlike the original benefactors of these taboos, we modern people aren't used to spending every spare minute spinning. We are no longer under social and economic pressure to do so, and for most of us nowadays, spinning is a hobby we choose to do. So to understand the taboos and, consequently, more about our goddess, we spend the month of December forcing ourselves to complete a specific fiber art project by Yule. Those of us who spin pledge an amount to be spun up by Yule, and those of us who do other fiber crafts pledge to do what we can, even if it is just braiding lengths of cord. There is room for all levels of fiber arts and ability within the cult.

The rules we keep are simple:

1. We spin or work on our pledged activity every day. Our labor is our offering.
2. We spin up everything we have pledged, or complete whatever activity we pledged to do by Yule.

As the taboo-alongs are devotional events that are done by individuals in their own homes, we make the following liturgy available for the pledging rite for participants to use should they so choose. Our taboo-alongs generally take place on a biannual basis, and run from the December 1 to Yule, as well as April 21 until Walpurgisnacht. The following ritual is the pledging rite used to declare what and how much we're going to do before beginning the work proper of a taboo-along.

⇢)⚬ Pre-Spinning Taboo-Along Rite ⚬(⇠

The Pre-Spinning Taboo-Along Rite is the beginning of what might be thought of as a ritual that lasts for anywhere from a week to roughly three weeks depending on the time of year. Due to this rite's role as the beginning of a greater ritual, what follows is incomplete, only fulfilling stages 1 through 6 of the Heathen ritual framework I use. At this time we come before the goddess and make an oath to perform a certain amount of labor as an offering to her in the hope that if we complete it, she in turn will bless us with good luck.

Before beginning any rites associated with the Cult of the Spinning Goddess, it's important to know of the custom to either bathe or perform some kind of ritual purification before every cultic rite (see chapter 11 for Sunna's Light Purification Visualization). The theme of cleanliness is quite important to one of the most well-known faces of the Spinning Goddess, Frau Holle/Holda, and I can think of at least one of her sites that is associated with ritual bathing.

If you take a physical bath before performing this ritual, I recommend first hallowing the water before bathing with the following charm:

> Over good water
> A galdor I speak
> With wise words I will it
> And my breath goes wholly in
> Making clean waters holy
> Fast flee the evil from it!
> Fast flee evil magic from it!

You will probably already recognize this charm from earlier chapters. As always, visualize your words imbuing the water with a golden holiness when reciting this charm while ensuring that your breath goes into the bathwater as you chant.

You do not need to spend a long time in the bath; just make sure that you fully submerge yourself before getting out, drying off, and dressing. Once purified, you are ready to gather your ritual and crafting tools and begin the rite.

You will need

The roving you are to spin/constituent parts of your project

Your tools (whatever you use for your devotional crafting)

An altar set up with a representation of the Spinning Goddess

Candle

Bowl of water

An offering

Ritual Procedure

1. Begin by setting up your altar. Place the representation in the center, the bowl before it, and the candle to the right of both. Have your offerings, project supplies, and tools to hand before starting. When ready, light the candle and say:

> Purified I approach the altar of the
> Mighty Goddess of Spindle and Staff
> May my presence cause no offense, and any
> Errors be forgiven as I make my pledge to honor
> The Spinning Goddess with my work.

2. Now take the candle and walk clockwise around the space. If your space is too small, simply move the candle at arm's length around you in a circular motion as you speak:

> Fire I bear in this space
> With fire I hallow this place
> Let all that is ill be driven away.

3. Now take some of the water and sprinkle in your space saying:

As the rainfall is a blessing to the parched earth
So is the water I sprinkle in this space
With precious water, I bless this space.

4. Return the candles and bowl to the altar before representation. Hold
your hand over the bowl of water and say:

With this bowl of water, I remember the
Ancient bog, the Hollenteich, and the waters through
Which one may meet the Spinning Goddess.

Hold your hand over the fire/candles and say:

With this flame, I remember the ritual fires built high,
The offerings sacrificed, and the coming light.

Hold your hands before the representation:

With this idol/statue/spindle, I create a
Seat for the Great Goddess in this space.

5. Return the candle and bowl to the altar before making the following prayer:

I call through the waters, I call through the fire,
I call to the most Sacred, the Spinning Goddess of many names.
I pray to a high and propitious Lady of many names
Celestial and chthonic
Of the high places and deepest waters
Lady of both hall and land
With gentle hands you protect the young
With deep wisdom you teach.

In your hands you hold mysteries
Bundled up on spindle wrapped with thread
Yours is the lesson of mystery in plain sight

Of how the greatest power can sit unseen
Yours is the mystery of childbed and hunt
Of a laboring mother's war cries
And wild witches shrieking in flight.

You are she who stands and remains
She who rose thrice from the ashes of her pyre
You are she of the Waters
The lady found in the bogs
The Spinner
The Lady of Venusberg.
You are she of many faces
Known to many lands
But here I call you "Lady"
And ask you, as your season approaches,
To bear witness to this rite and hear my oath.

6. Make your offering. Then take up the roving/supplies and hold them
before you to speak your oath:

Great Lady, I stand before you tonight with
An oath upon my lips and love in my heart
My hands are filled with my craft, and my mind with intent
I swear to you now, before your Sacred presence, that
Until Yule is called in my home/Walpurgisnacht, I will
Spin a portion of this wool I hold here in my arms
In honor of you. I swear that I will have this completed
By the arrival of the Raw and Holy Nights/Walpurgisnacht.
My labor in this endeavor, I give in offering to you. So be it! [329]

Extinguish candles, and then go start your spinning and don't stop
until Yule/Walpurgisnacht!

---

329. Delete/omit as necessary depending on time of year.

The Pre-Spinning Taboo-Along Rite is performed only once at the beginning of the taboo period. The taboo-along can be a difficult devotional practice, as participants typically spend many hours spinning or working on their chosen crafts on top of their usual daily commitments. And although we do not typically perform extra rituals throughout the taboo-along, many of us use at least a portion of our spinning or crafting time for contemplation and prayer to the Spinning Goddess.

⟶⟩◦ Post-Spinning Taboo Offering Rite ◦⟨⟵

When the taboo-along finally draws to a close, it's time to ritually close out that devotional period with a final rite to the Spinning Goddess. In the following ritual, we not only demonstrate to the goddess that we are capable of keeping our oaths, we show that we take her seriously enough to spend significant chunks of time working in her honor. In a taboo-along, it is the labor itself that is the main offering (although we give other offerings too during this rite). It is up to you whether or not you also choose to offer the fruits of your labor or keep it for your own use.

Once again, you will need to bathe and/or perform some kind of ritual purification before beginning this rite. You can follow the same procedures as before the "Pre-Spinning Taboo Offering Rite." This rite covers stages 1 through 11 of the Heathen ritual framework presented at the beginning of this chapter.

You will need

An altar set up with a representation of the Spinning Goddess

Candle

Bowl of water

An offering of a cup of wine and a bread roll (preferably homemade)

Your completed project

Ritual Procedure

1. Once again, begin by bathing or performing some kind of ritual purification. When clean/purified, dry yourself, get dressed, and then set up your altar.

2. Place the representation in the center of your altar, the bowl before it, and the candle to the right of both. Have your offerings and completed project to hand before starting. When ready, light the candle and say:

> Purified I approach the altar of the
> Mighty Goddess of Spindle and Staff
> May my presence cause no offense
> And any errors be forgiven as I make my pledge
> To honor the Spinning Goddess with my work.

3. Now take the candle and walk clockwise around the space. If your space is too small, simply move the candle at arm's length around you in a circular motion as you speak:

> Fire I bear in this space
> With fire I hallow this place
> Let all that is ill be driven away.

4. Now take some of the water and sprinkle in your space, saying:

> As the rainfall is a blessing to the parched earth
> So is the water I sprinkle in this space
> With precious water, I bless this space.

5. Return candles and bowl to the altar before the representation. Hold your hand over the bowl of water and say:

> With this bowl of water, I remember the
> Ancient bog, the Hollenteich, and the waters through
> Which one may meet the Spinning Goddess.

Hold your hand over the fire/candles and say:

> With this flame, I remember the ritual fires built high,
> The offerings sacrificed, and the coming light.

Hold your hands before the representation:

> With this idol/statue/spindle I create a
> Seat for the Great Goddess in this space.

6. Now it is time to call to the Spinning Goddess. If there is an invocation you like better, use it here instead. Usually by now, cult rite participants have plenty of ideas about what they'd like to say to her in prayer.

> I call through the waters, I call through the fire,
> I call to the most Sacred, the Spinning Goddess of many names.
> I pray to a high and propitious Lady of many names
> Celestial and chthonic
> Of the high places and deepest waters
> Lady of both hall and land
> You are she who stands and remains
> She who rose thrice from the ashes of her pyre
> You are she of the Waters
> The lady found in the bogs
> The Spinner
> The Lady of Venusberg
> You are she of many faces
> Known to many lands
> But here I call you "Lady"
> And ask you, as your season approaches,
> To bear witness to fulfillment of my oath.

7. When she has arrived and been made welcome with an offering, hold the yarn you spun/the work you did for her before her in a gesture of offering and say:

> For (number of nights) nights have I spun/created
> For (number of nights) nights have I worked my devotion to you
> Beloved and Propitious Goddess of Spindle and Staff

> I ask that you accept the labor I have given
> And bless my home with luck.

8. If it is your custom to perform divination to see if your offerings were received well, this is the time to do it. If not, thank her for coming. When you feel her presence leave, simply reverse what you did when setting up the ritual. Because of the way that the ritual space was set up, there is no need to "uncast" anything, but you will need to ritually declare the bowl of water to just be a bowl of water and the candle flame to just be a candle flame. Then blow out the candles and pour the water out onto the earth outside. The idol always remains a seat for the deity.

Rituals to the Spear God

From the rites of the Spinning Goddess, we turn once more to the Spear God, Óðinn. The Spear God can be a controversial figure in the modern Heathen community. He's often accused of being treacherous toward his followers, and many Heathens tend toward a policy of giving him a wide berth.

However, that has never been my experience with the god I affectionately refer to as "the Old Man." He's always brought change to my life, but he's also always brought the kind of luck that ensures that those changes end up working out for the better for me and mine. As I went from single to married and then to mother, his gifts have continued and he is now recognized as a luck-bringer for our family.

The rituals in this section are adapted from our family rites and reflect his role as *luck-bringer* in our lives. The first is a summertime ritual, to be held whenever it feels right. This ritual is focused on turning one's fortunes around if they are bad, or maintaining and growing luck if things are going well. The idea here is to approach the Allfather as the god of victory and ask him to bring us the kind of luck that will ultimately bring us victory over the obstacles in our lives.

The second ritual is to be carried out during the wild nights of Yule when the Wild Hunt is said to ride. The Hunt can be dangerous to the living, but it also brings blessings and growth to one's land if propitiated properly. Of these two rituals, only the first is suitable for the whole family. The second requires caution and a stout heart.

⟶꜀꜀ Summer Luck Ritual ꜀꜀⟵

The summertime luck ritual presented here is based on the idea of the *Sigr-blót* ("victory sacrifice") mentioned in chapter 8 of the *Ynglinga Saga*.[330] We are told nothing of the *Sigrblót* save that it was performed at some point in the summertime, and we can infer from the name that it was concerned with victory.

The Allfather has many *heiti*, or names, and no less than nine contain the compound *sig/r*, or "victory." He is the god of victory, and so for me, the *Sigr-blót* I celebrate in the summer is done in his honor. As previously mentioned, this is a rite that can be performed to help turn one's fortunes around if things are going badly, or grow and maintain one's luck if things are going well. The ritual presented here fulfills stages 1 through 11 of the Heathen ritual framework that I use.

You will need

A representation of Óðinn (statue or godpost/idol)

A candle

An offering bowl

A cup/glass for each participant who is of age plus one for the Allfather

Two bottles of wine

A bag of cornmeal or carton of cream for the wihta/Hiddenfolk (if working outside)

Incense (I like copal for this but anything suitably "kingly" like frankincense also seems to work)

Ritual Procedure

1. Set up your altar with the representation of Óðinn at the center and the offering bowl before it. Light and place the candle to the right and have the incense prepared and ready to be burned at the proper time. Open the bottles in advance and set the cups for participants to the side. Be sure to reserve the best cup for the god. Decide who will play the role of ritual leader and make an initial offering to the wihta if working outside.

330. Sturluson, *Heimskringla*, 12.

2. Begin by intoning together. This might sound strange, but not only can it help you get into the proper mindset for ritual, it can also be very appropriate for a god who is inherently connected with speech. Do this until it feels as though the group has reached a natural stopping point. From this point onward, the rest of these instructions are for the ritual leader.

3. Now pick up the candle and walk the boundaries of the space in a clockwise direction as you speak the following hallowing:

> With faithful heart
> I bear this flame
> Around this sacred space
> Sained within
> Yet wild without
> Þórr make holy this place
> Þórr make safe this space

4. Replace the candle on the table and call to Óðinn with the following words:

> Raven God
> God of the roads
> Tree-bound taker of runes
> Life breather
> Inspiration's breath
> Wise wanderer you ride the winds
> Wise wanderer ride your way to me.

5. Once you feel the presence of the god, offer one whole bottle of wine to him, saying:

> Welcome wise one! We are honored to have you at our rite!

Try to use a large enough bowl for the entire bottle, but if you do not have one, pour what will fit into the offering bowl that you have and set the rest to the side of the representation to signify that it has been gifted and no longer belongs to the world of men.

In your own words, explain why you have made this rite in his honor. Ask for his help in maintaining or bettering your luck and detail any specific problems that you are facing. Set out the cups and pour some of the second bottle of wine into each one, beginning with the Allfather's cup. Give him the most and share the rest among the rest of you as best you can. When you have done this, say:

> With generous hearts
> We give to you
> And bid you bless us in return
> Wine shared
> Shines with luck
> Luck-giving Wanderer make lucky these drinks
> Luck-giving Wanderer make lucky our lives.

If you have an idol or statue, wet the lips of the idol with wine and then drink from your own cups.

6. At this point, people may meditate or pull omens if inclined. Sometimes the Old Man may make a request or supply further information on how to further improve lives and maintain luck. Don't worry if you are unable to perform divination or communicate with the god. It's perfectly acceptable to move onto the next step.

7. Thank the Allfather for his help. This is best done in your own words as it's more heartfelt that way. If you are not sure what to say or cannot think of something at the time, you can say the following:

> Wish-giver, luck-bringer, cargo god of the roads!
> We thank you for honoring us with your presence
> This night, and give our most heartfelt thanks for any
> Help you give! May we all become luckier from this rite
> And may you always find a warm welcome in our home!

8. Finally, bow to the representation and step away. Allow the Old Man to leave in his own time. If for whatever reason you must move the altar and there is still a sense of presence, speak to him and explain what you need to do before moving him and his offerings somewhere safe. If the sense of presence is absent, simply pour out the offerings outside and return the representation to its usual position. Don't forget to drink your wine!

⟶⟫∘ Wild Hunt Rooftop Offering ∘⟪⟵

This offering can only be done during the twelve or thirteen nights of Yule when the Wild Hunt is said to travel the land.[331] You will not be calling up the Hunt in this rite; simply leave an offering for them in a high place so that they may partake of it should they pass over your land. Because of the nature of this rite, you can either perform it alone or include it as part of an indoor ritual with one participant taking the food offering outside and calling to the Hunt at the proper time. If you are interested in incorporating this rite into a larger seasonal ritual, this rite fits in with stage 7 of my Heathen ritual framework.

The Hunt can be unpredictable and move with the winds, capable of bringing both life and growth as well as death. You should be safe performing this ritual, but there is always the chance of attracting more attention than you would like when working with wild powers such as the Hunt.

Over the years, I have encountered the Hunt a number of times in ritual. There are several important warning signs that anyone working with the Hunt should be aware of. There is no safe way to interact directly with the Hunt. It is *always* best to leave before they arrive (if possible) and take apotropaic measures if caught outside.

In my experience, the first sign is the wind. It intensifies and becomes increasingly wild with every passing moment. You may also find that all the dogs in your neighborhood or area start barking. On rare occasions I've heard the sound of a hunting horn, and once I even saw a formation of clouds blow in that was shaped exactly like a group of riders on horseback. Please be observant when making this offering.

---

331. Some Heathens acknowledge twelve nights of Yule whereas others acknowledge thirteen.

You will need
A meal

A box of dirt

Ritual Procedure

1. Prepare a large meal for your family and make up an extra plate. The traditional way of making offerings to Yuletide spectral hosts is to leave them on the rooftop so that the host may partake of the offering if they pass overhead. However, not everyone has access to their rooftops in a safe way and so any high place on your property that is outside and safely accessible will do.

2. When you have your plate prepared, take it outside to the place you have chosen, and bring your box of dirt with you. Throwing dirt at the Wild Hunt is an effective apotropaic and I can confirm from personal experience that it works. So please do not forget it.

3. Once you get to your chosen place, put down the offering and speak the following prayer:

> From the warmth of my hearth to the cold of the night
> In the raw nights of Yule I make this offering
> Food in high places for any host that passes by
> I give so that you may bring blessings
> Heerfather, Valfather, wandering lord
> Wind-rider, wise one, hear my prayer
> A gift for a gift, accept my offering!

4. Retire promptly back inside and continue to enjoy Yuletide as it was meant to be enjoyed: inside, with family and friends.

⤐ Springtime Land Blessing and Ritual to Freyr ⤎

The following ritual is based on the Old English Æcerbót or "field remedy" charm from the *Lacnunga* manuscript. Although originally meant for farmers whose land had stopped producing as well, this land blessing is intended for gardeners to encourage a good growing season. In terms of timing, the best time to perform this ritual is before/at the first sowing, and preferably as the sun is setting during a waxing moon phase.

You will need
A bowl of water and a handful of salt

A spade (or a spade for each participant)

4 eggs

4 apples

Ale and barley

Whatever offering is traditional for the land spirits where you live

Some seeds or transfers you wish to plant

Ritual Procedure
1. Hallow the water and salt using the following charm:

> Over water and salt,
> A galdor I speak
> With wise words I will it
> And my breath goes wholly in
> Making clean waters holy
> Fast flee the evil from it!
> Fast flee evil magic from it!

2. Sprinkle the offerings and tools with the hallowed water. If there are any further prayers you wish to add to the tools and offerings, do so now.

3. Dig a series of four holes, one at each corner of your growing space. They each have to be deep enough for the offerings to fit. If your ground is hard then you may wish to dig the holes beforehand.

4. Once you have your holes, beginning in the east, deposit an egg for new life, an apple for the dead, and the appropriate offering for your local spirits. Then say:

> I pray to the god of peace and good seasons
> To Yngvi-Freyr, lord of the harvest

Grain-god, barley-god
Fertile, life-giving lord!

You who bring the rains and cause the sun to shine
Bringer of new life to the land
We ask you to descend to this land and bless it with fertility!

Pour some ale and scatter some barley into the hole, then get down to ground level and speak into the hole:

Be hæl, field, mother of men,
Grow full in the embrace of the lord
Filled with food for people to enjoy.

Then fill in the hole once more, saying:

Life-giver and life's mother, we leave you to your marriage bed!

5. Repeat the same process for each hole and begin planting. You do not need to do all your planting, just whatever you can do with what light is left.

⟶ Urð's Well ⟵

The final ritual of this chapter is actually a magical working in which we emulate the Norns themselves as they sit at the side of the well and choose fate. In the ritual presented here, the fates we speak into being are not scored onto slips of wood but the magic worked into fiber. As we saw in chapters 5 and 9, magic can be worked into fiber but only really becomes real in the world when spoken into being.

Because of the highly "localized" nature of this rite, I would begin this working (which fits in with stage seven of the ritual framework), with the method of casting a circle given at the beginning of this chapter. If you choose to opt for a different method of sacred space creation, then you need to be sure you include Urð's well within any sacred cosmology you create.

This ritual is best performed in a half-tranced state in which you also visualize yourself at the foot of Yggdrasill and crouched at Urð's well.

You will need

A large bowl of water to symbolize "Urð's Well"

Your magical embroidery or other magical fiber craft item

Your intentions or, if working with an embroidery, any text you have embroidered written out on paper

Instructions

1. Set up sacred space and invite any deities you feel appropriate for this work.

2. Kneel before your "well" and say the following:

> I kneel at the well and speak the law I have scribed
> With my breath I enlivened it
> And stitches gave color
> My words brought law to life
> This is the law I make in this place!

Read out loud what you wrote on the piece of paper, then submerge the embroidery in the well, saying:

> Law stitched
> And law spoken
> Made real in well waters
> A new layer I set
> A law I make
> A law to bind in all worlds
> A law to bind and change my world.

3. Thank any deities you have called to help you in your ritual and make any final offerings of thanks.

   If you performed this ritual in a half-trance, then this is the point when you should return to yourself. When you are sufficiently "back," declare the "well" and "tree" to be a bowl of water and tree representation, and thank any additional powers you invited. Finally, walk the boundaries counterclockwise, taking up any yarn as you go (if you used it). Be sure to ground afterward. Retain the embroidery and dry. Keep it on your shrine and speak its words often. Depending on the level of change you wish to make, you may need to set down a few layers of "law" in order to effect that change.

Making Old Magic Anew

One word found another word for me
One deed found another deed for me.
from *Hávamál*[332]

Heathen magic is founded in words and deeds. This is true of both magic in the Heathen period and magic now. It's true of the völva and helrune, as well as the charm-singing magician doing battle with a wolf-like disease, and the lawspeaker lying still under a cloak.

My journey into the words and deeds of Heathen magic began with a single word, *seiðr*. As magic workers, we inhabit a world in which some words are more powerful than others, and this one word is one of the most powerful words I've ever encountered. Like the magic it represents, it attracts and ensnares, then binds you to action. For me, a single word became the force that found me lots of other words—countless books and papers, in fact. But words are nothing without deeds to make them real. The charm must *always* be spoken or it remains little more than dead words on a page, and magic must always be tried out or it remains theory and never becomes practice.

The importance of practice cannot be overstated either, and in my experience, it's far more productive when inspired by those old words. There is a cycle here of words to deeds, and deeds to words. But it can be intimidating to begin the process of wading through historical sources and scholarly papers. Those waters can be downright unfriendly at times, and it can be hard to know if you're on the right track, especially when the theory you're building runs counter to ideas that are already well-established. It is here that practice comes in, because it isn't *just* about trying things out to see it they work. Practice can also be your guiding star. This is not a system in which words and deeds are separate. It is both a cycle and a feedback loop. Dreams and experiences can lead

332. Carolyne Larrington, *The Poetic Edda*, 34.

you to words hiding down previously unexplored avenues of research, and these in turn often lead you to yet more words and practices.

We may not have as much information as we'd like in the primary sources, and theory is a far more constant companion than anything resembling fact. But when you hit upon something that *works*, there's a spark to these practices that makes you feel like you're somehow pulling from that older vein of gold, albeit in a slightly different way.

The picture of Heathen magic that emerges from working in this manner is surprisingly coherent, and rooted in myth and worldview. Again and again, we see the same mechanics repeated, giving us a path for creating important new growth. Tradition without growth is like an insect trapped in amber. It's beautiful and a curiosity, but dead all the same.

In the primary sources, seiðr is often presented as magical chicanery, petty and troublesome. However, even within this narrative, there are hints of something deeper and lessons that go beyond the usual interpretations of Heathenry or the gods—especially when viewed through the eyes of a practitioner.

When Freyja wanders the roads looking for her "husband" Óðr, she is also in search of "mind" or "poetic inspiration," and as the thrice-reborn love goddess she demonstrates the supremacy of love over death. When Óðinn becomes a new person with each name, he demonstrates what can be done when not clinging to ideas of self, and as the giver of önd can be as expansive as the winds. Finally, as the dead god of the mound who continues to affect the prosperity of the land, Freyr teaches the kind of pervasive oneness that enables a person to go into the temporary mound of the cloak and experience the hidden land.

The magical path you stand upon is more than its spells and spindles; it is a path of inspiration that can only be won through knowledge and practice. This is an ever-evolving path, changing as words and deeds change you, and it's a path of striving to go beyond. So may you be rooted by ancient words, guided by the star of your practice, and eventually find your óðr.

GLOSSARY

ÆLF: Old English word for "elf" (plural form "ÆLFE").

ÆSIR: Old Norse word for "gods." One of the two tribes of gods (ÆSIR and VANIR). Were once at war with the VANIR. Generally concerned with order and keeping the cosmos together.

ÁLFR: ON word for "elf" (plural form "ÁLFAR").

ÁSYNJUR: ON word for "goddesses."

ASKR: ON word for "ash," the name of the first human man who was magically created out of a log of ash wood.

BLÓT: ON word for sacrificial ritual in the Old Norse sources. Commonly used by modern Heathens to denote Heathen offering rituals of any kind (both involving and not involving animal sacrifice).

CIRCUMAMBULATION: The ritual act of walking in a circle around a designated space for magic or settlement purposes.

CHARM: Can either refer to magico-medical remedy procedure, or spoken/chanted/sung spell.

EMBLA: ON word for "elm," the name of the first human woman who was magically created out of a log of elm wood.

FREYJA: ON goddess of magic (especially SEIÐR). Also associated with childbirth, death, and sexual promiscuousness. Sister of Freyr and one of the Vanir.

FREYR: ON god of "peace and good seasons." Brother of Freyja and ruler of Álfheimr (a realm of elves). Associated with fertility and harvest, burial mounds, and the Vanir.

FYLGJUKONA: A female spirit who acts and speaks as a guardian goddess and luck-bringer for the family line with which she is associated.

GÆFA/GIPTA: "Internal" forms of luck that manifest as good looks, beauty, physical prowess, and being "lucky."

GALDR/GALDOR: Spoken or chanted magical spells.

GANDR/GANDIR: A type of spirit emissary sent on a seiðrworker's behalf.

GOING UNDER THE CLOAK: Magical method of seeking wisdom as well as perceiving and possibly interacting with the hidden dimensions of a land.

GULLVEIG: A Vanic witch who was repeatedly burned alive during the Æsir-Vanir war by the Æsir, only to rebirth herself each time. Believed to be Freyja. Name has been variously translated to mean "woman made of gold," "gold-adorned woman," or "gold-adorned military power."

HAMINGJA: The externally-existing "personified luck" of a person.

HEATHEN: In the historical period, a Germanic/Scandinavian adherent of pre-Christian belief (ELDER HEATHEN). In modern day, a term commonly used by modern-day adherents of Germanic and/or Scandinavian deities (MODERN HEATHEN). Not to be confused with HEATHEN ELDERS, or elders within the modern Heathen community/communities.

HEIÐR: Archetypal Seiðrworker name.

HÆL/HÆLU (OE) or HEILL (ON): The quality of having physical health, but also luck, wholeness, and whole-making, as well as well-being, prosperity, mental or spiritual health, and auspicious omens.

HEITI: ON word meaning "names." Used to denote alternative names used by deities. For example, ÓÐINN has many different HEITI or "names."

HEL: Both the goddess and Old Norse land of the dead.

HELGRINDR: The gate to Hel, the land of the dead.

HELHEIMR: Another name for the Old Norse land of the dead.

HELRUNE: OE word for a female necromantic witch. Here: a witch who specializes in working with the dead and chthonic through intermediary technologies (including the body) as her/their main practice.

HIDDENFOLK: A word for the unseen beings with whom we share this world. Can be "nature spirits" or more like fairy-type beings.

HUGR (ON)/(HYGE): A part of the "soul." "Mind." Can also be understood as the "free" or wandering part that may be sent forth.

KENNINGS: Descriptive titles or labels given to deities, objects, places, and people within the Old Norse poetic tradition.

LUCK: Intrinsic quality possessed by every human. See: GÆFA/GIPTA for more on internal forms of luck and FYLGJUKONA and HAMINGJA for external forms of luck. MIÐGARÐR: ON word meaning "middle realm." In other words, the world which we inhabit—"middle earth."

MŌDSEFA/SEFA: OE word for the part of the "soul" that remains with the body. A "body-soul" associated with memory and possible source of spiritual power.

NORNIR: A triad of goddesses (singular "Norn") credited with choosing the "fates" of men.

ÓÐINN/WODEN: ON/OE name for Odin. God of magic (specifically galdr), healing, poetry, necromancy, and runes. Of the ÆSIR group of gods.

ÓÐR: "Sense," inspiration, mind.

ÖND: The "breath-soul" given by Óðinn. Both breath and inspiration.

SEIÐR/SĪDEN: ON/OE word for "magic," or more specifically a magic of binding or pulling that was connected with spinning in some contexts.

SEIÐKONA: ON word for a female practitioner of SEIÐR.

SEIÐMAÐR: ON word for a male practitioner of SEIÐR.

STURLUSON, SNORRI: Twelfth-/thirteenth-century Icelandic historian responsible for recording a large amount of what we know about the Old Norse myths.

SUNNA/SUNNE: ON/OE name for the sun goddess.

ÞING: ON word pronounced "Thing." Can refer to the "Alþingi," or parliament, or regional assemblies.

ÞÓRR/ÞŪNOR: Hammer-wielding god of thunder, hallowing, and fertility. Protector of mankind. Name anglicized as "Thor."

VANIR: A tribe of gods. Generally concerned with fertility, wisdom, and magic. Often credited with the ability to see the future. Once at war with the ÆSIR.

VÆTTIR: ON word generally used to refer to unseen inhabitants of the land.

VÉ: ON word meaning "sanctuary" or "temple."

VÖLUSPÁ: ON poem from the text The Poetic Edda that details the creation and destruction of the worlds. Title may be translated as "The Prophecy of the Seeress."

VÖLVA: ON word meaning "wand wed." Wand/staff-carrying seeress.

WIHTA/WIGHTS: OE word for any sentient being, but used here to refer to the unseen beings of the land.

YGGDRASILL: In ON cosmology, the world tree upon which all of creation exists.

OLD NORSE PRONUNCIATION GUIDE

Most of the terms pertaining to Heathen magic used in this book are written in Old Norse. This was, of course, the language of Viking Age Scandinavians, and the language in which the majority of the primary sources were written. Old Norse can be a difficult language to pronounce for Anglophones, and it's much easier to learn by hearing.[333] However, I have included a short guide here to help get you started.

Stress

Stress in Old Norse words typically falls on the first syllable of the word.

Vowels

Vowel	Old Norse Pronunciation
a	Like a in "father" but shorter
á	Like ow in "owl"
e	Like e in "met"

---

333. There are a number of helpful channels on YouTube produced by professors of Old Norse, such as Dr. Jackson Crawford from the University of Boulder Colorado or Dr. Mathias Nordvig of the Nordic Mythology Channel, that cover the pronunciation of commonly used Old Norse words.

Vowel	Old Norse Pronunciation
é	Same sound but longer
i	Like i in "thin"
í	Like ee in "screen"
o	Like o in "mole" but shorter
ó	Like o in "boat"
u	Like oo in "snuck"
ú	Like oo in "moon"
y	Like the German ü sound[334]
ý	Same sound but longer
æ	Like a in "cat" but longer
œ	Like ö in German
ø	Same sound as œ
ö	Like ow in "owl" but shorter than á
au	Like ow in "cow"
ei	Like ay in "day"
ey	Combined Norse e and y sounds

334. There really is no English equivalent for this Norse sound and the written descriptions are incredibly confusing, so I have opted for German equivalents instead, as more people have been exposed to German than Norse or Icelandic.

Consonants

Consonant	Old Norse Pronunciation
f	At the beginning of a word: like f in father. In the middle or at the end of a word: like v.
g	At the beginning of a word or after n: like g in "goober" Before an s or t: like Scottish ch in "loch."
j	Like y in "yes"
p	Like p in "pick" unless before s or t, then like f in "after"
r	Rolled
v	Like v in "vest"
þ	Like th in "thing"
ð	Like th in "this" or "father"
x	Like ochs in Scottish "lochs"
z	Like ts in "mints"

RECOMMENDED RESOURCES

The best place to find further resources in any book is the bibliography, and I recommend you take some time to go through the bibliography in this book. Many of the citations listed are available for free online and are well worth digging into. The resources listed here are the ones that I either wanted to reiterate, were mentioned at some point in the book, or were included because of their potential to help you continue on this path.

Historical Sources

The Poetic Edda (Carolyne Larrington translation)—This, along with **Prose Edda,** is one of the main sources of Norse mythology. Out of the two Eddas, the Poetic Edda is my favorite, and Larrington manages to strike a decent balance between accuracy and poetry. For the **Prose Edda,** I recommend the Anthony Faulkes translation.

The Sagas of the Icelanders by Jane Smilely. This is a mammoth collection of Icelandic sagas that won't break the bank. The translations are readable and the stories littered with intrigue and magic.

Modern Scholarship

Viking Age Iceland by Jesse Byock. If you're finding the world of the historical Heathen confusing and feel like you need some context, then you could do worse than to start here. This is concisely and clearly written, and overall an excellent introduction to the Viking Age society in Iceland.

Song of the Vikings: Snorri and the Making of Norse Myths by Nancy Marie Brown. As one of the main historical sources for Old Norse mythology and religion, it's important to understand the time and social context of Snorri's writing.

The Viking Way by Neil Price. More expensive but worth it if you have the cash. Price tackles the numinous, magical, and dead in a long-awaited new print run of this title.

Shamanism in Norse Myth and Magic by Clive Tolley. Again, an expensive title. However, this is one of the deepest scholarly dives into Norse magic out there on the market.

Modern Heathenry

A Practical Heathen's Guide to Asatru by Patricia Lafayllve. A clear and informative introduction to modern Heathenry from the point of view of a well-known *gyðja* ("priestess") in the Northeastern US Heathen community.

Languages

Viking Language 1: Learn Old Norse, Runes, and Icelandic Sagas by Jesse Byock. This is by far the clearest and best presented self-paced course in Old Norse that I've come across to date. It's still difficult because Old Norse is difficult. But at least it's not like trying to peer through mud.

Introduction to Old English by Peter S. Baker. The newer editions of this course are quite expensive. But older editions are much more reasonably priced and relatively easy to pick up. Good, clear explanations and plenty of opportunities to reinforce what you've learned with the Old English Aerobics website where you can find interactive quizzes and printable worksheets.

Herbs

Norse Magical and Herbal Healing by Ben Waggoner. The only translation of the Icelandic magico-medical manuscript AM494a on the market.

Leechbook III (https://leechbookiii.github.io/index.html). This translation of *Bald's Leechbook III* originally began as an undergraduate project but has become a resource in its own right. Even better, many of the herbs are hyperlinked to further resources!

Encyclopedia of Natural Magic by John Michael Greer. For those of you who wish to learn more about the world of herbal and planetary correspondences for baking into your magical tool-making endeavors.

Spinning

Respect the Spindle, Spin Infinite Yarns with One Amazing Tool by Abby Franquemont. Written by one of the key movers in the spinning revival, this book is a clear and inspiring guide to learning how to spin. Interested in learning how to spin but don't know which spindle to begin with? The Schacht Hi-Low spindle offers excellent value for money. It's well-balanced, and because of the way it's designed, can be used as either a top or bottom whorl spindle. I recommend getting the 3" diameter one.

Shadow Work

Feeding Your Demons by Lama Tsultrim Allione. This is by far the most effective shadow work technique I have ever encountered. I also have a deep appreciation for techniques that involve the personification of issues in order to deal with them more effectively. Very reminiscent of the magico-medical tradition!

Hiddenfolk, Fairies, and Elves, Oh My!

Fairies: A Guide to the Celtic Fair Folk by Morgan Daimler. This is one of the best guides out there on working with and surviving the Good Folk. A deep dive into the "fairy tale" rules I mentioned in chapter 11.

Pagan Portals: Living Fairy by Morgan Daimler. A truly unique book discussing the practicalities of working closely with the Other as well as laying down a manifesto for a better world.

BIBLIOGRAPHY

Adams Bellows, Henry. *The Poetic Edda, The Mythological Poems*. Mineola, NY: Dover Publications, 2004.

Aðalsteinsson, Jón H., and Jakob S. Jónsson. *Under the Cloak: A Pagan Ritual Turning Point in the Conversion of Iceland*. Reykjavik: Háskólaútgáfan, 1999.

Andersson, Gunnar. "Among Trees, Bones, and Stones: The Sacred Grove at Lunda." In *Old Norse Religion in Long-term Perspectives: Origins, Changes, and Interactions: An International Conference in Lund, Sweden, June 3-7, 2004*, edited by Anders Andrén, Kristina Jennbert, and Catharina Raudvere, 195–199. Lund, Sweden: Nordic Academic Press, 2006.

Bek-Pedersen, Karen. "Nornir in Old Norse Mythology." University of Edinburgh, 2007. https://core.ac.uk/download/pdf/153530959.pdf.

Bitel, Lisa M. "In Visu Noctis: Dreams in European Hagiography and Histories, 450–900." *History of Religions* 31, no. 1 (1991): 39-59. doi:10.1086/463255.

Bosworth, Joseph, and T. Northcote Toller. *An Anglo-Saxon Dictionary: Based on the Manuscript Collections of the Late Joseph Bosworth*. London: Oxford University Press, 1954.

Bosworth, Joseph, and T. N. Toller, eds. *An Anglo-Saxon Dictionary: Based on the Manuscript Collections of the Late Joseph Bosworth. Supplement.* London: Oxford University Press, 1955.

Boyer, Corinne. *Under the Witching Tree: A Folk Grimoire of Tree Lore and Practicum.* London: Troy Books Publishing, 2017.

Brady, Timothy, and Adena Schachner. "Blurring the Boundary Between Perception and Memory." *Scientific American,* December/January 16, 2008. https://www.scientificamerican.com/article/perception-and-memory/.

Bullock, Brooke. "Leechbook III: 123v." In *Leechbook III, A New Digital Edition.* Accessed November 12, 2019. https://leechbookiii.github.io/123v.html.

Cleasby, Richard, and Gudbrand Vigfusson. *An Icelandic-English Dictionary.* Oxford: Clarendon Press, 1874.

Cole, Susan G. *Landscapes, Gender, and Ritual Space: The Ancient Greek Experience.* Oakland, CA: University of California Press, 2004.

Cutchin, Joshua. *Thieves in the Night: A Brief History of Supernatural Child Abductions.* San Antonio, TX: Anomalist Books, 2018.

Cyr, Jon. "Skald Craft: A Practical Guide to Understanding and Writing Poetry in the Old Norse Meters." Óðroerir, no. 2 (n.d.): 125–138.

Daimler, Morgan. *Pagan Portals—Odin: Meeting the Norse Allfather.* Alresford, Hampshire, UK: John Hunt Publishing, 2018.

———. *Travelling the Fairy Path.* Alresford, Hampshire, UK: John Hunt Publishing, 2018.

Davidson, Hilda. *Gods and Myths of Northern Europe.* London: Penguin UK, 1990.

———. *Myths and Symbols in Pagan Europe: Early Scandinavian and Celtic Religions.* Syracuse, NY: Syracuse University Press, 1988.

———. *The Road to Hel: A Study of the Conception of the Dead in Old Norse Literature.* New York: Greenwood Press, 1968.

Dixon-Kennedy, Mike. *Encyclopedia of Russian & Slavic Myth and Legend.* Santa Barbara, CA: ABC-CLIO, 1998.

Daubney, Adam. *Spindle Whorl: Unique ID: LIN-D92A22.* Portable Antiquities Scheme, 2010. Accessed November 6, 2019. https://finds.org.uk/database/artefacts/record/id/409249.

DuBois, Thomas. *Nordic Religions in the Viking Age.* Philadelphia: University of Pennsylvania Press, 1999.

Eliade, Mircea. *The Sacred and the Profane: The Nature of Religion.* New York: Mariner Books, 1959.

Eriksen, Marianne H. "Doors to the Dead: The Power of Doorways and Thresholds in Viking Age Scandinavia." *Archaeological Dialogues* 20, no. 2 (2013): 187–214. doi:10.1017/s1380203813000238.

Ewing, Thor. *Gods and Worshippers: In the Viking and Germanic World.* Stroud, Gloucestershire, UK: History Press, 2010.

Gamkrelidze, Thomas V., and Vjaceslav V. Ivanov. *Indo-European and the Indo-Europeans: A Reconstruction and Historical Analysis of a Proto-Language and Proto-Culture. Part I: The Text. Part II: Bibliography, Indexes.* Berlin: Walter de Gruyter, 1995.

Gardeła, Leszek. "A Biography of the Seiðr-Staffs. Towards an Archaeology of Emotions." In *Between Paganism and Christianity in the North,* edited by Leszek P. Słupecki and Jakub Morawiec, 190–219. Rzeszów: Rzeszów University, 2009.

Gardeła, Leszek. "Buried with Honour and Stoned to Death? The Ambivalence of Viking Age Magic in the Light of Archaeology." *Analecta Archaeologica Ressoviensia* 4 (2011): 339–375.

GardenStone. *Göttin Holle: Auf der Suche nach einer germanischen Göttin: Frau Holle in Märchen, Sagen, Legenden, Gedichten, Gebräuchen und in der Mythologie.* Norderstedt: Books on Demand GmbH, 2006.

Giannakis, George. "The 'Fate-as-Spinner' Motif: A Study on the Poetic and Metaphorical Language of Ancient Greek and Indo-European (Part I)." *Indogermanische Forschungen. Zeitschrift für Indogermanistik und allgemeine Sprachwissenschaft* 103 (n.d.): 1–27.

———. "The 'Fate-as-Spinner' Motif: A study on the Poetic and Metaphorical Language of Ancient Greek and Indo-European (Part II)." *Indog-*

ermanische Forschungen. Zeitschrift für Indogermanistik und allgemeine Sprachwissenschaft 104 (1999): 95–109.

Grey, Peter. *Apocalyptic Witchcraft.* N.p: Scarlet Imprint Bibliothèque Rouge, 2016.

Grimm, Jacob. *Teutonic Mythology.* Translated by J. S. Stallybrass. Vol. 1. London: George Bell and Sons, 1882.

Gunnell, Terry. "Pantheon? What Pantheon?" *Scripta Islandica, Isländska Sällskapets Årsbok* 66 (2015): 55–77.

Hall, Alaric. *Elves in Anglo-Saxon England: Matters of Belief, Health, Gender and Identity.* Woodbridge, Suffolk, UK: Boydell Press, 2009.

———. "Research Article: Getting Shot of Elves: Healing, Witchcraft and Fairies in the Scottish Witchcraft Trials." *Folklore* 116, no. 1 (2005): 19-36. doi:10.1080/0015587052000337699.

Heath, Catherine. "Waking the Dead: A Comparative Examination of Ancient Ritual Technologies for Modern Rites Introduction." Last modified June 13, 2019. https://www.academia.edu/39821235/Waking_the_Dead_A_Comparative_Examination_of_Ancient_Ritual_Technologies_for_Modern_Rites_Introduction.

Heide, Eldar. "Spinning Seiðr." In *Old Norse Religion in Long-term Perspectives: Origins, Changes, and Interactions : an International Conference in Lund, Sweden, June 3-7, 2004,* edited by Anders Andrén, Kristina Jennbert, and Catharina Raudvere, 164-170. Lund, Sweden: Nordic Academic Press, 2006.

Henry, P. L. "The Cauldron of Poesy." In *Studia Celtica* 14, no. 15 (1980): 114–129.

Hyllested, Adam. "The Precursors of Celtic and Germanic." In *Proceedings of the 21st Annual UCLA Indo-European Conference: Los Angeles, October 30th and 31st, 2009,* edited by Stephanie W. Jamison, H. C. Melchert, and Brent H. Vine, 107–128. Bremen: Hempen Verlag, 2010.

Jochens, Jenny. *Women in Old Norse Society.* Ithaca, NY: Cornell University Press, 1998.

Joffe, Ben. "To See is to Call: Tantric Visualization, Summoning Spirits and the Mind As Petting Zoo." Last modified May 9, 2017. https://perfumedskull.com/2017/05/07/to-see-is-to-call-tantric-visualization-summoning-spirits-and-the-mind-as-a-petting-zoo/.

Johns, Andreas. *Baba Yaga: The Ambiguous Mother and Witch of the Russian Folktale*. Bern, Switzerland: Peter Lang, 2004.

Jolly, Karen L. *Popular Religion in Late Saxon England: Elf Charms in Context*. Chapel Hill, NC: University of North Carolina Press, 1996.

Jones, Mary. "Awen." In *Jones' Celtic Encyclopedia*. Accessed November 13, 2019. http://www.maryjones.us/jce/awen.html.

Kershaw, Priscilla K. *The One-eyed God: Odin and the (Indo-)Germanic Männerbünde*. The Institute for the Study of Man, 2000.

Larrington, Carolyne. *The Poetic Edda*. Oxford, UK: Oxford University Press, 1999.

Laurie, Erynn R. *Ogam: Weaving Word Wisdom*. Stafford, UK: Immanion Press, 2007.

Lecouteux, Claude. *Witches, Werewolves, and Fairies: Shapeshifters and Astral Doubles in the Middle Ages*. New York: Simon & Schuster, 2003.

Lincoln, Bruce. *Death, War, and Sacrifice: Studies in Ideology & Practice*. Chicago: University of Chicago Press, 1991.

Long, Charlotte R. *The Twelve Gods of Greece and Rome*. Leiden: Brill Archive, 1987.

Lund, Julie. "Banks, Borders and Bodies of Water in a Viking Age Mentality." *Journal of Wetland Archaeology* 8, no. 1 (2008): 53–72. doi:10.1179/jwa.2008.8.1.53.

MacLeod, Mindy, and Bernard Mees. *Runic Amulets and Magic Objects*. Woodbridge, Suffolk, UK: Boydell Press, 2006.

Mallory, J. P. *In Search of the Indo-Europeans: Language, Archaeology and Myth*. London: Thames & Hudson, 2001.

Markowsky, George. "Information Theory, Physiology." In *Encyclopædia Britannica*. Encyclopædia Britannica, Inc., 2017. Accessed November 13, 2019. https://www.britannica.com/science/information-theory/Physiology.

Maas, Michael. *Readings in Late Antiquity: A Sourcebook*. London: Routledge, 2000.

Mees, Bernard. "The etymology of rune." *Beiträge zur Geschichte der deutschen Sprache und Literatur* 136, no. 4 (2014). doi:10.1515/bgsl-2014-0046.

McKinnell, John. "Encounters with Völur." In *Old Norse Myths, Literature and Society: The Proceedings of the 11th International Saga Conference 2-7 July 2000, University of Sydney. Supplement*, edited by Geraldine Barnes and Margaret C. Ross, 239–251. Odense, Denmark: University Press of Southern Denmark, 2000.

McKinnell, John. "On Heiðr." *Saga-Book* 25, no. 4 (2001): 394–417.

Mierow, Charles. *The Gothic History of Jordanes (1915)*. N.p: Literary Licensing, LLC, 2014.

Motz, Lotte. "Freyja, Anat, Ishtar and Inanna: Some Cross-Cultural Comparisons." In *Mankind Quarterly* 23 (1982): 95–212.

———. "The Winter Goddess: Percht, Holda, and Related Figures." *Folklore* 95, no. 2 (1984): 151–166. doi:10.1080/0015587x.1984.9716309.

North, Richard. *Heathen Gods in Old English Literature*. Cambridge, UK: Cambridge University Press, 1997.

North, Richard. *Pagan Words and Christian Meanings*. Amsterdam, NL: Rodopi, 1991.

Osborn, Marijane, and Stella Longland. "A Celtic Intruder in the Old English 'Rune Poem.'" In *Neuphilologische Mitteilungen* 81, no. 4 (1980): 385–387.

Owen, Gale R. *Rites and Religions of the Anglo-Saxons*. New York: Dorset Press, 1985.

Pálsson, Herman, and Paul Edwards. *Eyrbyggja Saga*. London: Penguin Books, 1989.

Pendell, Dale. *Pharmako Poeia: Plant Powers, Poisons, and Herbcraft*. Berkeley, CA: North Atlantic Books 2010.

Pollington, Stephen. *Leechcraft: Early English Charms, Plant Lore, and Healing*. Hockwold-cum-Wilton, Norfolk, UK: Anglo-Saxon Books, 2003.

Price, Neil S. *The Viking Way: Religion and War in Late Iron Age Scandinavia*. Uppsala, Sweden: Dept. of Archaeology and Ancient History, Univ. Uppsala, 2002.

———. "The Archaeology of Seiðr: Circumpolar Traditions in Viking Pre-Christian Religion." *Brathair* 4, no. 2 (2004): 109–26.

———. "Dying and the Dead: Viking Age Mortuary Behavior." In *The Viking World*, edited by Stefan Brink, 257–273. New York: Routledge, 2011.

———. *The Viking Way: Religion and War in Late Iron Age Scandinavia*, 2nd ed. Oxford: Oxbow Books, 2019.

———. "Nine Paces from Hel: Time and Motion in Old Norse Ritual Performance." *World Archaeology* 46, no. 2 (2014): 178–191. doi:10.1080/00 438243.2014.883938.

Rafnsson, Magnús, and Museum of Icelandic Sorcery & Witchcraft. *Tvær galdraskræður: Lbs 2413 8vo : Leyniletursskræðan Lbs 764 8vo*. Hólmavík: Strandagaldur, 2008.

Schnurbein, Stefanie. "Shamanism in the Old Norse Tradition: A Theory Between Ideological Camps." *History of Religions* 43, no. 2 (2003): 116–138.

Simek, Rudolf. *Dictionary of Northern Mythology*. Suffolk, UK: Boydell & Brewer, 2007.

Sejbjerg Sommer, Bettina. "The Norse Concept of Luck." *Scandinavian Studies* 79, no. 3 (2007): 275–294.

Skoglund, Peter. "Stone Ships: Continuity and Change in Scandinavian Prehistory." In *World Archaeology* 40, no. 3 (2008): 390–406. doi:10.1080/00438240802261440.

Storms, Godfrid. *Anglo-Saxon Magic*. Gravenhage, NL: Martinus Nijhoff, 1948.

Sturluson, Snorri. *Heimskringla: History of the Kings of Norway*. Translated by Lee Hollander. Austin, TX: University of Texas Press, 1964.

Sturluson, Snorri. *Prose Edda*. Translated by Anthony Faulkes. London: J.M. Dent, 2003.

Sundqvist, Olof. "The Temple, the Tree, and the Well." In *Old Norse Mythology—comparative Perspectives*, edited by Pernille Hermann, Jens P.

Schjødt, and Amber J. Rose, 163–190. Cambridge, MA: Harvard University Press, 2017.

Timm, Erika. *Frau Holle, Frau Percht und verwandte Gestalten: 160 Jahre nach Jacob Grimm aus germanistischer Sicht betrachtet.* Stuttgart, Germany: Hirzel, 2003.

Tolley, Clive. *Shamanism in Norse Myth and Magic.* Helsinki, Finland: Academia Scientiarum Fennica, 2009.

Waggoner, Ben. *Norse Magical and Herbal Healing.* Morrisville, NC: Lulu.com, 2011.

Westcoat, Eirik. "The Goals of Galdralag: Identifying the Historical Instances and Uses of the Metre." *Saga-Book* 40 (2016): 69–90.